LIVING LEGACIES

Compiled by Loreen Coons and Brittney Stutz.
Book design by Loreen Coons. Printed in 2025.
livinglegaciesbyloreen.com

Table of Contents

Foreword

Written by Loreen Coons, Life Historian

I feel fortunate to have been in the home of Dick and Fay Wheeler almost every week for close to two years as we worked on their life stories together. Dick and Fay are one of the most inspiring couples I've ever met, and my life has been enriched because of the time I've spent with them.

Laura (Dick and Fay's daughter) and her husband, Bill Gregory, hired me to help Dick and Fay write their life stories. Dick and I started meeting together once a week in April of 2023. We originally intended to write a book for Dick and a book for Fay, but we didn't know how we would write about their life together. Eventually, we decided to do one volume for Dick from his birth until after his first wife, Joan, passed

2024—Fay, Dick, Loreen

away; one volume for Fay from her birth until after her first husband, Evan, passed away; and this volume of Dick and Fay's life together from 1981 to the present. We hope you love all three!

Many people helped make this book a reality. Dick and Fay were very diligent about being prepared for each of our sessions together. They were always present and helpful. My daughter, Brittney Stutz, helped by transcribing and editing the interviews, scanning and cleaning up pictures, and making the final document look better. Dick and Fay's children helped a lot as well. Dale (son) spent so much time in the background working on pictures. Laura, Pam (daughter), Meilyn (daughter), Kristen (daughter), and Summer (granddaughter) read the final draft and gave input. Kristen wrote the introduction. This book wouldn't be as enjoyable or complete without each person's contribution!

I have learned so much from Dick and Fay. They live life intentionally. They don't just let life happen; they plan and teach and make deliberate choices to help their loved ones know of their concern and share what has brought them happiness. They have long-standing traditions to bring their family members closer to each other and to God. They both exemplify Christlike qualities of charity, faith, and endurance each day. Their love for and commitment to God, each other, and their family is evident in everything they do.

All the effort they expended to write this book was for you—their loved ones and friends. They love you and care about you. Thank you to Dick, Fay, Laura, Bill, and all the family for the honor of getting to know such remarkable individuals. It was a pleasure!

Introduction

Written by Kristen Reber (Dick and Fay's daughter)

I've heard it can be difficult to blend two families together. In my experience, it's actually pretty easy. The trick is to show up after all of the hard work is done, and then give yourself full credit for smoothing out any rough edges that remain. I know I was too young to recognize many of the bumps and bruises that were a natural part of putting two families together, but I think there were a few things that helped us make two families into one.

First, we worked together. Many of our Saturdays were spent doing yard work for people that struggled to do it themselves. We moved loads of palm tree trimmings from the ground to the trailer. We could set up and take down a wedding reception in record time. We sorted thousands of mismatched socks that piled up in the laundry. (Could there have been thousands? In my memories the sock piles covered the entire family room floor, several feet deep in places. Why did we own so

About 1986—Wheeler/Eagar Family
Back: Josh, Becky, Laura, Larry, Dale, Rick, Kari, Tami, Bryan, Meilyn, Michael
Front: Julie, Pam, Fay, Dick, Kristen, Sheri

many socks?) Even keeping the house clean and the family fed required all hands on deck. We learned that many hands make light work.

Second, we played together. We went to National Parks, and theme parks, and our own tiny cabin in the woods. We played games together, and we played jokes on each other, and some of us even thought they were funny.

Third, we sang together. Every time we were in the car, we were singing. When I was young, I thought this was just because we loved music so much. As I got older I realized it was probably to stop us fighting in the car, but it was impressive either way. So many of my best memories involve singing with my family. Whether it was at a wedding, a funeral, or just standing around the piano in the living room, music brought us together.

And lastly, we showed up for each other. We went to concerts and plays of all types. We showed up for birthday parties, baptisms, and celebrations. Anytime family was required (and a lot of times when they weren't), we were there. And we continue to be there for each other day after day, and year after year. I'm grateful I get to be part of it.

Timeline for Dick and Fay Wheeler

Dick and Fay's Homes		*Significant Events in Dick and Fay's Lives*
	1980	**Oct. 7, 1980**—*Evan H. Eagar passed away.*
		Nov. 9, 1980—*Betty "Joan" Wheeler passed away.*
1981—*1501 E. Glade Avenue, Mesa, AZ*		**Mar. 24, 1981**—*Dick & Fay went on their first date and became engaged.*
		Apr. 17, 1981—*Dick and Fay were married in the Mesa Arizona Temple.*
		Dec. 11, 1981—*Rick married Debra "Debbie" Jean Cluff.*
		Oct. 30, 1982—*Beniah Wheeler (Dick's father) passed away.*
		1983—*Dick became Principal of Poston Junior High School.*
		Apr. 22, 1983—*Kristen (daughter) was born.*
		May 12, 1983—*Dale married Tracy Lee Singleton.*
	1985	
		Jul. 2, 1987—*Meilyn married Robert "Rob" Lasel Bushman.*
	1990	**Oct. 26, 1990**—*Larry married Michelle Poplin (divorced).*
		Sep. 4, 1991—*Edith Hamblin Eagar (Evan's mother) passed away.*
		Nov. 22, 1991—*Laura married William "Bill" Harrison Gregory.*
		Nov. 22, 1991—*Becky married William "Bill" Edward Cox, Jr.*
		1994—*Dick retired.*
		Dec., 1994—*Mike married Jackie Sherwood (divorced).*
	1995	**Oct. 14, 1995**—*Josh married Kristie Lynn Polke.*
		1997—*Mike married Cindy Halls (divorced).*
		Feb. 7, 1997—*Bryan married Jennifer Hammon (divorced).*

Dick and Fay's Homes		Significant Events in Dick and Fay's Lives
		Feb. 1, 1998—*Thomas Wiley Dorathy, Jr. (Joan's step-father) passed away.*
		Nov. 25, 1998—*Tami married Devin Todd McCoy.*
2000—1305 N. Porter Place, Gilbert, AZ	**2000**	**May 1, 2003**—*Julie married Jonathan "Jon" Michael Spahr (divorced).*
		Jul. 2004-Jan. 2006—*Dick & Fay served a Leadership/Activation mission in Olongapo, Philippines.*
	2005	**Mar. 31, 2005**—*Paul Brown Eagar (Evan's father) passed away.*
		Jan. 23, 2006—*Willie Mae "Dude" Rutherford Coombs (Fay's mother) passed away.*
		Aug. 25, 2007—*Kristen married Ty Pace Reber.*
		Sep. 2007-Mar. 2009—*Dick & Fay served an ITEP (International Teacher Education Program) mission in Suva, Fiji, teaching courses for college credit through BYU–Hawaii.*
		Apr. 3, 2009—*Beniah "Benny" Cutler, Jr. (Dick's brother) passed away.*
	2010	**Apr. 14, 2010**—*Lovel Wheeler (Dick's mother) passed away.*
		Jul. 26, 2010—*Jay Ballard Coombs (Fay's father) passed away.*
		Jul. 22, 2011—*Bryan married Christina Elaine Ingram.*
		Dec. 23, 2013—*Season Hale (granddaughter) passed away.*
	2015	**Oct. 22, 2015**—*June Denham Dorathy (Joan's mother) passed away.*
		May 15, 2017—*William "Bill" Ronald (Dick's brother) passed away.*
		Jun. 2, 2017—*John Phillips (Dick's brother) passed away.*
		Apr. 29, 2018—*Mike Hale (Sheri's husband) passed away.*
		Feb. 15, 2019—*Lovel Louise (Dick's sister) passed away.*
	2020	**Sep. 30, 2020**—*Sheri (daughter) passed away.*
		Nov. 6, 2021—*Mike married Cindy Ellen Eaves.*

Part 1: A New Start

1. Some Family Background

By Dick:

I was married and sealed to Betty Joan Holt on September 4, 1954, in the Mesa Arizona Temple, and we brought eight children into the world. Joan was an excellent wife and mother. She loved her family, served her Heavenly Father, loved her extended family, and was very involved in genealogical research and record keeping. She passed away following complications from a gallbladder surgery on November 9, 1980, at Desert Samaritan Hospital in Mesa. She was buried in the Mesa City Cemetery on November 12, 1980.

1981—Dick & Fay

Fay was married to Evan H. Eagar on June 14, 1968 in Eagar, Arizona. They were sealed in the Mesa Temple the next year on June 27, 1969. They brought six children into the world. Evan was an excellent husband and father and was very involved with the young men's program and other church service. Evan was a superintendent at the Farnsworth Construction Company, drew house plans, and successfully built several homes for his family and others. He passed away on October 7, 1980, at St. Joseph's Heart/ Neurological Center Hospital in Phoenix, following complications from a surgery to correct his double aortic arch (a birth defect), and was buried in the Mesa City Cemetery on October 9, 1980.

The Wheeler/Eagar family began with the marriage of myself, Richard Wallace Wheeler, to Fay Ellen Coombs Eagar, for time in the Mesa Arizona Temple on April 17, 1981. We affectionately call ourselves the "Wheagars."

Our marriage was the result of a three week, whirlwind romance several months after the death of both of our spouses and under the direction of the Holy Ghost. In fact, in conversations with Sheri, Rick, Pam, and Dale, they all stated they had confirmation of our marriage before either of us had even really given it consideration.

Contrary to a question asked by one of Sheri's friends, this was not a "marriage of convenience." The "facts" and "water under the bridge" make it clear that there have been few conveniences and many challenges and problems coupled with lots of joy, happiness, fond memories, and shared love. This is our story.

2. Our Courtship and Marriage: Fay's Perspective

By Fay:

My husband, Evan Eagar, died on October 7, 1980, the day before our oldest daughter's birthday. All of my kids were 12 and under. It was a surprise to all of us and very hard to deal with! As the months went by, I tried to find ways to get back on track.

Early Interactions with Dick

My temple recommend was getting close to expiring, so I went to the stake center during the time the stake presidency had set aside for temple recommend interviews. When I walked into the foyer, I saw a lot of women waiting and the stake president (President Woolf) and his counselor (President Lindblom) just standing there. I asked, "What's going on?"

And they said, "These women don't want us to renew their recommends. They're all waiting for President Wheeler." I guess they were hoping to be the next Sister Wheeler.

President Woolf looked at me and said, "Hmmm, you may be interested too."

I said, "I just want my temple recommend renewed. Would one of you please help me?"

They asked, "Are you sure you don't want to wait?"

I said, "No. I've got kids waiting at home for me." So one of them did my interview. We came out at about the same time as Dick came out. His eyes were so big just looking at all the women. He looked at the stake president and the other counselor just standing there, then he just sighed and invited the next lady in for her interview. I felt so bad for him.

At one point, my bishop asked, "Have you ever thought about Brother Wheeler?" And then he said, "Oh I guess he's too old for you, isn't he?" I didn't say anything.

Around that time, I was working for a couple in our ward, the Archibalds, who had a company that catered weddings and receptions. They invited me to help them. It gave me a place to be, gave me a little money, and gave me a break from my kids (and my kids from me).

One weekend, we were catering a big wedding, and I really wanted to go to the adult session of stake conference that Saturday evening. Going to church meetings was really important to me, and I knew I needed more divine help. The Archibalds knew that I wanted to go, and they finally said, "Just go ahead and go." I was in charge of making the champagne punch, so I almost didn't go because I had champagne all over me and didn't have time to change before the conference. I thought, "I'll just sit in the back where nobody is."

The meeting had already started when I walked in, but the very last bench was empty, so I slipped in there. Dick was conducting that meeting. I looked up at him and thought, "He knows how I feel. He's the only one here that really knows how I feel." I was very touched as I listened to the speakers. When the meeting was over, I went home, heaved a big sigh, and went to bed.

The next morning, I went back to conference. I was singing in the choir, so I sat in the choir seats —back then, they had primary classes for the kids, so they were taken care of. Dick spoke about how to get by when God pulls at your heartstrings. He gave a beautiful talk that really touched me. I thought, "That is exactly true, and then you have to figure out a way to come back. You have to get yourself put together and be there for your kids."

After the meeting, I went down from the choir seats to shake Dick's hand. He said, "You know how I feel."

I said, "I do, and you did a good job." About that time, a lady fell down the choir steps—she was fine—so Dick ran over to help her. I picked up my kids and went home.

The kids and I had a really easy day. That evening, Dick called me and asked, "Would it be okay if I came over and visited with you for a few minutes? I have some things to talk to you about."

I said, "Okay."

He said, "I'll be over in about 20 minutes."

I said, "Okay, goodbye." My journal entry below explains more.

Monday, March 23, 1981 Journal Entry about Sunday, March 22, 1981

I was singing some beautiful songs this evening, about 9:15 p.m., that Meilyn is learning for a special chorus. I was really enjoying myself when the phone rang. It was President Wheeler, and he wanted to come over to speak to me for a few minutes. My heart really started racing. I was frightened for some reason, and yet I said, "Sure, come over. That would be fine."

I madly rushed to pick up a few things in the family room and wished I could have changed my clothes. We'd been to the park and played kickball and cooked hot dogs, and I think I was a mess.

But he arrived, so I somehow calmly invited him in, and I really felt panicky until he sat down and he began to make some polite conversation. Then I felt a really calm feeling come over me. He began to tell me that since his wife had died, he felt like he had a really good handle on things. He is very strong and capable, and he and his children all felt this. He figured he would never remarry or even need the association of dating, but that just recently, since the Saturday evening meeting I believe, he had felt very strongly about me. About needing to talk to me, see me, etc. That he had prayed about it and even asked for a stupor of thought if these feelings were wrong.

It's so strange to me to hear him voice these same feelings I've been having. I'm truly frightened by them when I'm alone, and yet when he calls and speaks to me, I feel a real calm, and I seem to say the right things and not sound foolish. He assured me that he had not had any revelations or visions, just these very persistent feelings.

When he left, the calm I felt left with him. I read from Proverbs, and I exercised, and I wandered around in circles until about 11:20 p.m. when he called again. I knew it was him, and I was almost afraid that he'd called to take back all he had said, but instead he had called to tell me he'd been by to visit his two married daughters and tell them his feelings. Again, when I heard his voice, even knowing before that it was him, I felt very calm again. He asked me to dinner Wednesday. I'm excited and very scared.

I feel so in awe of him and his ability to do what's asked of him by our Heavenly Father at all times. I've wondered if maybe he is on a spiritual level that is too far above mine, and yet I know I have grown too in these past months. I've been on my knees tonight too, and I know I will be again. I need the Spirit to guide me now more than ever. I called Claudia about 11:50 p.m. I just needed to talk. I couldn't explain things to her or really tell her anything, and I know she is frustrated now too, and yet she knows so well when not to push but just to listen and support. I promised him I would keep the things he told me in confidence for now, and I will. I need that security myself.

Our First Date and the Proposal

On Wednesday, he stopped by the house during school hours. I had my little curlers in when he knocked on the door. I was so surprised! He said, "I'm just making sure that we're still going tonight. I'll come pick you up at five o'clock." Then he leaned in and gave me a kiss! He said, "I'll see you then," and he closed the door.

I just stood there for a minute, then I ran next door to my friend's house and said, "He kissed me! What am I supposed to do with that?" She just laughed and laughed. I was really shaken up, and I didn't quite know what to do. I went upstairs in the afternoon before he came and talked to my kids. I told them Dick and I were just going to dinner.

Dick picked me up in the evening in a little sports car he had borrowed so he could have a nice car to take me on a nice date. We decided to go to the Black Angus in Tempe in hopes we wouldn't see anyone we knew. The server seated us at a table that was clearly visible from the entrance. The worst part was that the light cover was broken, so it was like we had a spotlight on us. We only ate a few bites because we kept looking at the door every time it opened, like we were getting caught doing something we shouldn't be doing. It was so awkward. Finally, he said, "I thought we'd go over to the park where my son, Rick, is playing baseball."

And I said, "Okay."

When we got to the baseball park, Dick drove around and around and around in the parking lot until he found a place under a light. He explained, "I want to talk to you for a while, and I don't want people to think we're doing things we shouldn't be doing." He talked for a little while and then he said, "I really, really feel like we're supposed to get married." As you can imagine, there was nothing but silence for a few seconds.

Then I said, "There's one thing I need to know. What should I call you?"

And he said, "Well, my name is Richard, and my friends call me Dick."

I asked, "And so what should I call you?"

And he said, "I hope you'll call me Dick."

And I said, "Okay."

He asked, "Are you saying yes?"

I said, "Yes, I'm saying yes." We just sat there for quite a while and never did go to see the baseball game. Then he drove me home. He says I kissed him at the door, but I did not. He kissed me. Anyway, when I got home, my kids were all asleep, so I didn't wake them up to tell them.

Telling Our Families and Friends and Setting a Date

I called my parents that night at about 10:30 p.m. I said, "I've been asked to get married."

My mother said, "What?"

5

I replied, "Yes. Bishop Wheeler asked me to marry him." Dick was in the stake presidency at that time, but they knew him as Bishop Wheeler. I told them, "He asked me to marry him tonight, and I said yes."

My dad asked, "Fay, are you sure?"

I said, "Dad, I've never been more sure of anything. I know this is the Lord's plan. I've never felt this strongly about anything in my life. I know this is what He has in store for both of us. He wants us to raise our families together. I can't say no."

He asked again, "Are you sure?"

And I said, "I'm sure, Dad. Pray about it, and talk to me tomorrow."

He said, "I will."

I guess they stayed up all night talking about all the positives and all the negatives. Then first thing in the morning, I got a call from my dad. He said, "It's going to be okay, Fay. We'll be behind you. We will support you. When do you want to let your brothers and sisters know?"

I hadn't even told my kids, so I said, "Not yet!"

When the kids came home that afternoon, I had them all sit down. We talked about their dad for a while. I knew how much they missed him, and I told them I missed him, too. Then I said, "But I'm going to marry Bishop Wheeler. He's actually in the stake presidency now. You know who he is."

Meilyn said, "That's Laura's daddy."

I said, "Yes. He asked me to marry him last night, and I told him that I would. I feel very very good about it, because Heavenly Father wants you to have a dad here as you grow up. He wants you to have a father and a mother, and this is what He has told me we need to do."

They all cried. The little ones didn't even know why they were crying. When all was said and done, they said, "Okay," so I had their permission and my parents' permission.

Next, Dick and I had to tell the other in-laws and parents (Grandma Dorathy, Grandma Wheeler, and Grandma and Grandpa Eagar). That Sunday was fast Sunday, so we told them all we had some things to talk about and asked them to fast to be able to understand the things we were going to say. We started with Grandma Dorathy (Joan's mother). She smiled and said, "I'll just gain another daughter." That's how she treated me from then on!

Then we went to Dick's mom and dad. When we told them, his mother said, "The king is dead! Long live the king!" We kind of looked at each other but had no idea why she said that. His dad didn't say a word.

We left there and went out to Edith and Paul Eagars's (Evan's parents) house, and we told them. They just sat there with their arms folded, kind of ruffled. Edith, my mother-in-law, said, "I know it's the right thing to do, but that doesn't mean I have to like it." That was her answer, and Paul's was basically the same.

Our friends had various responses, as you can imagine. One of our friends in Provo wrote a letter telling Dick he was making a mistake. Dick told his friend that we had prayed about it and felt it was right. Dick told him we'd love to have him at the wedding if he felt good about it, and he and his wife did end up driving down from Provo for the wedding.

The day after our first date and Dick's proposal, my visiting teaching companion and I went to see our sisters. She said, "I need to talk to you. I have found my husband!"

I said, "Oh wonderful! Who is it?"

She said, "It's President Wheeler. I just know it. The Lord revealed that to me."

I didn't know what to say. I had told Dick, "Yes," so we were technically engaged, but we hadn't even told all our family members yet. I just said, "Great! Good luck! I have to go get my kids."

That same day, Dick came over to my house to talk to the kids and tell them his feelings. The kids listened to what he had to say and tried to understand, but they were all pretty young. I knew that they would love him.

That evening, Dick and I went to the young women's standards night together and created quite a stir. People were breaking their necks turning around to look at us. They weren't sure if we were actually together or if we were just sitting together. We were just trying to be very cool, but it was pretty hard. I saw my visiting teacher partner, and I mouthed the words, "I'm sorry."

She said, "Don't be." She was so cute.

After standards night, we went to Dick's home to visit with all of his children. I was pretty nervous. His children were older, and even though the things he told me about their reactions were all positive, I was still feeling a little like I was entering the "other camp." Stupid, but real, feelings.

Late 1981 or early 1982—Back: Pam, Kari, Larry, Rick, Sheri, Dale, Laura, Meilyn
Middle: Dick, Fay, Becky, Tami
Front: Mike, Bryan, Josh, Julie

He told me to go ahead. I just stared at him and said, "You're kidding, right?"

He said, "No. You made me tell your kids, now you tell mine." So I finally proceeded to tell them my side of the story. I could really feel their warmth and their feelings for me. It amazes me still to think how receptive and welcoming they were to me. I could tell his children were really special. They had a sense of humor, and even more impressive to me was their sense of responsibility, not only to themselves but to each other, and also to their family as a whole. I wanted my children to develop those same traits.

Dick and I didn't set a date right away, but as the first few days went by, we could see that waiting a long time wouldn't work. We were all on edge all of the time. If I was at his house, my kids were calling. They didn't

1982—Fay & Dick

know what was going on. If he was at my house, his kids were calling. Dick finally said, "This isn't working. We just need to do this and get them all together." He was right. We looked at the calendar and picked a date three weeks out, so our engagement was about three and a half weeks.

Our Wedding

We asked the temple president where we should be married. Should we be married in our church or our house? He said, "Oh, no! You come to the temple and we will do a civil ceremony." So the wedding was performed in the Mesa Temple "for time."

When we were kneeling at the altar, the sealer said, "This isn't the kind of marriage we like to do," meaning he liked doing sealings, not civil marriages.

He kind of went on and on, and I was sitting there thinking, "Maybe this isn't what we were supposed to do." Then I got an amazing feeling, and the thought came, "Just ignore him. It's exactly what you're supposed to do." So we did.

When we stepped outside, there were 50 people there to greet us—all of our kids and many loved ones—which was great, because we wanted our kids to recognize that weddings should be performed in the temple.

Everyone wanted a celebration, but we didn't want it to be all about us. We didn't want a reception and all that hoop-la. My son had turned eight and hadn't been baptized yet, so we decided to have his baptism in the afternoon, so that's what we focused on. People kept saying they wanted to do something for us, so I said, "You could put on a luncheon for my little boy's eighth birthday and his baptism." They asked him what he wanted to eat, and he wanted Chinese fried rice. That's what he loved, so that's what we had. It was fun! Our loved ones felt good about being able to do something for us, and the kids had a good time.

Our Honeymoon

Sheri came to the house and stayed with the kids while we went on our honeymoon. Dick asked me, "How would you like to go to our cabin in Pinedale? It's not anything spectacular, but would you mind going?"

I said, "Sure I'd love to go." We stayed there for a few days. For me, it was great. I loved every minute of it. We walked and talked.

Dick kept telling me, "We need to make some plans."

I kept telling him, "No."

He asked, "What do you mean?"

I said, "No. I'm not ready to make plans." So he let it go.

Then the next day, we went through the exact same thing. I did that the whole week. At the end of the week, he was so frustrated that he asked, "How about if I make some plans and you can look at them?"

I said, "Okay," so he wrote some things down.

One of the things that was important to him was to let the kids know that I wasn't a maid, and that every one of them was going to have assignments. We assigned the six oldest kids six duties, such as vacuuming, working with me on the meals, setting the table, taking care of the yard, taking out the garbage, etc. He made a chart with everyone's name and a dial in the middle so each person had a different job each week. He did the same with the little kids. So we had some plans and went back home to start our new life together.

3. Our Courtship and Marriage: Dick's Perspective

By Dick:

After Joan's death, I was dubbed the "most eligible widower" in the stake, which turned out to be a big mess. It wasn't that I was such a great catch; it was the fact that there were so many women who weren't sealed to anybody and wanted that so badly. They knew that if they weren't aggressive, they wouldn't have a chance. It was very upsetting to me. I had concluded that I was going to stay single.

My wife died a week before Thanksgiving. Immediately, women started coming to the door with pastries and things. When one of the kids answered the door, they didn't say, "Would you give this to President Wheeler?" They said, "I want to see President Wheeler," so I had to go to the door and see who it was. It got so bad.

One of my friends said, "Dick I've got five people who want to date you."

I told him, "I'm not interested, but if you want to write their names down, you can do what you want." I told myself I wasn't interested in getting remarried, but God had other plans. My journal entries from that time give a more detailed account of the deep feelings of my heart, so I share some of them here.

Promptings From the Spirit
Sunday, March 22, 1981

I realize, finally, that I was not able to be effective in all of my callings or assignments alone. I was busy during the day at school as the principal, I was busy several evenings a week in the stake presidency, and more importantly, I was not fulfilling my calling as Father and Mother to my family. I had given some thought to the available special interest sisters that I knew of. The only name that came to me was Fay Eagar. I thought of all of the reasons why it was not the right thing to do. I thought about our age difference, and knew that Fay would not be interested in marrying an old man 13 years older than her. I thought of the six kids we each had at home, and I thought of the closeness of the deaths of our spouses and knew that it was too soon. I knew how beautiful she was, that she loved to sing and often did with her husband, and that I couldn't even carry a tune. I didn't know if my salary could sustain both families, and I knew that I would want her to be a full-time mother and wife and not have to work outside the home.

I spent a great deal of time on my knees in prayer and asked the Lord to help me with my concerns or for a stupor of thought if it was not to be. The feelings continued.

The next Sunday was stake conference. A lady came up and put her hand through my arm. I was repulsed and said to myself, "I'm not going to remarry."

On Sunday night after I saw Fay again at conference, I said to myself, "I need to call her and visit with her." She was at home and invited me to come over. We talked for a few minutes and we agreed to get together with our families sometime in the future so my two sons who had served missions could share their slides and mission experiences since she had two young boys. My feelings for her continued.

I contacted my older kids that evening to see how they would accept Fay as their mother. They were all in agreement, and asked me why it had taken me so long to recognize it. When I talked to Sheri and Pam, they said they had seen Fay at a stake event at the junior high. One of them nudged the other and said, "Wouldn't it be neat if Dad married Sister Eagar?" Then I called Dale. He asked, "Why did it take you so long? I've known since Mom's funeral." Rick and he had seen Fay at Joan's funeral and one said something like, "I think Dad is going to marry her."

Monday, March 23, 1981

After I got things under control at school, I stopped by Fay's house to see if she would go out with me on Tuesday evening for dinner and a date.

Our First Date and the Proposal
Tuesday, March 24, 1981

I got up with the 4:45 alarm and woke Laura and Bryan. We went to Dale's, got him and Brother Slider, and jogged over to Mesa High. Then we ran the track for a couple of miles before going home.

The day was long and the time passed very slowly.

Laura asked where I was going in the evening. I told her I was going to take someone to dinner. She asked who and I told her, then she got a worried look on her face. I could tell she was uneasy about it and tried to assure her it was all right.

I picked Fay up at 5 p.m. We went to the Black Angus restaurant in Tempe. I thought the Black Angus would be neat because each table has a separate booth. I figured if we went to Tempe, we wouldn't attract too much attention from Mesa people.

I didn't see anyone I knew, however, the booth we were placed in was open to the entrance and main lobby. We had a good meal, although neither one of us was very hungry. Then I drove toward Mesa trying to figure out where to go to sit and talk where we wouldn't be bothered.

We went to Kleinman Park. There was a ball game in progress, and we parked a good distance away from it but still in the parking lot where there was the security of lights and people. We talked about lots of feelings and timelines, etc. We continued to feel good and positive, so I officially proposed to her and she accepted. We sat at the parking lot until the game was over, then when the lights began to go off, I felt it was time to move on. I drove slowly in the direction of home, and guess what. The car knew its way. We decided to go into the front room of my house and talk.

Laura heard us and came in to kiss me good night. I could see that she was upset, so in a few minutes, I excused myself and went in to talk to her. She got up, threw her arms around me, and cried. I asked her what was wrong. She said, "Dad, I'm so confused!" I told her that I too had been confused, but that I now understood everything, and what I was doing was right. That assurance gave her the ability to calm herself.

Fay and I talked and visited until midnight, then I took her home. I went in and told Becky and

Laura what I was feeling and what led up to the dinner date. After I talked, they both got a sweet, warm glow, and they went to sleep.

Sharing the Good News and Making Plans
Thursday, March 26, 1981

I slept in this morning. After baths, sleeping late, etc., we all got off to school. Before we left, I told the little boys about the proposal. Everyone seems to really be supportive and excited.

At 11, I met with Fay and her parents. They are from Eagar and teach school in Round Valley. They were down this week on spring break. They were very nice and were supportive and encouraging. The rest of the school day was fairly routine.

At 5:30 p.m., I met with Joan's folks. They too were happy for us and seemed to accept it well.

1980s—Dude & Jay Coombs

June & Tom Dorathy (Joan's parents)

At 6:45 p.m., I dropped Laura off to practice and I went to meet with Fay's kids and explain to them how we felt and what was happening. They were receptive and supportive. She has a lovely family. Then we went to the Beehive standards night with our daughters. It will probably start an avalanche of gossip, but we are ready. The standards night was well done but a bit too long.

Afterward, we went to our home to meet the family and discuss our feelings and plans. The kids were thrilled and seemed to understand. We had a family prayer together. The kids went towards bed and we shared a few precious moments together. We knelt in prayer together. It was a super spiritual feeling for us. I look forward to the special times and feelings together as we kneel as husband and wife.

Fay is a really special, beautiful, caring, appreciative, spiritual, conscientious, special, special, special person. I feel truly blessed to have this special second opportunity for a choice marriage. I know that the Lord is looking over me and blessing me. She makes me feel so important and special and, in doing so, challenges me to be better. I only hope I can live up to her expectations and treat her as a queen and goddess. I also hope I can give her the help which will enable her to carry out the load that will be expected. I truly love her dearly and know that this love will grow. It's also hard to believe that my feelings for Fay have grown so strong in such a short time.

I know that Heavenly Father has brought us together and that He has a purpose for us to fulfill. I know that he has increased our capacity to love. I know that he will continue to bless us and give us the strength needed to unite our families as one. I only hope and pray that I might possess all of the qualities that my family and Fay seem to feel I have. I feel they overrate me, but I also feel the challenge to do better and to be the person I need to be to set the perfect example. I love Heavenly Father and feel that I am eternally indebted to Him for life itself and for all of my many special blessings.

Friday, March 27, 1981

Fay talked to Evan's parents and then later in the evening to his brother and wife. They both were receptive and supportive.

I visited on the phone briefly with Jonnie, Mom, all of my brothers and sisters locally, Presidents Woolf and Lindblom, Floyd Judd, Bob Potter, and Arlene Smith. They all seemed pleased and supportive (almost).

It was a long day, but everything seemed to work out perfectly. Obstacles are being removed daily. We are looking at a late April date for the wedding.

1970s—Edith & Paul Eagar

Saturday, March 28, 1981

Today was our stake family fun Olympics. It was held at Mesa Junior from 8 to noon. We had a fun time, and 24th Ward took first place and the trophy. I ran the 2-mile and mile run, not too fast, but I did complete them.

I attended the young women's broadcast from Salt Lake via cable with Laura, Fay, and Meilyn. It was a very good conference. Then Dale Garner talked to us for a while about the Ninth Drive property. We are now looking at April 17 as a wedding date. I am hopeful that we can get prepared for then. I will sure try anyway. Whatever we don't complete, we will have to work out after we are married.

Sunday, March 29, 1981

Today is fast Sunday because next Sunday is general conference. Fay and her family were over this morning for a home evening activity. Rick and Dale showed us the slides and talked about their missions. It always inspires me to see them and hear them talk about their two years while serving others. I am sure that the younger brothers and sisters are also impressed. The seed for missionary work must be planted very early in life.

Fay took her kids home and then we went to my folks' home to visit with them for a few minutes. Later in the day, we went to Grandma and Grandpa Dorathy's and visited them and Alan and Maryann. We were well received and felt inspired. Not only were we touched by the Spirit, but many others have been testified to also. It has been a very beautiful and strengthening week for me. I have felt the Spirit strongly and know that the decisions we have made to unite our families are the right ones, and that Heavenly Father had a part in it. It was necessary for me to have a strong witness. Otherwise, I'm afraid I would not have heard properly.

I have a deep love for Fay. I know it is not as strong as it will be years from now, however, it is very strong. I know we have had a big and busy week, but I wouldn't trade it. It has been one of the choice experiences of my life. Many obstacles which seemed insurmountable have just melted before us, and many hearts have been touched by the Spirit. There seems to be a strong feeling of excitement and support from everyone.

I truly hope I can be the kind of person Fay feels she is marrying. I want to be a good companion and show her the love, respect, kindness, and attention which she deserves. She is a choice spirit and has lived close to Heavenly Father. She has a beautiful personality and is beautiful in every way.

Monday, March 30, 1981

Today Tim and I ran 4 1/2 miles safely to Guadalupe and back, then I fixed breakfast and got the day going for everyone. School was a drag. I guess I just felt too tired to really get going. I did meet with a Mexican/white group to discuss communication and social problems. It didn't bring the desired outcome, but we did challenge them to give it some more thought.

Tonight we went to the Eagar's for a barbecue. Sheri and Pam and family were also there. We had a home evening. We sang a few songs, and each of us told a little bit about ourselves.

Thursday, April 2, 1981

Today Fay and I went to Phoenix and got our marriage license.

Friday April 3, 1981

This morning Alan, Tim, and I ran four miles. Dale was sick, and Steve got to bed too late. Today Fay called Evan's sister. She is overwhelmed with our marriage plans. Her own plans call for her going through the temple for her own endowment on the same day as our wedding. We have moved the wedding to 11 a.m. so we can go through the temple with her. Evan's mother is also having some problems accepting it. All of this naturally causes us anxieties and worries. We certainly don't want them to feel bad and not accept it, so we knelt in prayer and asked for direction and confirmation of the Spirit that we were truly doing the right thing. A feeling of peace came over me, and I have no questions that we are doing the right thing. I know that in time, they will accept us and overcome their feelings. In the meantime, we must continue as we have planned.

I went to dinner with Fay's family at the Top Shelf Mexican restaurant. We had a fun evening. Her mother and sister were here from Eagar, and her brothers and their wives were all there.

Saturday, April 4, 1981

I didn't run this morning. I attended four sessions of general conference via satellite at the stake center. The 1st was the welfare session. Then Laura and I attended the first general session. Then Fay, Laura, Larry, Becky and I attended the 2nd session. Then I attended the priesthood session at 7 p.m. with the boys.

When I picked Fay up to go to the afternoon conference session she has just received a call from her sister-in-law, Judy. Fay had expressed her own feelings and then said to Judy yesterday that she hoped she would pray about it and receive her own answer that it was the right thing to do. Well Judy called back to tell her that she had gotten an answer and that she now really feels good about it. As I have stated before, both Fay and I have felt strongly the Holy Ghost as He has answered our prayers and the prayers of our friends and loved ones. We have felt closer to this Spirit than I can ever remember before and feel that each concern and prayer has been answered.

After the second session, I went shopping with Bryan and Becky. We bought Bryan and Michael a ball glove. We also bought a few groceries. I'm sure tired this evening. I would like to catch a few winks, but feel I had better not. The time is getting away just too fast.

Sunday, April 5, 1981

Today was a busy day. We started at 7 a.m. The kids and I attended the first session of conference and the Spoken Word broadcast. It was a choice session. Becky had the chills, however, and has not felt good all day. Laura has been sick also.

At noon the Eagars came over and we went to Grandpa Wheeler's for dinner. All of my family was there to meet Fay and her family. Bill, Ben, John, Karen, Diane and their families were there. We had a super meal and a choice visit. It was the 1st time we have been together for several months. Then we took the kids to the Eagar's and Fay and I attended the 2nd session. The total conference this year was especially good and the spirit strong. There were several choice emphasis'. 1st and foremost was the importance of a strong family unit. Boy this really hit home hard. I realize its importance and hope I can really be a strong dad and develop the love, unity, and celestial life that we so need in our home. Another emphasis was on financial security and sound purchases. Moral standards were also stressed and emphasis was placed on strengthening our relationships with Jesus and Heavenly Father. I sure feel motivated and hope I can put this enthusiasm into my everyday living and that of my family.

After a full day with the family, I feel my responsibility strongly and keenly and, I feel inadequate to tackle it, but I know Heavenly Father will bless me with strength and the ability to succeed.
After the second session we all went to Wilkins' for ice cream and to get acquainted. Grandma Dorathy was there too.

Then we took the kids to my home for a couple of hours, and Fay and I went to visit Evan's parents. We had a good visit. I think we have now met most all of the families. Boy there sure have been lots to see and meet.

April 6, 1981

Well we got up and ran again this morning. Becky and Laura were both sick today. Fay wanted to have them over so she could take care of them and get to know them better. They both had fevers, and Becky was chilling part of the time.

Today is Michael's birthday. He is eight. We decided to have a picnic so we left at 4:00 to go to Usery Pass Park. We roasted weenies and had potato salad, chips, dip, punch, and cookies. Then we hiked up the mountain. After the hike we found a large parking lot and played a game of softball. We had just about enough to have two full teams. We played until dark and then went to Eagar's and played hide-and-go-seek for a little while. It was a fun evening.

April 9, 1981

Dale, Tim, and I ran five miles non-stop this morning. Then I fixed oatmeal mush for breakfast. The kids like it and pretty well cleaned up all I made.

Sheri was over today. She fixed supper and then helped get some dishes and things packed to be moved. When I came in from my room, I noticed Sheri was crying. I asked Sheri what was the matter. She said that as she was getting the dishes out, she thought about her mother. Then she said, "Dad, I really miss her!" Well, we both cried for a minute as we embraced and comforted each other. We really do miss her. She was such a sweetheart and such a part of each day of my life for 26 years.

I took the younger kids to Eagar's for an hour tonight. I painted two walls in the boys' bedroom. The other two still need to be taped and textured since the walls were remodeled. Fay's brother, Steve, is going to do the texturing.

I hope to be able to paint the front room and dining room tomorrow plus Saturday and Monday of next week. Then I hope to be able to get some new carpet down in the small downstairs bedroom. We will try to get most of the important things moved on Wednesday and Thursday. The time is fast approaching. I hope we will have most everything ready. But if we don't, we'll have time after we are married.

April 10, 1981

In the evening, I went to the Eagar's to paint. It went well, and I was able to paint the whole front room plus the entryway from the front.

After that, Fay and I walked two miles. She likes to walk and I do too, so hopefully it will become a regular part of our schedule.

I spent an hour with Fay. She is sure a sweet, special person. I love her very much and feel blessed that she feels the same about me. I know that I now need her and love her beyond my strongest imaginations. I truly felt that my life was complete, and that I would never fall in love again. I am truly grateful for such a special change and blessings that I have received.

April 11, 1981

Dale and I ran seven miles today. That's our longest in some time.

Then I went to the Eagar's to get the small downstairs bedroom ready for John to carpet. The wallpaper was torn on one wall, so Fay and I removed it completely, then I painted the bedroom.

Later in the day, John came by and laid the carpet. Then I began moving furniture. I got most of the front room moved. It really dressed up the front room to have the newly upholstered furniture over there. I also moved some of the other things. It was a big and tiring day.

Steve Coombs also came by and taped the large downstairs bedroom. He and Craig Coombs and Reuben Eagar have really been super to remodel, put in the wall, cupboard and doors etc. for us. They are all really super guys.

April 12, 1981

I have the early ward assignment this week, so I attended 7th Ward priesthood meeting at 8 a.m. Then I went to the 45th Ward sacrament meeting. After these meetings, I signed temple recommends at the stake center.

Then I went home and Larry gave us the home evening lesson. I held personal interviews with all of the kids. These are special moments for me and, I hope, for the kids. I try to get them to feel free to talk and ask questions. They often respond well, and I always feel good about the experience.

At 2:45, I picked Fay and her kids up and we attended 24th Ward as a family.

At 6 p.m., we all went to my house, and I fixed some muffins and crackers for the kids. Fay was fasting, so we didn't eat until later in the evening.

Then we went by to visit my folks and Joan's folks. We had nice visits, and they seemed pleased to see us. June impressed me and told me how happy they were for us and how much they were supportive of the marriage. She also loves Fay and told her the same thing.

Then we took the kids home, had family prayer, and then I took Fay and her family home while Sheri stayed with the kids at my house for a while. After the Eagar kids were down, Fay

About 1979—Ben & Lovel (Dick's parents)

fixed us a cheese omelet for supper. It was really good. I then spent the evening with her.

Fay is a beautiful person, and I am finding it hard to believe that the Lord has blessed me again with such a choice sweetheart, friend, and perfect spirit. She is so uplifting and seems to have such a choice spirit. She motivates me to set higher goals and to strive harder for perfection. She is also so close to the Spirit and we have felt closer to the Spirit than I have in a long time. We both feel the need to always feel this closeness and this strength, especially as we combine families and accept this added responsibility of 10 children. We love each other's children and feel the challenge to have their full acceptance of us. I can already feel the changes in them and the acceptance. I know we will be pulling together as a family very soon.

April 14, 1981

Today was another day of moving. Wow, it's getting old. I did run five miles with Dale this morning also. Sheri and Pam helped here at home with organizing, boxing, cleaning, etc. I moved the washer and most of the beds. We are going to sleep on the floor for the next few days. Sheri fixed spaghetti for everyone, so we came to our house for that.

I had a presidency meeting at 6:30. At 8:30, Fay and Michael interviewed with the bishop for their recommends (Fay for the temple and Michael for his baptism).

April 16, 1981

Got up at 5 a.m., and Dale and I ran 5 ½ miles. Then I went to the Eagar's to paint some doors so they would dry before evening. After the painting, I got cleaned up and then went back over to help get other things in order. We got the boys' room arranged. It turned out real well. It looks so good that the girls sound like they would like to trade the boys. The room is about 18 x 40 with a fireplace. We have a set of bunks plus two twin beds. Reuben was over this evening to finish up the trim and closets. All we lack now is the trim and second coat on the closets.

Evan's sister, Judy, came by this afternoon. She is 37 and is going through the temple for her own endowments tomorrow at 9 a.m., so we will go with her and then be married as soon as the session ends. Fay's parents and Shannon also came in from Eagar today, and we had a good visit with them.

April 17, 1981 (written April 24, 1981)

This was a busy and exciting day for us. I finished packing my things, got ready, and picked Fay up at 8 a.m. She was ready when I got there, as she always is. She has a strong desire to be places on time, which is super. She was dressed in a beautiful new pink dress. She really looked lovely. We went to the temple an hour before the 9 a.m. session so we could be instructed as needed.

Then we attended the 9 a.m. endowment session in the new endowment room. We went through this session so that we could be with Judy (Evan's sister) as she received her endowments today.

Our wedding was planned for 11 a.m., but it was 11:45 before it got started. This made us an hour late for the baptism of Michael, Fay's eight year old. The wedding went well and there were many relatives and friends present.

We held Michael's baptism at the ward building at 1:15 p.m. I baptized Mike, and his Grandpa Eagar confirmed him a member of the Church, assisted by about 20 brothers (uncles, grandparents etc.). Laura and Meilyn sang a duet, and then we went to the cultural hall for a birthday meal that the ward sisters prepared.

After visiting with the families and friends, we went home to change before we headed out. We spent the first evening at the Roadway Inn on Grand Avenue and Indian School Road. It was a nice motel, and we spent a very enjoyable evening there. We went to Bill Johnson's Big Apple Restaurant for an evening meal.

We got up in the morning and decided to go to Pinedale instead of waiting until Monday. The weather was good and we truly had a beautiful week there. We were the only ones around and it was so quiet and peaceful. We hiked every day. We made plans for our combined families. We just really had a beautiful opportunity to get to know each other better and to begin to make plans for the future. I can say that it was one of the most beautiful weeks of my life. Everything went so well, and we had a tremendous week together

Fay is truly a beautiful person. She is very spiritual and loves the Lord and wants to serve Him. She is a sweet mother and shows genuine concern for each of her children and their welfare. She strives for perfection in all she does. She is very mature in her actions and thoughts. She is active and loves to do things to keep herself in good shape physically. She loves the out-of-doors, including camping, hiking, and sports. Fay is very conscientious of others and strives to meet their needs, especially those of her companion. Each day I realize more fully what a blessing she is to me and how fortunate I am to be her husband. I count my blessings regularly as I find out new things about her. She has truly made me feel important and grateful for life itself, and I only hope that I may be able to enjoy at least another 50-plus years with her. I truly love her and am grateful to Heavenly Father for blessing me with such a special companion. I know I will grow stronger in the gospel and as a father with her by my side.

4. Merging Our Families

Dick's Perspective:

Our Home on Glade Avenue

After our marriage, our two families were combined, and my four youngest children (Larry, Laura, Becky, and Bryan) and I moved into Fay's family home at 1501 E. Glade Avenue in Mesa, Arizona, with her children (Meilyn, Kari, Mike, Josh, Tami, and Julie). At that time, Sheri and Pam were already married, and Dale and Rick did not live at home.

When Fay's first husband, Evan, was called to be the young men's president, he added a large family room with a fireplace on the south end of the house for firesides, etc. This was a real blessing to our larger family.

After my kids and I moved into the house and, with the help of Reuben Eagar (Evan's brother) and Craig Coombs (Fay's brother), we were able to make the original family room that was downstairs into a large bedroom. We added a partition to the open stairway and added a door. The room had a fireplace, but it was never used as such. We also enclosed an area on the east end so the girls would have a large closet. With the new bedroom, we had five bedrooms, three upstairs and two downstairs.

There was a 1/2 bath downstairs (it did not have a bathtub or shower). There were two full bathrooms upstairs. The main bathroom had a tub and shower. The second one had just a shower and was part of the master bedroom.

1501 E. Glade Ave. Mesa, AZ
Our first home together

1990s—Grandkids on the trampoline in the backyard of the house on Glade Ave.

There was a large deck outside the master bedroom. It was the roof of the toy room which had a low ceiling and was called the "kiddie corner." Later on, we put a roof over the deck, walled the room up half of the height, and screened the upper portion.

The main problem we had later was that there was no bathroom or bedroom on the main level. After the replacement of my knees in about 1986, the stairs were a challenge, but the house served us well for many years. We lived there together from 1981 to 2001.

Journal Entry from April 23–26, 1981

This has been a beautiful week. Fay gave me a new set of scriptures for our wedding day plus a beautiful letter expressing her feelings for me. Both gifts were super special. I really cherish a letter of love and appreciation much more than any gifts, probably with the exception of the scriptures. Both were so special and so uplifting. This has been her greatest gift to me. She has uplifted me, given me new hope and desire and direction, and made me feel so special and important. She, in turn, experiences the same feelings from me.

Putting two families together as one is not without problems. There are adjustments to make on everyone's part. The kids seem to make the adjustments rapidly. They can take discipline, get really upset at times, and yet get over the feelings soon and move forward. I am certainly amazed at the intelligence of the kids. They are able to pick out the best rules and schedules and activities of each family and suggest we accept the best of both families for our new family. Not too shabby. They want to stay up late, get up late, watch TV whenever, play whenever, work as little as possible, etc. All in all, they are really just good old typical kids who have great capacities to love and be loved. It's going to be fun being their dad and mom. We are sure enjoying the challenge. We are also ready to put them to bed when the time comes so we can enjoy an hour together in quiet. We usually are about ready by 9.

I try to run five miles each morning with Tim and Dale. Some weeks this works out better than others.

On Saturday we spent a large part of the day at the stake fair. I was in charge of the prizes and prize booth and getting the booth. It was a fun day for most of the family. Some of the kids were in

1982—Back: Meilyn, Larry, Laura
Second row from back: Becky, Kari, Michael
Sitting: Tami, Dick, Fay, Josh
Children in front: Julie, Bryan

21

the talent parts of the program. Laura and Meilyn both had pillows in the cultural arts section. Laura and Meilyn worked in one of the booths, and most of the kids worked with me in the prize booth for a while. It was a fun but tiring day. I was glad to see it come to an end.

Transitions

The summer after we got married, I had the month of July off, so we went to the cabin. We had electricity, but we had to carry in all our water from the Forest Service, and we had about fifty milk cartons to do that job. At the cabin, we had no phones, no radio, and nothing to disturb us. We just spent a full month with the two families, and that helped them to begin to bond really well.

Rick and Debbi were soon engaged and married on December 11, 1981. Pam and Dale sold their home two blocks away and moved into my former home, and Rick and Dale (my sons) lived with them until Rick got married and until Dale bought a home of his own in East Mesa.

Sometime in late 1982, we had a family council and asked the kids how they would feel about adding another baby to the family that was "ours." The immediate response was a resounding, "No! We are already the biggest freaks in the ward."

We told them, "Well, it's too late. We are having a baby in April." The idea took some getting used to, but everyone was certainly happy when the baby finally came.

On April 22, 1983, Kristen was born into our new family. She made the family complete and added joy and happiness to all. She was blessed with a sweet smile, a lovely disposition, lots of intelligence, and the ability to act as a glue or bond to bring both families together as one. She is the little sister to all of our children. She was also born as an aunt, and has many nephews and nieces. She is extremely patient and understanding and has a great relationship with all the family.

1984—Kristen & Dick

22

About 1983—Back: Bryan, Becky, Meilyn, Kari, Larry, Laura, Michael, Josh
Front: Julie, Fay, Tami, Dick, Kristen

23

Fay's Perspective:

Like Dick said, merging our two families was not easy. I'd like to share a few of the many experiences we had as Dick and I transitioned to being married and the kids figured out how to navigate our new family.

Marriage Transitions

We got everything moved to one house. The older kids helped a lot and had the younger ones pretty much all settled when we got home from our honeymoon. That night, we all had prayer together, and

Dec. 11, 1981—In front of the house on Glade in Mesa
Back: Pam holding Mandy, Larry, Debbie, Rick, Kari, Sheri, Fay, Mike H., Dick, Dale, Laura, Meilyn
Middle:, Tami, Mike, Josh, Bryan, Becky
Front: Dale holding Nathan, Summer, Julie, Tara, Aaron

everybody went to bed. In the morning, my four year old, Tami, climbed up the stairs and woke me up. I said, "Hi, honey. How are you?"

She looked astonished and said, "Mommy, Mommy! Bwutho Weeloo (Brother Wheeler) is in you bed!"

I said, "It's okay, honey, he's your daddy now." That was the one of many adjustments we all made.

After our fifth or sixth week of marriage, Dick got up about 4:15 a.m. so he could get ready and go jogging. I heard the garage door close, and I assumed he had left. After a while, I heard a noise, looked at the clock, and saw that it was close to 5 a.m. I thought maybe one of the kids was up, so I got out of the bed and started down the stairs.

As I got near the bottom of the stairs, I could see that Dick was mopping my floor. I sat down on the step, and the tears started falling. I thought, "He must think I'm a horrible housekeeper, so he has to do my job." I was so embarrassed.

About that time, he turned around and saw me crying. He came over to me saying, "I'm sorry it took me so long to remember to mop the floor." We both stopped, and then he started laughing.

I asked, "You're supposed to mop the floor?"

He said, "Yes. That has been my job since I was big enough to hold a mop stick." I finally laughed, and he hugged me and said, "I am so sorry."

"Don't be sorry," I said, "I thought it was my job."

Later in the day, I told my friends who lived next to us about what happened. They told me how lucky I was, which I knew. Several days later, their husbands asked me to please not tell their wives any more of what Dick did for me in the house. They didn't want all that pressure.

Merging Families

One time we were having some particular problems with the kids meshing together and becoming a family. They were fighting and saying things like, "We had to give up our house. You didn't have to give up your house," and, "We had to give up our bedroom. You didn't have to give up your bedroom," and that kind of thing. Things were just getting worse and worse.

One night, Dick said, "I think I have something that will help." He got pictures of him and Joan, me and Evan, and him and me. Then he got pictures of him and Joan and their kids, me and Evan and our kids, and a picture of him and me and all our kids together.

He had all the kids sit down and look at the pictures. He pointed to the picture of him and Joan and asked, "Who is this?"

The Wheeler children said, "That's OUR mom and dad."

He pointed to the picture of him and Joan and their kids and asked, "Who is that?"

The Wheeler kids replied, "That's OUR family."

He pointed to me and Evan and asked, "Who is this?"

And the Eagar children said, "That's OUR mom and dad."

He pointed to the Eagar family and asked, "Who is this?"

They replied, "That's OUR family."

Then he put his finger on the picture of him and me and asked, "Who is this?"

It was kind of quiet for a little bit until finally somebody said, "That's our parents now. You are our parents now."

He pointed to the picture of him and me and all the kids and asked, "And who is this family?"

They replied, "That's our family now." He pointed to the Wheeler family and the Eagar family and said, "Your goal is to get back with the Wheeler family and the Eagar family, and you're not ever going to get back to those families unless you make this new family work."

What he said really resonated with the kids. It made an impression on me as well because I had not looked at it that way before. I don't even think he had thought about it like that until then, but it made a difference for all of us. We had to change and just love each other no matter what.

Motherhood Transitions

We had kids in elementary, junior high, and high school. It was kind of good for me because I could help each group as they got home, then be ready for the next group.

When they first walked in the door, I told them to grab an apple or an orange or whatever I put out for a snack. Then they needed to look at the chart and figure out what their chores were. When chores were done, then they needed to do homework. If that got done, they could play with friends on our street.

Shortly after that, I started putting together supper and Dick got home. Sometimes he came in and tucked a hand towel into his pants and asked, "How can I help?" Other days he opened the door and heard, "Mom needs a date!" That meant that I had not been the best mom that day. He then walked up the stairs and said, "I'd like to take you to the movies today if that's okay," or, "I'd like to go to the temple with you tonight. Will that work?" It always worked. Sure enough, when we got home I was nice again.

Merging our two families was not easy. Sometimes I thought, "What am I doing wrong? Why can't I get this right? Why can't I be a good mother to all these kids? I just don't have it in me."

After a few months, my mom took me aside and said, "Fay, you need to lighten up. You've got to see the humor in all of this that's going on around you, or you're not going to make it."

I asked her, "Well how do I do that?"

And she actually gave me some examples of things that I had done that would have gone better if I had just been a little more chill and not so serious. She said, "Laugh at yourself. Laugh at the situation. Laughter will get you through this." I really worked at it, and honestly, that advice really changed my life at that time.

Extended Family

One year we decided to have each extended family over to visit with us so that we could get to know them better. We had the Coombs (my family) one time, the Eagars (Evan's family) another time, the Wheelers (Dick's family) once, and then the Dorathy's (Joan's family).

When the Eagars came, my kids wanted to hear about their dad. Everyone started talking about Evan, and that went on for quite a while. Eventually, Dick started feeling really upset, and he went upstairs to the bedroom. I got up and followed him and asked, "What's the matter?"

He said, "They just keep talking about Evan. Do you know how that feels?"

I said, "Yes, I do. I get that every single Sunday when your kids come over and talk about Joan. The thing is, your kids need to hear about her, so after a while, I go find something else to do. This is the first time my kids have had a chance like this to talk and hear about their dad."

He asked, "You feel like this?"

I said, "I sure do."

And he said, "I'm sorry." Then he came back downstairs because he recognized that it was true; the kids needed to hear about Evan. I didn't spend a lot of time talking about Evan, so it was nice for them when they were around the Eagars. It all turned out fine.

Nov. 1982—Back: Bill, Dick, Benny, John, Doug
Front: Karen, Diane, Lovel, Lovel

A Hospital Scare

When we had been married almost a year, I was serving as the Primary chorister for stake conference. The Primary children were divided into two groups by age, and I taught one group after the other, beginning with the youngest ones. I started feeling a cramp in my right side. It wasn't too bad, and I figured I had stretched it while I was getting the kids to get dressed and do their hair so we could make it to church. I did okay teaching the Primary kids in the first half with a little pushing with my hand. During the second half, I had to bend forward a little to keep it from hurting too much. Before it was finished, I was bent clear over and another sister had to finish leading the music.

When we got home, Dick said I needed to go to the ER to find out what was happening. They couldn't find anything significant except that my white blood cell count was just barely up. They decided to do a surgical procedure to see what was happening. I asked, "What happens if nothing is found?"

The doctor answered, "We will take out your appendix either way."

They went in and found adhesions around my intestines that were almost closing them down. They also said that my appendix was pulling up behind my intestines, kind of hiding. They took care of the adhesions, removed my appendix, and said everything was okay.

Our kids were pretty upset from the time we left for the hospital until Dick came back and told them that I was okay. However, they didn't quite agree with him that everything was okay. They had all sent a parent into a hospital before, and they didn't come home again. We recognized that something had to be done.

I called several times every day and spoke with every child, but it wasn't enough. Dick decided they needed to be able to see me. They came to the parking lot at the hospital, and we got someone to open the window so I could be seen standing and be able to talk to them and answer their questions. That made them believers that I was coming home, and it worked out okay.

About 1986—Wheeler/Eagar Family
Standing in far back: Meilyn Eagar, Dale Wheeler, Mike Hale, Rick Wheeler, Justin Wheeler, Debbie Wheeler
Standing: Aaron Hale, Joshua Eagar, Michael Eagar, Larry Wheeler, Dale Garner, Tracy Wheeler, Kari Eagar, Laura Wheeler, Tami Eagar, Bryan Wheeler, Becky Wheeler
Sitting: Julie Eagar, Tara Garner, Pam Garner, Benson Garner (lap), Fay Eagar Wheeler, Sarah Wheeler (on lap), Spring Hale (on lap), Dick Wheeler, Trevor Wheeler (on lap), Sheri Hale, Winter Hale (on lap), Summer Hale
Front: Nathan Garner, Mandi Garner, Kristen Wheeler, Tanner Garner, Autumn Hale

Working Together

We had home evening every week. Sometimes we had it on Sunday when school things interfered on Monday. We started with just Dick and me doing the lessons, but the kids thought it was too long and never really fun. So we talked it over and decided we would let them all have a turn. They would give the lesson, choose the activity, and decide what was for dessert. They really liked that idea.

We started with Mom and Dad, and then the kids got their turn from oldest to youngest. The lessons got a lot shorter, and Dick added to them each week to make the lessons as long as when he taught. Finally, we had to talk. I said, "I think if they get the point of the lesson pretty well, we should let them be done, move on to the activity, and bring the dessert in." He agreed that would be a really good idea too. As we implemented that strategy, we had a lot of activity time and fun, and we were together longer for family home evening than we had ever been. Plus the lessons were done better and better.

Elder Oaks was the visiting authority for stake conference soon after we were married. We had a dinner with the stake presidency and their wives at the home of President Woolf. Those in charge of seating arrangements thought it would be funny to put me right by Elder Oaks. During dinner, he asked if he could ask me a few questions about my husband. He asked, "Do you have home evenings?"

I told him, "Every week."

He said, "Let me ask you another thing. Is your husband one of those "tidbit" guys or is he the "fullness of the gospel?" I told him Dick was definitely the fullness of the gospel. He told me that his family had home evening every Monday night. They started with a prayer and a "tidbit," then had refreshments and went to the family room for Monday night football. It was a fun evening!

1985—Julie & Tami during FHE

2013

5. Fifteen Children

Introduction Written by Dick:

When Joan and I had our first daughter, Sheri, we loved her with all our hearts. When we anticipated the birth of our second child, we wondered if we would have to love Sheri less in order to love Pam. Guess what? Our capacity to love increased, and we didn't have to love one any less in order to love the other completely. We found we had an abundance of love for both. This principle has continued throughout my life with the births of our other children. I love each of them abundantly.

This principle of love has also applied in my married life. I loved my wife, Joan, with all my heart. We had a great life together and certainly had no thoughts of that being terminated after her surgery.

When I married again, I wasn't sure I could love another person. Guess what? I was wrong. Fay and I love one another and enjoy each other. I often pray for more years together.

When Fay and I married, I gained six children, and that same feeling of love for each of them

Richard "Dick" Wallace Wheeler: Dec. 7, 1935
Betty Joan "Joan" Holt: Aug. 17, 1936–Nov. 9, 1980
Married: Sep. 4, 1954

Sherilyn "Sheri" Hale: Aug. 28, 1955–Sep. 30, 2020
Pamela "Pam" Gale Garner: Oct. 15, 1956
Richard "Ricky/Rick" Wayne: Nov. 26, 1957
Dale Brent: Sep. 4, 1959
Lawrence "Larry" Todd: Aug. 17, 1965
Laura Lee Gregory: Oct. 5, 1968
Rebecca "Becky" Amy Cox: Jul. 10, 1971
Bryan "Buckwheat" David: May 2, 1974

Fay Ellen Coombs: Mar. 14, 1949
Evan H Eagar: Sep. 17, 1949–Oct. 7, 1980
Married: Jun. 14, 1968

Meilyn Eagar Bushman: Oct. 8, 1968
Kari Eagar Earlywine: Nov. 24, 1970
Michael "Mike" Evan: Apr. 6, 1973
Joshua "Josh" Coombs: Feb. 16, 1975
Tami Eagar McCoy: Sep. 27, 1976
Julie Eagar Spahr: Jul. 7, 1978

Richard "Dick" Wallace Wheeler: Dec. 7, 1935
Fay Ellen Coombs: Mar. 14, 1949
Married: Apr. 17, 1981

Kristen: Apr. 22, 1983

continued. To take on six children that aren't your flesh and blood was a challenge, and unless you've been through it, you won't realize how challenging it was. It was never quite like, "You're my dad." They had a hard time accepting the fact that I loved them like they were my own. That feeling was not easy to project to them. I worried about them and loved them as much as I did my own, and some of them did not realize that. I know some of them are realizing it now, and I hope they all will someday.

Some of the kids like to say, "I'm Dad's favorite son (or daughter)." The truth is that I have no favorites. I love them all equally. I don't always love everything they do, but I still love them. After experiencing this love, I can better understand Heavenly Father's position with each of His children. He loves each of us, knows us, and wants us to return and live with Him forever. I'm sure that at times He's disappointed in our decisions, but He still loves us unconditionally.

Love is a great gift and needs to be handled with care, kindness, consideration, and affection. I want to be sure my children understand this.

Here are some character sketches on each of our wonderful children that Fay and I have put together with much love. The comments are from both of us, unless indicated.

About 1988—Wheeler/Eagar Family
Back: Mike, Dale, Josh, Rick
Middle: Larry, Sheri, Pam, Becky, Meilyn, Bryan
Front: Kristen, Tami, Laura, Fay, Dick, Kari, Julie

By Dick and Fay:

Sherilyn "Sheri" Wheeler Hale

Sheri was the first child and always tried to do what was right. She led out and set an example of obedience, cooperation, and support for everyone to follow. She always loved all her siblings, including the new ones that came into the family. She was very family-oriented. She was a dependable, loving, dedicated, committed, and an appreciative person.

When it was time for Sheri to go to third grade, Holmes School had opened up and the boundaries changed, so she attended school there. Being a new school, the principal didn't know better and just opened up the election for student body leaders to any of the grades. Whoever was running and got the most votes became student body president. Sheri was in third grade, and she had a really cute skit. She got the most votes and was student body president as a fourth grader. She was conscientious and sharp, and she did a good job. After that, the school changed the rules and only sixth graders could be president.

Sheri excelled in school, worked at the bank, and earned enough money to pay for college. She went to BYU for one year and then ASU. She married Mike Hale. She raised seven children—one boy and six girls.

Sheri liked to sew, like her mother. She and Pam bought nice sewing machines at the same time and learned to do a lot of sewing. Her mom always made matching outfits for all of the kids, but Sheri found that she could go to JC Penney's outlet and get cute matching clothes on clearance for cheaper than the cost to sew them.

Sheri was always frugal. For example, even though Mike was a CPA, she was the one who did their income taxes for a lot of years, and she took care of all of the bills and finances for the family. Sheri's kids learned to be very frugal from the way she lived and taught them to spend their money responsibly.

I (Fay) felt like Sheri accepted me from the beginning and always seemed to know when I was having a hard day. On many of those hard days, she gave me a call, which always lifted my spirits. She just oozed with praise and told me something that was wonderful about me. She would say how grateful she was that I was the mother of the family now. She was so supportive and lifted me up and helped me feel like I could keep going. Sheri was really good at knowing when someone needed a phone call.

Sheri was always conscientious of doing her own part to help others. She gave lots of service to those in need. She would never have been the one to say, "Sorry, I can't possibly participate in that service project."

When Sheri was Relief Society President, she knew if an assignment was given, it needed to be filled. When she was handed a stake welfare assignment to line up volunteers for the cannery, Bishop's storehouse, etc., she wrote down all of the assignments that her ward had for that year on a piece of paper, then she handed copies out to the sisters and said, "Look at all of these projects and times. It should be possible for everyone to serve sometime this year, so plan ahead according to your schedule." As a result, she was prepared ahead of time instead of waiting until the week before the assignment.

Sheri attended the temple weekly. Even if Mike wasn't able to go with her, she still went with a friend. She even had a room in her house that she decorated nicely and had white couches so that it would feel special like the temple. The kids knew that wasn't the place to roughhouse. Sheri also had a real desire to keep her home organized and looking nice.

When we got together once a month with all of our children, Sheri regularly came early with her kids. She and the kids helped make sure everything was set up and ready.

Sheri would always help her kids, even traveling to help kids who lived out of town. If a baby was being born, or if a family was going on a trip and needed extra help, she would go and stay a week or two or whatever they needed. After Mike died and she sold her house, all of her kids wanted to take turns having her live with them because they loved having her in their homes. I'm sure she helped them and gave them advice about how they could help their kids more.

Sheri helped Summer's kids with tutoring when they were struggling with dyslexia. Sheri researched on her own what she needed to do to help them overcome that, and she spent hours helping those grandkids.

When Sheri got cancer, it seemed like the doctors did everything that they could and gave her as much time as they could. They didn't find out that she had it early enough to save her, and that wasn't something that we had control over. Before Sheri died, we used to go to her house every other

Hale Family 2010—Back: Ian Barnett, Kyle Freebairn, Cory Theobald, Mike Hale, Aaron Hale, Nate Schlink, Jason Crawford
2nd from back: Season Barnett, Winter holding Owen Freebairn, Spring holding Freddy Theobald, Sheri Hale, Becky holding Haleigh Hale, Summer holding Faith and Liberty Schlink, Autumn holding Leah Crawford
Middle: Rainy & Brandon Christensen (bride and groom)
Kids in front: Ethan Schlink with George Theobald in front of him, Aceson Hale, Mary Freebairn, Maggie Theobald, AJ Hale, Abby Theobald, Hannah Hale, Aro Hale, Belle Schlink, Nathan Schlink

day to visit her. There were always a lot of people there visiting. She appreciated everything that people did to serve her. She was very compassionate to the end. In fact, Summer said that, even bedridden, she asked Heavenly Father every morning who she should contact that day. Time after time, she had just the right conversation with the people who needed to hear from her.

One of Sheri's neighbors joined the Church shortly before Sheri died. The neighbor told Sheri that she and her husband weren't getting along, so Sheri counseled with her on how to make compromises that could make her marriage work. Sheri was never hesitant to suggest to people she loved that they make changes to improve their lives and bring them closer to God. It might have been offensive coming from someone else, but coming from Sheri, it was always well received because they were friends and family that she contacted regularly, and they knew she loved them.

It got to the point that Sheri couldn't communicate anymore. When people visited at that time, sometimes they would just sing. Laura stood by her bed and sang for her, and Sheri smiled and was so thrilled.

Sheri passed away in 2020. When she went, it was time; she had accomplished everything that she could.

Sheri with her grandkids in 2019—Back: Freddy Theobald, Belle Schlink, Ethan Schlink, Aceson Hale, Nathan Schlink holding Hyrum Christensen, George holding Henry Theobald, Aro Hale, Owen Freebairn
2nd from back: Mary Freebairn holding Annie Christensen, Leah Crawford, Maggie holding Eleanor Theobald, Abby Theobald, Sheri Hale holding Watson Barnett & Michael Theobald, Haleigh Hale, Liberty Schlink, Hannah holding Heavenly Hale
Front: Vaughn Crawford, Blake Freebairn, Sawyer Christensen, Brecken Barnett, Oliver Christensen, Carter Freebairn with London Barnett in front of him, Harper Hale, Dylan Freebairn, Ander Hale, Alice Crawford, Hinzlee Hale, Faith Schlink, Hope Schlink

Pamela "Pam" Gale Wheeler Garner

Pam followed closely on her older sister's path. She was obedient as a child, did well in school, and was family-oriented. She always wanted a big family.

She saved up enough money to go to BYU for college. She attended for a year, then graduated from ASU.

Pam married Dale Garner. They are the parents of nine children—four boys and five girls.

Pam always made sure her kids were good students and turned in all of their assignments completed. She worked with them and helped them to achieve their goals. Six of her kids chose careers in the medical field.

Eight of Pam's children served missions. The ninth got a mission call as well, but pivoted when she found her eternal companion before her mission started.

Pam and Dale served a mission in the Dominican Republic. They also served a mission in the Fort Collins Colorado mission, while living with their daughter and her husband in Laramie, Wyoming. Pam and Dale work closely together doing their missionary work. They have made big sacrifices to serve multiple missions.

2024—Back: Jake Garner, Spencer Rowland, Clint Acedo, Ezra Acedo, Nick Hansen, Marshall Hansen, Tanner Garner, Brody Garner, Hunter Garner, Colter Stewart, Tommy Stewart
Second row from back: Benson Garner, Sarah Garner, Heidi Garner, Nate Garner, Mikah Garner, Catcher Boynton, Brittany Boynton, Tara Rowland, Aubrey Acedo, Mandi Acedo, Brookley Hansen, Shelly Garner, June Garner, Natalie Garner, Kourtney Stewart, Sawyer Stewart
Third row from back: Ellie Garner, Abby Garner, Maesyn Garner, Whitman Garner, Jayden Boynton, Noah Garner, Allie Garner, Henry Garner, Emery Stewart, Bridger Stewart
Front: Rockwell Boynton, Ben Garner, Quincy Garner, Harper Garner, Morgan Boynton, Scout Boynton, Lincoln Acedo, Dale Garner, Pam Garner, Bridgette Hansen, Graham Hansen, Addie Garner, Indy Garner, Brody Garner, Heber Stewart

Pam and Dale also love the temple and are very dedicated to temple work. They attend regularly wherever they are—at least once a week, sometimes more. They also babysit grandkids so that their kids can go to the temple more often. They are temple workers and are always happy to substitute for the other workers.

Pam is very thorough and conscientious. She's a hard worker and is always doing something big. She has so many talents! She loves to sew and goes all out. She has made all kinds of costumes for Halloween and the Nativity. She's good at helping with anything—including helping with costumes, schoolwork, decorating for weddings, or anything that her ward or family needs her to do. We're proud of Pam's church service and her generosity.

Pam is a wonderful gardener. She can make anything grow. Pam is a super good cook too! She can make anything taste great, and she's so quick. She also keeps a clean house and puts a lot of effort into decorating to make holidays more enjoyable.

Pam loves having her kids together, and they gather often. Every week, she and Dale go to one of their kids' homes for a family dinner. She is also an amazing grandmother.

Pam is supportive of our monthly home evening nights. She always makes extra food so there is enough for everyone.

Pam and Dale have been staying with us for a time so that she can help serve an aunt, meanwhile, she and Dale have done a great job building shelves and organizing here as well. They both say that they just love the work. They have so much energy for service. Having Pam and Dale living in our home has been such a blessing for us; not just because of their service, but because we love being around them and growing even closer to them.

Richard "Rick" Wayne Wheeler

Rick was born in California. He has been an obedient, faithful son, and has always followed his parents' teachings in keeping the commandments and living the gospel. He followed his sisters in many of their strong characteristics. He is quiet, very patient, helpful, and straightforward in his opinions. He is also responsible, appreciative, and gives thanks easily. He has a great love for his parents and his brothers and sisters. Likewise, we have a great love for him.

Rick is good at serving. He's a strong example and a strong follower. He is very devoted to the Church.

Rick is a hard worker. When he puts his mind to something, it gets done.

Rick served a faithful mission for the Church in Johannesburg, South Africa. He called it! He always told us he was going to go to Africa. He learned Afrikaans, but he mostly spoke English. On his mission, he gained a stronger testimony of the gospel. He also gained a great deal of confidence in himself and in his abilities.

Rick and his three siblings—the ones that were out of the house when we got married—were always so good to come over every Sunday to visit with us and let us be a part of their family. Eight months after we married on December 1, 1981, Rick got married to Debbie Cluff who is so sweet. We've had some really great times with them and their three boys.

Rick takes good care of his family and often brings them with him if he has an out-of-town job so that he can keep them close. He and Debbie worked a lot with Trevor, who has Down Syndrome, and helped him graduate high school. Rick also helped his other boys get their Eagle Scout Awards by working closely with them.

He currently works as a supervisor for Porter Brothers Construction. He's a building supervisor—the company turns whole jobs over to him. He builds difficult buildings, such as the San Carlos High School, elementary schools on the Indian reservation, a number of church buildings, as well as four and five-story hotels. He worked on the Mesa Temple during the remodel. He does it all well! I was really proud to hear someone say, "We know if Rick Wheeler is on the job, it will get done right!" He taught his son Justin to do the same, and Justin is now doing great and following in his dad's footsteps. Rick is loyal to both work and his family. Rick has let some family members work under him so that they could benefit from his contracting knowledge and skills and grow their own construction businesses.

We love having Rick and Debbie come over with all of their kids and grandkids and watching them all interact. Rick and Debbie are fun grandparents. They love to tease and play with the kids. When Rick noticed that I (Dick) could use a ramp, within a few days he had figured out the best plan and installed it for me.

Back: Ashley, Justin, Trevor, Rick, Debbie, Hadley, Sarah, Chase
Front: Brooklyn, Gunnar, Indy, Beau, Piper, Graham, Cooper

Dale Brent Wheeler

Dale Brent Wheeler, our fourth child, was mine (Dick) and Joan's anniversary baby born on our fifth anniversary. He was very close to his mother. He has a very sharp mind and is easy to be around. Dale is dependable, responsible, humble, resourceful, clever, and fun! He stays busy all the time. He's quick to jump up and help, whether that's pushing a broom or clearing a table. He always does his share. Once Dale did service helping a company that rounded up wild horses for troubled teens to take care of and train.

Dale served his mission in Portugal, returning only a short time before his mom went to the hospital and passed away. He attended at least two years of college at BYU.

Dale knew my (Fay's) husband, Evan Eagar, from Farnsworth Builders, so I knew Dale pretty well, too. He was very accepting of mine and Dick's marriage. In fact, he saw me in the cultural hall at his mother's funeral, leaned over to his brother Rick, and said, "Look back there. It's Sister Eagar. Can you see her? Wouldn't it be neat if Dad married her?" Shortly after we got married, Dale got sick and didn't have any place to stay or anyone to take care of him, so we asked him to come live with us for a while until we could get him well.

Dale was married in the temple to Tracy Singleton. They bought a home in Apache Junction and fixed it up. They have four children—two boys and two girls—and we're proud of them.

2023—Brent, Sidney, Ashleigh, Emmett, Zoey, Austin, Dale, Tracy, Sarah, Carter, Kenny, Ella, Laura

Dale and his good wife, Tracy, are active in the gospel, and Dale is a leader in the Church. He feels the Spirit strongly and is very spiritual. He has a strong testimony and the Lord blesses him. He's done a lot of family history work and has added a lot of pictures and stories and memories.

Dale has a good singing voice. His whole family is musical, and they share their talents.

Dale has always worked hard to provide for his family. He worked in the construction trade for several years. He worked for Farnsworth Construction Company, and he and a friend ran a sheetrock business. He is an entrepreneur and has started several businesses and ventures. Dale started working with a cruise line timeshare company and continues to work for them. He also occasionally drives for Uber or Lyft.

Lawrence "Larry" Todd Wheeler

Larry Todd called himself Larry "Toad," and it stuck. He was really close with his mom. He has a great brain, and did well in school. He was the oldest child in our combined home. Larry is loving, sensitive, and intellectual.

As a child and even into his teenage years, Larry had a lot of health problems. Quite often when he was in junior high, he had severe asthma and could not breathe properly at all. Frequently, we would pound on his back and stay up with him all night doing breathing treatments. He and I (Dick)

Larry, LaRisa, Bethany, Kiri, Jordan, Kyrene, Prezley (front), Kinzley, Michelle

had a series of tests for allergies. The doctor figured out what we were allergic to and developed a serum for each of us (I was allergic to bees and wasps). We had weekly injections, which were beneficial and gave us some relief.

Larry could do as much school work in four weeks as it took most kids to do in nine. In high school, he would come home during the fifth week of the quarter with failing grades in every class. Then he would get to work for the next four weeks and miraculously pull off straight A's in the end! Larry served a mission in the Tokyo North Mission in Japan. He didn't have any background in the language before he left. During his second week in the country, he gave a really intelligent answer in Japanese, shocking his companion with his fluency.

He married Michelle, and they became the parents of five children, one boy and four girls. They are divorced. Larry is loyal to his children and really loves them deeply.

Larry wanted to become an insurance agent. He hardly even had to study to be able to pass the insurance license exam with flying colors!

Larry is presently living in Cottonwood, Arizona. He performs custodial services for a charter school and other businesses there.

Laura Lee Wheeler Gregory

Laura was 12 years old when her mother died. It was hard for her to have another mother, but she and Fay both tried to help each other. Laura is sixth in both the Wheeler and the "Wheagar" (Wheeler + Eagar) family lineups. She is three days older than Meilyn, who is Fay's oldest, so we called them our twins—they were both 12 when Fay and I got married. Laura is responsible, dependable and generous. She likes to make meals to feed others and shares what she has.

Laura attended Holmes School. She always did her best in her studies and was a good student. We don't remember ever having to ask her to do her homework. She enjoyed school. She also loved running. Laura and Meilyn attended Taylor Junior High together.

Laura is very musical and sings beautifully. She and Meilyn were both in choir and occasionally sang together, which we loved! It sounded so good. I (Dick) called on them to sing in meetings at the last moment many times, and Laura was glad to make me happy. Laura also loved playing the violin.

Laura saved some money and went to BYU-Provo for a time. Then she went on a mission to Calgary, Canada, where she served for 19 months. Being cold is not her favorite thing! She even had to plug in her car during the winter to keep it from freezing up. Laura was a good missionary and sent us letters every week to inform us of what was going on. She sang "Via Dolorosa" at many conferences as a missionary and even sang it for her mission president's homecoming in Salt Lake City, Utah.

Following her mission, Laura married Bill Gregory. They are the parents of two girls and five boys.

Laura helped her husband, Bill, get his teaching degree, and he taught for a charter school. After their kids were all in school, Laura went back and got her Bachelor's degree.

Bill and Laura teamed up with Aaron and Becky Hale and started their own charter school business. The name of their school is Legacy Traditional, and the business has really grown. They started with a school in Maricopa and had a lot of struggles, but then were able to separate from the guy who was causing trouble. They then expanded to lots more places in the valley and in Nevada. Laura and Bill eventually sold their interest in the schools, and Aaron and Becky have continued to develop the business. The Legacy Traditional Schools have grown to 30 schools of 1,200 students per school. They have campuses in Arizona, Nevada, and Texas. Laura has continued her education and has a Master's Degree in Counseling.

Laura and Bill bought a ranch in Heber, Arizona, which they made into a family retreat for their seven kids, and built a big lodge there where our extended family can gather. They also built a big house across the street from the Gilbert Temple and have always generously offered it to others for their showers, receptions, luncheons, and other events.

Laura does a lot of counseling. I don't think she does it formally, but just out of kindness. She's been in Relief Society presidencies and has had a lot of opportunities to use her counseling skills. Laura co-founded a non-profit organization where she brings women to her ranch to do retreats. She works hard with kids with challenges.

One of Laura's favorite things to do is play games. She loves to play and likes to win. When you play with her, you either get one star, two stars, or a pity smiley face.

Laura's having problems with Parkinson's, but she's working hard to keep it from going into the later stage by staying active. Laura's family likes to travel, and they've done a lot of traveling together.

2023—Bill & Nancilee Gregory, Kelton, Kyler holding Wyatt, Ashley, Kazlan, Ellen, Kutler, Laura, Bill, Kianna, Kallen, Kaden, Dick & Fay Wheeler

Meilyn Eagar Bushman

Meilyn was the oldest of her first family and the youngest of our "twins." As we mentioned above, she is the same age as Laura. It was hard for her to go from being the oldest to being in the middle, but she learned that we still depended on her a lot. She was a typical oldest daughter and was always there for her brothers and sisters. Meilyn has always been an obedient daughter, a good student, and an accomplished pianist and organist. She is always available to help her neighbors, the people in the church, and especially her family. We still lean on her often.

Meilyn is very musical and has continued to develop her musical talents. She loves to sing and loves the piano. She accompanied the choir in junior high and high school.

One day she came home from school saying, "We heard a beautiful song in choir this morning. It's a different tune than I've ever heard." It was the song, "Oh What a Beautiful Morning," that I (Dick) always sang to wake the kids up every morning. Apparently, she had just learned that it could actually be enjoyable to listen to.

Meilyn had a great time at BYU even though she broke her arm there doing push ups. After her freshman year of college, she married Rob Bushman, who had been in her family home evening group. Rob and Meilyn are the parents of one daughter and two sons.

2024—Molly, Zac, Jon, Rob, Meilyn, Chelsea, Andrew, Gabe (shoulders)

After Rob's graduation from college, he became a teacher in Mesa. They have lived in the valley ever since. Meilyn tended kids often, including the children of her siblings.

Now, Meilyn teaches piano lessons, leads choirs, arranges musical numbers, and plays the piano and organ for everybody. She accompanies school choirs and often plays special numbers at wedding receptions and funerals, even for people she doesn't know. She uses her music mostly to serve, playing in sacrament meeting as the ward organist and accompanying in Primary. She's always happy to serve.

Whenever anyone in our family is performing or has some special event, Meilyn always attends and supports them. She is at every single one of her son Zac's performances, but also at any of her niece's and nephew's as well.

She once wrote in a card to me (Dick), "I've always admired you, ever since you healed my mother's heart." It made me feel good. She's loyal to her dad (Evan) and has been very supportive in keeping her siblings together.

While we served our missions, Meilyn and Rob moved into our home. The first time, they helped Shannon take care of my (Fay's) folks. The second time, it was just Grandpa and Shannon, but Grandpa had Alzheimer's by then.

Meilyn and Rob love dogs and have recently gotten into breeding puppies, which has been a blessing during Rob's transition to retirement. Meilyn has been grateful that it gave her more financial freedom to do extra service, like making big meals to feed the cast at Zac's performances.

Kari Eagar Earlywine

Kari was my (Fay's) second child. I was so happy that she would be a sister for Meilyn. I always wanted a sister, but I had to wait nine years to get one.

Kari was 10 when we got married and she gave us the opportunity to develop several new parenting skills as she grew to maturity. Kari is such a good person and is really smart. She is patient and tries to be a peacemaker and mitigate problems. She is very responsible and diligent with anything that needs to be done. She's innovative and ambitious. She's courageous, strong, and successful.

Kari was not turned on by school and struggled to get through high school, but she did okay when she applied herself. We didn't know until the afternoon of graduation if she was going to graduate! She just had a lot of energy and was very active and was involved with boys and cheerleading at the football games. She was on the Bunnies squad at Mesa High School. Then, when she took college online, she got all A's!

After high school, she married Kevin Earlywine, grew up fast, and became responsible quickly. Kari and Kevin had one boy and three girls. They are divorced now. Kari keeps her kids close and takes great care of them. She is loving and accepting and supportive of them, no matter what. She's trusting and allows her kids to make their own choices.

Kari has had to overcome a lot of trials, but her struggles have created good qualities of responsibility and the ability to stand up for herself. She has grown to be able to stand on her own two feet and recognize what needs to be done.

Back: Evan, Bryauna, Chandler, Paityn, Kari, Nick, Taylor (holding Loretta Fay), Ciara, Ryann, Tyler (holding Everleigh)
Front: James Dean, Kannon Dean, Bradleigh, Millie, Kyson

Kari has always had a testimony. She is sensitive and feels the Spirit. She recognizes that people are good and are trying their best.

Kari works for a group of doctors as a medical bill collector supervisor. She learned how to do billing and took over billing for a lot of offices. Now, she's starting up her own business. She helps us with all the things we don't understand about the Medicare system. She spent a lot of time helping us with some of our confusing, medical billing issues.

Kari adopted and is raising several of her grandchildren. Even though she's divorced, she shares a house and responsibilities with Kevin.

Rebecca "Becky" Amy Wheeler Cox

Becky was mine (Dick) and Joan's seventh child and was about nine when we got married. She used to spar with her new mother, and occasionally, they locked horns for a battle royale. But, we could usually get Becky to do what we needed her to do. Becky grew up close with Kari. Becky was one of the funniest kids. We love to hear her laugh. She is also someone you can count on to be on your side when you're right. She's very dedicated. When given an assignment, she'll jump on it right away and get it done. She is very respectful and supportive. She is cute and always has something sweet to say. Becky is very musical. She often sings at family events.

Becky married Bill Cox. They lived in Provo for a while as they both attended BYU-Provo. Then they moved to Arizona, and Bill started a successful flooring business. Becky helped run the business side of things, and they built it into a very successful company.

Becky and Bill have one boy and one girl. Becky is a devoted and supportive mother. She follows her kids wherever they want to go. She loves her husband, Bill, and their kids.

Becky worked nights at Southwest Airlines, then she went to work for Allegiant Airlines until she completed her college teaching degree. She, then, became a second grade teacher at Legacy School in the SanTan Valley. Becky's a great teacher and is very conscientious. She doesn't put up with a lot of monkey business. She tells it like it is and isn't afraid to speak her mind.

When Becky worked for the airlines for a number of years, it made it possible for us to travel all over. Becky and Bill love to travel and took us to Ireland. They took me (Fay) on an Alaskan Cruise. I (Dick) didn't go on that one, but did go to Alaska when I was helping move Josh back. One year, we got a SeaWorld pass with them and another year, we got a Disneyland pass. We had a lot of fun trips with them.

When Becky's kids had a dream of living on a ranch, she and Bill bought over 20 acres in Texas, got Longhorns, Deseret cattle, and a Shetland pony. I (Dick) tried to talk them into buying a Zonkie—a donkey crossed with a zebra—but it didn't happen. They also got a lot of horses and took horseback riding lessons and all learned horsemanship. They had chickens, geese and ducks, and worked really hard tending to all of the chores.

2023—Back: Josh holding Barrett, Bailey, Becky, Bill, Ashley
Front: Brantley, Jaxon

Michael "Mike" Evan Eagar

Mike is my (Fay's) oldest son and was a new toy for his sisters when he was born. They loved him and always wanted to hold him, and he smiled and rubbed their faces. He was sweet and very much a daddy's boy. He loved it when Evan learned to draw house plans because he could do that at home and have more time with the kids. Mike was often under Evan's feet at the drawing board, driving his little cars up and down and around and on his dad and on the plans. I (Fay) would tell Mike he needed to leave his dad alone, but Mike said, "He likes me to be here!" Evan loved it too!

As Mike grew, he started eating from the table. He really loved vegetables, especially broccoli, cauliflower, and peas. His dad only ate green beans and corn. When Mike was eating the other veggies, his dad said, "Mike, yuck."

Mike answered, "Da, yum!"

Mike has a strong love for his mother. There were days when I (Fay) would go to his school to help, but I was exhausted and run-down and didn't feel like I was very presentable. Mike never acted embarrassed like some kids might have. He came running to me and announced to everyone that I was his mom and was just thrilled to have me come to his school! Mike was popular at school, especially with the girls.

Mike was baptized the day we got married. We had the wedding at the temple, then went to the church building for his baptism.

2024—Hayden Palmer, Posey Palmer, Ashton Palmer, Josh Smedley, Alexa Smedley, Ethan Lawlor, Cindy Lawlor Eagar, Mike Eagar, Cole Eagar, Jason Eagar, Dakota Roberts, Aubrey Roberts, Chase Lawlor

Mike earned his Eagle Scout award. I (Dick) was his Scoutmaster part of the time. When Josh was a brand new Scout and backpacking for the first time, we were at a Scout outing and were crossing the Aravaipa River. He fell in the river face first with his pack on his back and couldn't get up. Mike jumped in and rescued him, pulling Josh and his pack up before he drowned. That was commendable! Mike is a protector!

Mike served a mission in Taipei, Taiwan; learned to speak Mandarin; and learned to love the people he served. While he was out, his cousin Dustin Coombs, who was also on his mission, was killed in an accident. Mike had an option to come home, but he said, "No, I need to stay and finish mine and Dustin's missions." He also had success as a missionary after he came home, teaching a family and baptizing them.

Mike married Cindy Halls, and they have a daughter and two boys together. They divorced. Mike's new wife Cindy Lawlor had two girls and two boys when she married Mike. Mike loves his family, and they do a lot of things together. He's a great dad. He is a good caregiver of his kids and always makes sure their needs are met.

Mike is so good to help those that need help. He is very dependable, responsible, ambitious, hard-working, determined, and independent. He really tries to please people. Mike is busy. He has a lot to do, but he's not afraid to work, and when people come to him for help with repairs or whatever, he always makes himself available.

Mike's father, Evan, had perfect pitch, played the guitar, was a lead singer, and had his own Western band which performed often. Mike has also developed his voice, plays the guitar, and enjoys family songfests.

Mike started out working in the concrete business and did well, but then he decided he wanted to be an auto mechanic. He went to school for that and scored well. He was hired by a high-paying company and received even better training from them. He was fast and did the jobs well. He was a good mechanic and the work paid per job, not by the amount of time it took to do the job. Because he was fast, he could make more money. The company ended up hiring too many mechanics though, so he didn't get enough work, and in the end, he decided to leave. He bought a bug spray business called Pest Experts; it has been successful and has branched out to include weed control. He services about one-half of all the Legacy Schools and numerous clients as well.

Bryan "Buckwheat" David Wheeler

Bryan David was my (Dick) last boy, but when Fay's family joined with us, he went from being the baby to being a middle child in a big family. He turned seven shortly after we were married and ended up with four siblings younger than himself. It changed his role, and he had to learn to adjust to that. Uncle Marvin called him "Buckwheat," and it kinda stuck as his nickname. Bryan had the cutest smile and was always happy.

Bryan was always ambitious and intelligent. We never had to prompt him to do his school work. He did well in school. Bryan earned his Eagle in Scouting. He had an aura about him that people were impressed with. For instance, when we had a fundraiser for Scouts, we sold flag subscriptions. The people subscribed at almost every door Bryan knocked on. All the kids begged him to go door-to-door and sell for them when they had to do fundraisers for school so they could get prizes. He was happy to do it—for a small cut. He was so good at selling anything because of that smile and those twinkling eyes.

Bryan went to Japan on a mission and did well there. Sendai, Japan, is very far north, and we had a really hard time finding clothes here that were warm enough to send with him. We looked everywhere to find boots (it was summertime when he left). One man told us he could get him the kind of boots he needed. When Bryan got to Japan, his mission president said, "We need seven or eight more pairs of boots just like this!" So we were able to help them get more pairs.

Bryan and Christina were sealed in the Gilbert Temple. Together, they have nine children. Bryan is a good dad. He's loving and does everything that he can to keep his family together.

When Bryan was first married, he worked for AT&T. While he was working for them, they paid for his schooling at ASU, so he got his bachelor's and master's degrees. I (Dick) was really proud of him for going so far in college and doing it without any debt. The master's degree was in computers, and that's how he got his current job with FedEx in the computer field. He is an asset to them. Now, Bryan does a lot of working from home. He's very dedicated to his job and has continued to get promoted and do well. He and his wife have started a business raising Goldendoodles. They usually get a litter of ten, and they get $3,500 per dog! I think they've earned enough now to put a downpayment on a home.

Bryan is appreciative. For example, when he goes up to visit Laura's ranch, he pitches in to help and is very grateful.

Bryan likes to sing. He sings in the Millennial Choir. He took his daughters with him, and they learned to love to sing as well.

Slade, Austin, Amelia, Kinley, Kassidy, Bryan, Christina, Lorelei, Blake, Brynn, Baily

Joshua "Josh" Coombs Eagar

Josh was Fay's second son. We (Fay and Evan) were so happy that Mike would have a little brother. Josh never ate baby food. We tried pretty hard to get him to eat his food. But, no, he insisted on eating what was on the table for the rest of us. So, we put the food in the blender and let him eat it, but we could hardly stand to watch him. He continued eating until everything had been cleared off the table.

Josh's nickname became "Grumpy" because he thought it was a fun name. Then he saw the movie, Snow White and the Seven Dwarfs. He said, very loudly with eyes full of madness, "I is not gwumpy!" He decided he wanted to be friends with the other kids, and he worked at it by being "not gwumpy."

Josh was very smart. He was a good student, but hated to do his homework because he thought it was a waste of time. He always aced his tests, but the math teacher would say, "I need to see your work to prove that you know how to do it." Josh thought his grade should be proof enough, but she wrote a hard problem on the board and wanted him to show that he could do it. He still wouldn't show his work on the board, but he was able to do it in his head. She was shocked that he knew the answer.

Josh enjoyed singing in the school choir. He has a beautiful voice!

When Josh was in Scouts, on his first hike down Aravaipa Canyon, his older brother Mike saved his life. The group had to cross a river, and he went down into the water, pack and all. Truth is, the water was only about 18 inches deep, so it wasn't like he was going to drown, but he was exhausted and under the weight of the bulky pack, and he thought he was going to die. His brother lifted him out and was always credited for saving Josh's life.

In high school, Josh dated Kristie Polke from Mesa High. Most of her friends were LDS, but she wasn't a member of the Church. She always appreciated the commandments like the Word of Wisdom and kept learning about the Church. She tried to take the missionary lessons before she and Josh got married, but it was too much pressure. They were married by the bishop and had a nice reception. After that, Kristie asked the missionaries to teach her.

Not very long later, Kristie called me (Fay) and said, "Mom, could you help me with something on Friday evening?"

I said, "Sure, what do you need?"

Kristie said, "Would you give the Holy Ghost talk at my baptism?"

I said, "'WHAT!?!?" We had no idea that Kristie was even taking the lessons again. She didn't want anyone to know because she wanted to make sure that she was just doing it for herself because she truly believed it was right. She's been such an amazing member ever since. She is a wonderful person.

Josh and Kristie have two girls and one boy.

Josh worked for Alaska Airlines when they were living in Anchorage, Alaska, near Kristie's folks. After returning to the valley, Josh worked for a cement contractor and later took employment with a vending company—Accent Food Source. He's been with them for a long time now and has worked his way up in the company. He is now number two at the Arizona facility.

Every time I (Dick) need a new shirt, I instruct Fay to get one of Josh's shirts. I now own six of them. They're my favorites!

Josh served in the temple baptistry. He is presently working with the young men in the Primary, doing activity days. They come over to our house a few times a month for that.

Josh likes being outdoors. He's a hunter and loves hunting both with archery and a rifle. He likes fishing as well, but he likes hunting best. He loves to go four-wheeling, including mudding in one of his Jeeps. He's a Jeep man. He also likes paddle boarding.

Josh is one proud grandpa! He will stop by the kids' apartment on his way home from work just to hold and play with his granddaughter for 45 minutes. When they come over here, Nova is mostly on his shoulders. He loves being a grandpa.

Josh is very very responsible and dependable. We've traveled with him, and he usually makes all of the arrangements (airfare/rental car/hotel) and takes care of me (Dick) with my handicap needs and my heart condition. Once we get to where we're going, he's always right where I need him, helping me.

Back: Jacie, Kristie
Front: Kylie, Josh, Jacob

Josh and Kristie moved into the mother-in-law apartment connected to our house. He does a great job taking care of the lawn and irrigation on our property, and anything else we need.

Josh is very loving to his mother, always checking on her and making sure she has whatever she needs. He's always doing whatever he can for her.

Tami Eagar McCoy

Tami's birthday was at the end of September, but because she was tested and got 100% on everything they threw at her, she got to start school early. She was tall and fit in with the girls in that grade. She was such a good student, but didn't like to be in the spotlight. She was very reserved. We always had to tell the teacher that Tami would be glad to lead the pledge, but not to say to the class, "Tami's going to lead us." It was best to just let her stand up and do it. Tami is amazing.

Tami was young when we got married and very reserved in her relationship with me (Dick). I admit, I am a pretty scary guy. I interviewed the kids every month, and she'd always end up crying. She just could not handle it. She became more comfortable with me over the years.

Shortly after high school, Tami was working at Water and Ice. She was introduced to Devin McCoy by her friend, Kelly, who also worked there. Devin and Tami were together from then on. Tami started working at 3 Day Blinds. She learned really quickly there and was good with the customers. She got to know Devin's mom really well because they worked together.

Tami and Devin were married in November 1998, and a year later, they were sealed in the Mesa Temple. They now have three children—two girls and one boy. Tami is very much family-oriented. She's a good mother and focuses on her kids.

After Tami left 3 Day Blinds, she started tending kids. She's really good with children. She's patient and they really like her. She's done a super job of babysitting and takes care of young children during the week.

Tami and Devin are very active in their ward. At one time, Tami was called to be the Primary pianist in their ward. She had taken piano lessons for years, but she wasn't very confident in her ability to fulfill the assignment. She felt strongly that she should accept the calling, however, and made sure to be set apart right away, desiring for the Lord to bless her efforts. Tami practiced and worked really hard and gained a lot of confidence.

Tami has taken up cooking and baking and is always willing to make good food for church and family events. She bakes lots of bread, cookies, and pastries. She's gotten so good at what she does that people now often hire her to make food for private events as well. She makes a lot of sugar cookies that are decorated so special, and they are often ordered for receptions. She also makes sugar cookie kits for Christmas. Her daughter Ryleigh also takes after her. They make cinnamon rolls and bread and anything you want,

2023—Ryleigh, Tami, Meghan, Devin, Liam

including dehydrated candy and all other goodies. Everything she makes tastes great!

Tami is not afraid to try anything. For example, when Megan was born, she wanted to make her some clothes, so we found a sewing machine that was like her mom's and she figured it out. She sewed Megan's clothes for a long time after that. Tami is a good seamstress. Tami always carries her load and takes her responsibilities seriously. She has changed from being shy to being stable, mature, and outgoing.

Tami's family enjoys traveling, camping, and often visits family in Idaho and Utah. They also enjoy Disneyland, the beach, and cruises.

Tami and her family visit us often. Their visits are very much appreciated and looked forward to.

Julie Eagar Spahr

Julie's dad died soon after she turned two years old. She was really close to him and loved to sit on his lap. Julie was still two when we got married. She was excited to have a dad again. She fit in with the family as the little sister. Everybody loved her and she liked them.

Julie is our only redhead. My (Fay's) mom and dad, Grandma and Grandpa Coombs, were so happy to have a redhead.

I (Dick) remember once when Fay and I were first married, Julie was sitting on my lap during church. I began singing along with one of the hymns. She listened for a few minutes, but then she turned around and put her cupped hand over my mouth and let me know that I didn't sing very well. We all just laughed!

Julie loved ice cream like her dad. She could never sneak it because it would get all over her—all around her mouth and even up on her nose. It took a long time for her to grow out of that, and we loved it!

Julie was a great student and a real helper. She is a good friend to everyone. In elementary school, she befriended a handicapped boy who needed a friend, and she stayed in the cafeteria with him through her entire lunch recess. She would play games or just talk to him. She never told us about it, and we only found out at the end of the year when the school contacted us because she was being honored for being such an exceptional citizen. When we asked her why she did it, she said, "Well, he's nice."

Julie had her own unique system of organization. For example, she called me (Fay) one day and asked me to find a certain piece of clothing for her. I said, "None of your dirty clothes are in the laundry room."

Julie said, "I know, Mom, but what I need is in the second pile of clothes in my room, third thing down." I went downstairs, found the pile, counted "one, two, three," and there the item was! I took it out and ironed it for Julie so she could go on a date that night. Julie did indeed have her own "system," because she always knew right where to find things!

Julie has a knack for doing hair—styling and color. On the last day of high school, she met with her counselor who told her she had a scholarship available for beauty school and asked if she might be interested. Julie accepted it and excelled in cosmetology school.

Julie worked her way into a high-end hair stylist position and has been very successful. She was employed by Rolf, who was a hair stylist in the Phoenix Valley who catered to the rich and famous. In

2024—Gavin, Gunner, Grady, Julie, Griffin, Gage

fact, they would go up every year to Flagstaff and do the hair of the Arizona Cardinals baseball players for free, who would then become clients. Julie became one of the top stylists at Rolf's Salon. After some jealousy, she was fired, so she went to another salon where she quickly became their head stylist with the highest pay. Julie and some of her co-workers decided to go out on their own and started a successful business. They have a salon on Higley Road in Gilbert and are doing well.

Julie makes twice as much money as I (Dick) made when I retired—it's unreal! I cannot believe that people will pay $50 or $60 or more just for a haircut. I'm used to giving five bucks to a barber to cut my hair. Julie had one client who spent $1,400 between getting her hair done, buying some products, and leaving a tip.

Julie loves to sing and has a beautiful voice. She took to the piano at a fairly young age and is a very accomplished pianist. When she moved out on her own, one of the first things she bought was a baby grand piano. She also played the cello and got one of those too.

Julie has five boys and provides well for them as a single parent. She has carried the responsibility of finances in her family.

Julie is dependable, responsible, hard-working, considerate, patient, kind, and loving. She worries about other people way more than herself. She wants everyone to be happy and goes out of her way to make it so. Julie serves her family and friends and is always willing to pitch in and do anything she's asked to do. She thinks of thoughtful things, like recently for Father's Day, she met us at Dairy Queen with all of her boys and bought us a treat. She seems to be on top of things like that. She's glad to cut our hair every six weeks, so we don't have to go to Great Clips.

Kristen Wheeler Reber

Kristen was number 15 in our family and the ninth girl. She is the "ours" in the "yours, mine, and ours" family. She was the mortar that bonded the two families together. She was "Aunt Kristen" to seven nieces and nephews when she was born, and that number has grown to 67 (we have 71 grandchildren, and four of them are Kristen's children).

When Kristen was born, the doctor handed me (Dick) the baby. I talked to her a lot and kind of bonded with her. She was born with a full head of black curly hair. I (Fay) actually asked the doctor if he was sure she was my baby. He said, "You're the only new mother in the whole hospital!" The kids were not happy when we first told them we were having another child, but once we got Kristen home, they all loved her. She is everyone's sister. Kristen loved her dad so much. When she heard his voice, she automatically stopped nursing, wiggled, and twisted her head around until she could see him. I (Fay) was pretty jealous!

Ty, Leo, Ari, Jack, Jay, Kristen

Kristen was a great reader. She started reading the scriptures with us in the morning when she was three and was good at reading and understanding. I (Dick) suggested that all of the kids read at least three books a day to her. She would always bring a stack of books to me. If I ever started to just tell her the story instead of reading it, she would stop me and say, "Dad, read!" She loved to read on our road trips while we traveled. We would often go from a Walmart in one town, to a Walmart in another town so we could get more books for her. She asked for a book by Neal A. Maxwell for one of her birthdays. He was very scholarly and it was about three inches thick, but she read and understood it. Reading was her love, and is still.

Kristen was studious in school and got A's in all her classes. We didn't have to pressure her to do her homework. She just took care of it. She also played the string bass in orchestra in elementary school.

Kristen had tons of really good friends in high school who were such silly and fun girls. Most of them were the oldest kids in their families, while Kristen was the baby. When we were worn out and didn't want to stay up waiting for her to come home late after outings with her friends, we would ask her to stay home instead of going out, and she didn't mind! Her friends would say, "Doesn't that make you so mad?"

She would just say, "No, my parents are old, and I don't mind staying home with them." She would just go find a good book and read. She never complained or fussed about it.

When Julie got married, that left Kristen as the only one home. Some of the older kids started to give her a bad time about being spoiled and getting privileges they didn't get. They would say things like, "Kristen gets all of the attention!" Her response was, "Why do you think I waited to be the last?"

We waited to go on our mission until Kristen finished her associate's degree in college. After she graduated from Chandler Gilbert Community College, she followed an impression to go on a mission and served at the same time we did. While we served in the Philippines, she served in San Antonio, Texas, where she got to use the Spanish she had learned in school.

After her mission, Kristen attended BYU–Provo and married Ty Reber, who was serving in the military. After they married, he joined the Army National Guard and is still in it. Kristen and Ty have three boys and one girl and live in Hanover, Maryland.

Kristen has a good voice and loves to sing. She also really loves movies. She loves dressing up. She often gets all dressed up for the movies. For Halloween, I (Fay) was always happy to make the kids exactly whatever costume they wanted. Kristen really had fun with that. She and Ty dressed up together as well.

Part 2: Raising Children Together

6. A Typical Day and Temple Service

By Dick:

A typical day for me usually began about 4:30 a.m. I got up, dressed, and then went jogging for several miles. I was usually home by 5:30. I had started the fire earlier, so by 5:30, the family room was pretty warm. At 5:30 each morning, I sang, "Oh What a Beautiful Morning," loud enough for everyone to hear—and on key (my key, that is). The family all came into the family room for scriptures, where we each took turns reading. Then I read one to three topics of Bruce R. McConkies's *Mormon Doctrine*. Then we had family prayer, the kids began getting ready for school, and Fay prepared breakfast.

We ate at about 6:30, and I tried to get to school by 7:30. The only change in the weekly schedule was on Wednesday morning. That was temple time for me. The temple had a 5:30 a.m. session each Wednesday morning. I left home about 4:30, picked up Floyd Judd, and we usually sat on the front row for the session. One problem that I have always had is that I don't like to see the same movie over and over, so I closed my eyes and listened attentively. The officiator, Brother Fish, a shop teacher at Powell Junior High, accused me of sleeping through the session. I asked him, "Does anyone have

2003—Back row standing: Kari, Larry, Pam, Dale, Sheri, Josh, Rick, Becky, Tami, Laura
Sitting: Dick, Fay
On the ground: Bryan, Michael, Julie, Kristen, Meilyn

to nudge me when it's time to stand or make clothing changes?" Then he realized that I was really being attentive.

Fay went to the temple each week with friends and performed initiatory work when all of the kids were in school. We felt that we needed to attend the temple weekly to really feel the Spirit of temple work.

We later served as temple workers twice weekly for twelve or more years, and served as trainers and coordinators. We even were able to serve as temple workers on Saturday mornings at the Fiji Temple. These have been cherished times. Floyd Judd was called to serve as a temple worker about seven years after he retired, and I remember him saying to me, "I have wasted seven years of my life."

Mesa Temple

Suva Fiji Temple

7. Raising Our Family in the Gospel

By Dick:

Making the transition to 15 kids was not easy and took many years, but Fay and I really tried to do everything that we were supposed to do as a family. After we got married, we developed a family crest to remind us about some of the most important things.

This crest speaks of missionary work, education, and returning with honor. It emphasizes Christ, family, the temple, service, prayer, scriptures, and the importance of letting your light shine. The flags represent some of the different countries where over 70 members of the family have served missions. The eagle represents the 36 Eagle Scouts we have in our family, and the young women's medallion represents our 42 girls who have received that award.

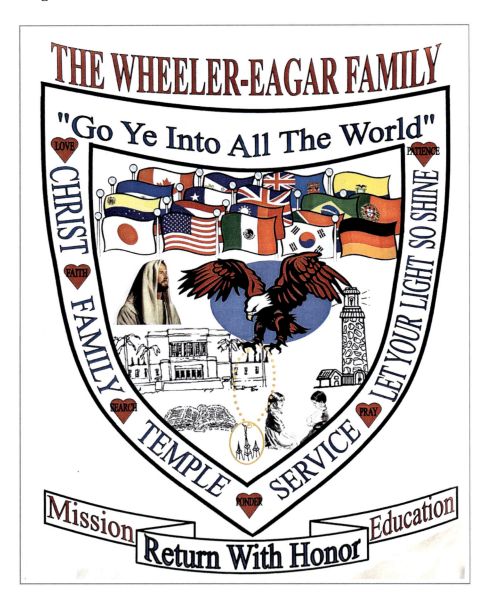

Some of the kids are not active and some don't belong to the Church anymore. That happens. We pray for them and love them and try to let them know we care for them. But as we look back on it, we can say that at least we tried to do all the things we thought we should do. All of these principles are important, and when a person starts neglecting any one of them, he begins to lose his testimony and begins to question the truthfulness of the gospel. We emphasized each of these principles regularly and tried to live them carefully.

About 1988—Chris Christensen, Dick, Josh, Fay

- We had family and personal prayer every day, communicating with Heavenly Father and thanking Him and requesting blessings from Him.

- We read the scriptures every morning except Wednesday. That was the day I went to the temple because it was open early, and the kids got to sleep in that day for 30 minutes.

- Fay and I went to the temple as often as possible.

- One of the things I thought of early was that the kids needed to know the doctrine of the Church. I got hold of Bruce R. McConkie's book *Mormon Doctrine*. It talks about the doctrine from A to Z and he has scripture references with each subject.

FHE Activity
Back: Mike, Bryan, Laura
Middle: Julie, Tami
Front: Kristen, Josh

Every morning before we started reading the *Book of Mormon*, I read one or two topics from Bruce R McConkie's book. I didn't read the whole thing, just the parts I had highlighted earlier. Recently, Josh told Fay that he really appreciated that we went through that with them.

- We went to church and sat together each week to take the sacrament and renew our covenants. We even went to church when we were traveling. When we were gone for a month, we'd find a church to attend. One time in all those years we couldn't find a church, so we pulled over and had a Sunday School lesson with just our family and Fay's parents.

- We had home evening every week.

- I held father's interviews every month on fast Sunday and kept a calendar of it so I knew what I had talked to each child about. I used the Especially For Youth pamphlet as a guide to the interview questions.

- We counseled together as a family.

- We fasted at least monthly.
- I gave blessings to family members.
- We taught our children to be morally clean.
- We paid tithes and offerings, avoided debt, and were honest in our dealings. The Lord's blessings always poured out abundantly.
- We accepted callings willingly and performed them to the best of our ability.
- We taught our children to listen to and follow the promptings of the Holy Ghost.
- We have home evening with the extended family on the first Monday of every month. Sometimes, we have to adjust the day or the time. Some people's schedules or their kids' schedules don't allow them to come, and that's okay. We've had as many as 120 people—especially at Christmastime when we do the nativity; we set up a stable and a manger outside. Some of the girls have sewn costumes for Mary and Joseph, the cow, the sheep, the angels, the wise men, and all the other prominent figures. It's a fun time together.
- We have dinner together every family night. We used to have a signup, but now everybody just brings their own food. It's simpler that way. Getting together also gives an opportunity for us to share some feelings, and for the kids to share feelings. We take turns. It's nice to hear the things that they loved from conference or how they feel about a particular subject. It gives us a little bit of a peek into how they're doing too. It's a good thing. Some Monday nights we don't get as many people. Even though sometimes not as many can come as we'd like, we have continued to have family dinner. . They still say, "Thanks, Dad. We appreciate having it."
- We served those around us. The kids and I helped people with their lawns and trees, paint jobs, and whatever else they needed help with. I tried to teach them the value of hard work and service.

2003—Wheeler family in front of the Mesa Temple

Additionally, we always tried to follow the church handbook for youth, titled *For the Strength of Youth*. Specifically, I'm referring to two areas at this time.

• Modesty in dress and grooming. Fay sewed many of the girls' dresses and accompanied them as they shopped for clothing. We felt very strongly that the body should be appropriately clothed. If, for instance, they were going to a swimming or boating activity, they put their suit on under their other clothes. That way they were not going to the event in their swimming suits. They were expected to go to these particular events appropriately clothed and or dressed.

• We followed the dating guidelines closely. That included no dating until age 16. We also did not allow dates to drive up to the curb in front of our house and honk their horn for their dates to come to the car to meet them. We insisted that their dates come to the door and knock. Then we were not only able to meet their date, but to ask about their event or activity and the approximate time they would be home. If there were reasons they would not get back on time, they were always expected to call home and explain the delay. If the activity or event did not meet our standards or church standards, we were not afraid or hesitant to say so. We became known as the "bad guys" by our kids' friends and the whole ward. If kids asked their parents if they could go to a particular activity, they always said to their kids, "If the Wheeler kids' parents let them go, then you can go also." Some parents, rather than be the bad guy, chose to put the blame on someone else.

8. Holiday and Birthday Traditions

By Fay:

As you can imagine, our family has a lot of traditions associated with holidays and other special occasions. We love to get together to have fun and celebrate whenever we can. Here are a few of my favorite memories.

Birthdays:

We had so many kids that we tried to make them feel extra-special on their birthday. We always had fun. They got to choose whatever they wanted for breakfast, and we didn't say no. They got to eat their breakfast on a red plate and drink their milk or juice from a wine glass. A lot of kids asked for biscuits and gravy. Sometimes they asked for waffles with strawberries and whipped cream. There were times when we had to make a second breakfast because the other kids didn't like it. For example, one year when Kristen was about three, she wanted red licorice and potato chips for breakfast. So every kid came downstairs for breakfast and found about five pieces of red licorice and a bag of potato chips on their plate. Their reaction was, "We don't want this for breakfast. Do we have to eat this?"

Kristen said, "I'll take it," and she got all of it. She had stacks of bags of chips and all of the licorice, and she was perfectly happy and thought it was the best birthday ever. We pulled out the griddle and made pancakes and eggs or something. Then everyone was happy.

They didn't have to do any work on that day at all, and the other kids were always willing to do their jobs. Everybody helped with the extra jobs that were left because they knew their turn would come.

A lot of times we were on vacation when it was someone's birthday. Julie and Becky were born in the summer, and we were always on vacation during July. They didn't have jobs like at home, but they got treated really special. We stopped at Walmart, and everybody got them a little gift or something for a dollar or so. It was fun. We really loved birthdays.

The kids didn't very often have birthday parties. I think we got to a point where we said they could have one with the family one year, and then the next year they could have one with their friends, but it didn't last very long. It was hard to have friend birthday parties, but we tried to do good parties with the family. Sometimes the older sisters and brothers that had already moved out came over and helped us celebrate in the evening. We really tried to make it fun.

Children's Day:

Once we were talking about Mother's Day and Father's Day, and the kids protested by saying, "We don't get a special day. Why isn't there a Children's Day?"

My response was, "Every day is kids' day," but we decided to have a special day for them that summer and continued that tradition for many years. We gave them some summer shorts and a t-shirt or a swim suit. The kids felt pretty special because none of their friends got to celebrate Children's Day. Later, we found out there really is a Children's Day on the calendar!

Valentine's Day:

The thing I remember about Valentine's Day is that we used to get a heart box of candies and a little card for each one of the kids. That was about it for Valentine's Day.

Easter:

When the kids were little, we got them really nice baskets for Easter. We also hid Easter eggs out in the yard, both when we lived on Glade and in our current house. As the kids got older, we decided they didn't really need all that candy and stuff, so they woke up to an outfit, like shorts and a top or something nice like that. They still got some candy, but it wasn't quite the same. They usually needed clothes anyway, so I think they enjoyed that.

Over the years, we've done a lot of celebrating and hunting for Easter eggs with grandkids in our current house, and we all love it.

Fourth of July:

We always had ice cream—usually homemade—for July 4th no matter what. We were usually traveling around the United States during the month of July, and we always found fireworks wherever we stopped on the fourth. One year, we were at Mount Rushmore. It was so fun! They even had a Navy band and a program. The last living man who worked on Mount Rushmore spoke a few words. I had wanted to go there my whole life, and I was in heaven. They had wonderful, wonderful fireworks that went on and on. I loved it!

We went up to Eagar a couple of times for the Fourth of July parade, rodeo, and fireworks. One time Devin brought some fireworks and lit them off on my parents' property, and the police came. My mother was so mad, but we all lived through it.

Thanksgiving:

Of course we always had lots of turkey, ham, tons of pie, and everything that goes with it for Thanksgiving. Now that the kids are married and have their own families, they go to their in-laws' house every other year or have Thanksgiving with their own kids and grandkids. We always tell them we'd love to have them at our house, and sometimes we have quite a crowd. One year we had 80 people here at the house! We always move the furniture around and set up lots of tables so we can eat inside. Sometimes the grandkids eat outside together so they can visit. It's so fun to see them all being nice to each other and having a good time, just like they did when they were young. I really enjoy it.

The Christmas Season:

One year we were up at Grandma and Grandpa Coombs's house in our motor home for Thanksgiving, so we figured we could cut real Christmas trees for ourselves and other people and put them on top of the motor home. We were told we could cut trees that were 10 feet or shorter, so we went out looking. We didn't have any real way to measure, so we cut some of the shorter trees and strapped them onto the motor home. When we got home and tried to put them in the house, we found that most of them were way taller than 10 feet. We were shocked! We hadn't cut big trees on purpose. They looked small among all the tall ones, but if anybody would have stopped us and measured, we would have been in so much trouble. The trees we cut wouldn't fit in the house, so we had to put them in the yard. We had trees everywhere that year!

Service has always been a very big part of Christmas for our family. We did different things over the years. We often picked a family and provided Christmas for them. We went to the cannery at the Bishop's Storehouse in Mesa and packaged beans. The kids loved it because everyone had a job they could do.

We loved caroling door-to-door every year. The kids each held a candle and sore a white shirt with a red bow. They were real candles at first, but that caused too many problems with the little ones, so we switched to using candles with a battery. We loved singing together, so caroling was a very fun tradition for us.

During the Christmas season, the kids looked at the ads every Sunday and checked things they liked, then picked some items from among their choices. They didn't know what they were getting, but we knew it would be something they liked. They were still surprised. With about three gifts apiece for 11 kids, we had a mountain of packages under the tree. People saw them and told the kids, "Oh

Dec. 1996—Christmas
Star: Brookley
Nativity: Josh, Trevor, Jonathan, Chelsea, Kyrene, Papa, Tami, Winter
Camel: Nathan
Sitting on right: Sheri, Brittany, Mandy

my gosh, you guys are so lucky." I loved wrapping the gifts and making beautiful bows for them. I wrapped and decorated packages for days. I loved seeing all the beautiful presents, and the bows made the kids as happy as what was inside. One year I just used black and white newspaper so I could decorate with any color ribbon I chose. It was fun for me. I enjoyed it.

Christmas Eve:

We got everyone matching pajamas for a few years and let the kids open them on Christmas Eve. At some point, we realized they didn't like them and didn't really want pajamas, so we stopped doing that. We had too many kids to just throw money away for that.

On the other hand, reenacting the Nativity was always a Christmas Eve tradition for us. We still do it with our extended family here at the house. We have it outside if the weather is nice, and inside if it's raining or too cold. We've had up to 120 people, but we usually have about 70 or so. Pam made many elaborate costumes over the years, and the kids love dressing up. One of the costumes is a cow with an udder. Some of the boys love that, and others say, "I don't want the udder." We have an old manger that looks very rustic and pretty realistic. We have scaffolding that we set up behind the manger so the little angels can get up there and do their part. They like that. We have a written dialogue that goes through the scriptures and a number of songs. Usually Mandy, Tara, Summer, or one of the other grandkids is the narrator. We used to give each child a part to say, but they got where they didn't want to do it if they had to talk, so the reader just reads their lines. The kids love it. They really do, and we love it. We feel like it has been a good thing for our family.

Dec. 1994—Christmas
Back (sitting): Jonathan, J.C., Mike, Kevin, Kari
Middle: Winter, Brookley
Front: Mandy, Justin, Chase

1998—Christmas
Kristen & Jacie Lynn (Josh's daughter)

Christmas Morning:

Every Christmas morning when the kids were little, Dick gathered them all together and told them, "Santa didn't come this year, so you can go back to bed."

They all said, "Daaaaad!" He had everyone kneel down and have family prayer, then let them go in to see what Santa brought.

Christmas Now:

Christmas these days is obviously different, but we still have traditions. Dick and I stay here at the house, and I have a big potato salad, ham, rolls, a big fruit salad, and homemade peanut brittle and candy for anyone who comes by on Christmas day. I always hang a lot of candy canes on the Christmas tree so the kids can each take one off the tree. Last year not one was taken off the tree, so I had candy canes until Easter. For months, I asked everyone who came to visit, "Would you like a candy cane?" Liam, Tami's son, would take one every time he came.

Those are just a few of our Christmas traditions. It's a wonderful time of year!

New Years Eve:

We always stayed up for New Year's Eve and played games and ate popcorn. At midnight, we took pots and pans outside and banged on them as loud as we could. We wanted to wake up the neighbors if they had gone to sleep. Once the kids got older and went to parties, we just went to bed.

That's a pretty good summary of some of our holiday traditions. We sure have had a lot of fun together over the years. I'm grateful for every year and for every person who has been part of our lives.

Peanut Brittle

1 C. sugar
½ C. Karo
¼ tsp salt
1 T water
1 T butter
1 C. peanuts

Cook until light brown. Like the color of the peanuts. Ten add 1 tsp soda and stir well, and pour on a buttered 12" pizza pan & spread a little. Let cool then break as you like it.

Canned Milk Candy

Carmelize 2 C. sugar when all the sugar is melted.
Add ½ lb butter — let it melt.
Then add 1 can evaporated milk a little at a time! & stir constantly ~~little~~ stream
Then add 4 C. sugar and
Cook to a soft ball.
Let set for 30 min to cool a little.
Then beat until it loses it's sheen and has thickened some.
Then add 1½ t vanilla + 2 C. nuts Pecans or walnuts
Pour into a buttered 9 x 13 pan.

9. Some Journal Entries from 1984

By Dick:

September 10, 1984

I 'll try to summarize some of the events and feelings I have had since Fay and I got married. This section will be like Mormon's condensed version. I'll try to remember some of the important events and impressions I have had and try, in a weak way, to express these thoughts.

Fay and I have been married now for almost 3 ½ years. This has been a very special relationship. As we sat together on the porch of the cabin on our honeymoon, we made plans and discussed our future. Although it was hard to plan after our other plans seemed destroyed by the death of our spouses, we made commitments and set goals.

One of the important commitments that we both felt strongly about was that life was too short and too precious to spend any of it fighting, criticizing each other, or finding fault. I can truthfully say that there has been none of that—or so very little that it could be considered none. Fay has been a perfect wife, companion, and sweetheart. She has treated me with such kindness and always makes me feel like I am someone special. She is always so complimentary and so encouraging.

Our marriage has truly been an "ideal one." I could not wish to change even a minute of it. I truly feel that the Lord directed me to Fay and that this relationship has been a great blessing to me. Fay is a perfect individual, wife, sweetheart, companion, mother, neighbor, and friend. She is so concerned about others and truly gives of herself to others. She is so unselfish, and her own needs are usually last in her thoughts.

Now, I'll summarize some of the thoughts about our family. We are truly blessed to have 15 of the most choice spirits Heavenly Father has. Each one of our children has been so special, and not one of them has in any way been rebellious and not wanted to serve the Lord and strive to keep his commandments. Now, don't misunderstand me; I don't mean that they are in any way perfect. I don't believe anyone of them is about to be translated. They all have room for growth. What I am saying is that not one of them has shown, in any way, that they are not desirous of being good. They are all trying to improve and striving to do the things they are being taught. I feel so blessed to have such fine children that challenge and encourage me to do better by their thoughts and actions.

Since we have been married, Rick and Dale have both married, and the four married children have blessed us with 10 grandchildren.

Sheri and Mike Hale now have four: Aaron, Summer, Autumn, and Spring. Mike works for Continental Homes as an accountant and is into computers in a big way. He has graduated from college and is now working on his CPA recognition and also on a real estate license. They presently live in Tempe and are extremely active in the church. Sheri and Mike set a neat example for the younger children. They are special people and we were pleased that they chose to accompany us this summer on our trip for 17 days. They were neat to travel with, seemed to really enjoy themselves, and carried their load in every way. Sheri has always been a "model child" and has shown such concern and affection for all.

Pam and Dale Garner now have four: Tara, Nathan, Mandi, and Tanner. Dale is a Real Estate Broker and has his own agency (Regency West). He works hard, reads a lot, and is very positive in his desires to do well. Pam is very much the same, and they will succeed in all they do. Again, they are tremendous people and set a fine example for the rest of the family. They live close and are always available when we need them. They are both very active it the Church, and both are extremely interested in helping others whenever there is a need.

Rick and Debbie (Cluff) have one son, Trevor, and are now expecting another. Trevor has been such a special son and spirit. He has Down Syndrome but has been blessed with good health and a sweet spirit. We are so pleased to have him in our family because he brings so much happiness and joy into all of our lives. We thrill as we see him grow and achieve; this week was his second birthday. Rick and a friend have their own framing business. They keep busy and seem to be doing well. Rick and Debbie recently bought some new furniture for their living room. Rick worked on some extra jobs for several weeks so that when the furniture arrives, it will be paid for. It now is paid for. I like this kind of example and attitude. Rick and Debbie are fine examples to their brothers and sisters. The kids feel they are so special. Debbie gets double duty often as the girls go to her for haircuts, etc.

Blacker's Home in Idaho
Fay & Trevor

Dale and Tracy (Singleton) now have the newest grandchild, Sarah. She was born this summer while we were on our trip. Dale and Tracy too are neat kids and great examples. They live east of town and have to drive quite a ways to work etc. Dale is a framer also and works for Farnsworth Construction. He serves as an assistant scoutmaster in his ward. Dale loves life and, like Rick, enjoys hunting, fishing, and sand railing. We are pleased with their example also.

All four of the married children have been married in the temple and all of them are extremely active in the Church. We are fortunate to have them all live so close. On the first Monday night of each month, they all come over and we have a special meal and home evening. We now number 30, so it is an eventful evening. I can truly say my quiver is full and my cup runneth over. These are always choice experiences.

September 13, 1984

Larry Todd turned 19 this summer (August 17) and left on August 22 for the MTC (Missionary Training Center) in Provo, Utah. He has been called to serve in the Tokyo North (Japan) Mission. He is still in the MTC learning the Japanese language. His letters home indicate that he is really having a choice spiritual learning experience. In just a few weeks—in fact, even in the second letter—we could really feel the Spirit that he was feeling. He is thrilled with the opportunity that is his.

Larry worked as a plumber this past year for Earl White and earned all of his mission money. He also attended Mesa Community College in the evenings and earned over 20 college credits. During High School and college, he studied the German language for three years. He wrote home after his second week and said that he already has learned more Japanese than he learned German in three years of school. The church training program is really good, and the gift of tongues truly blesses these young men in their study of the language.

Larry is a special son. He was number three at home when his mother died, but Rick and Dale were adults (home from their missions), so they didn't move with us after I married Fay. Larry became the oldest of 10, and then 11 when Fay and I had Kristen. The role change was a biggie. He went from little brother to a big brother overnight. Larry has a very bright mind.

10. Children Who Got Lost

By Dick:

I never got lost as a child, but I have lost children and left behind some of the kids when we were traveling. Four memories in particular stand out.

The first time I lost a child was when my oldest daughter, Sheri, was little and Joan and I still lived in the apartment at my parents' home. I took Sheri to the back room to take a nap and decided to lie down with her. I must have fallen asleep before she did, and when I woke up, she was gone. Joan and I were very worried because a big, wide, irrigation ditch was out in front of the home, and beyond that was the road. The family all went out looking for Sheri. We looked and looked but could not find her anywhere. That is when we realized that Sheri was too little to open the door. We started looking harder inside the house and finally found her fast asleep inside the cupboard under the kitchen sink.

After I married Fay, our combined families made 15 children, so we really had to keep an eye on everyone and count heads. Once we went to Yuma in our motor home and then to California to the sand dunes. After the tour of the old Yuma Territorial Prison, we loaded up to go to the sand dunes. Fay asked on several occasions, "Where is Laura? I don't remember seeing her get in." Everyone assured her that Laura was in the back. When we got to the dunes about an hour and a half later, the kids got out and ran to the tops of the dunes and started playing. They were having a

*Early 1956—Powerhouse Rd/Stapley Home
Sheri, Dick, Joan*

ball. Fay didn't remember Laura getting out of the motor home. The kids pointed to someone wearing something similar to what Laura was wearing, but Fay told one of the kids, "You go closer and make sure it is Laura." Well, it wasn't Laura, so we headed back to the Yuma Prison. When we got there, a very angry Laura was sitting on a large rock. She had gone to the bathroom and didn't get back to the motor home in time, then waited alone for our return for several hours.

The third time we lost someone was at the Los Angeles beach. Fay, Julie, and I stayed in the motor home to prepare lunch. The rest of the family went ahead to the beach and was within eyesight. When we got lunch fixed, we sent Julie, who was about four years old, to go get Grandpa and Grandma Coombs and the rest of the family. They didn't return quickly, so Fay went to check on why everyone didn't come to lunch after Julie went for them. Julie never got to them, so in a panic mode on a crowded beach in LA, we immediately started a search for her. One lifeguard called to the other lifeguard towers down the beach. Three towers down, the guard said he thought he spotted someone that fit the description. Sure enough, it was her. When she got to her mother, she was very unhappy. Fay asked her why she was so angry. She said, "He lifted up my shirt!" Julie didn't understand that the lifeguard was verifying that the swimsuit under the sweatshirt matched the description of the missing child's. She must have gotten over her fear of the lifeguard, since she allowed him to carry her the mile and a half back down the beach.

Another time we lost someone was in San Francisco. We got tickets to ride the Bart train to San José. The sites on the way were San Francisco Bay (which goes to San José), Oakland, the Oakland Temple, the airport, miles and miles of neighborhoods, the bridge across the bay side of San Francisco, etc. If you just stay on the train and get off where you got on, there is no extra cost and it is just $1 apiece. When Fay gave everyone their ticket, she had one left over and we realized that Mike was missing. I went up the stairs to the main street where we had been watching a man with no arms playing an accordion-like instrument. Sure enough, there was Mike wrapped tightly around a light pole. Boy, was he glad to see me!

11. Wedding Decorations

By Dick:

When Meilyn was planning her wedding in 1987, we decided that we would make some decorations that could be used over and over because we had six more girls to get married. We began to make and purchase some items that could be used numerous times. I will try to describe the wedding decorations as I remember them.

- I built eight backdrops to be used behind the wedding line or wherever else the decorator wanted. With all eight backdrops tied together, the backdrop length was thirty feet wide by eight feet high. We then covered the trellis with a large drape and tied it up at different heights. We usually attached a bouquet of flowers at each gathered spot. At weddings when we were expecting a smaller crowd, we only used four or six trellis sections for the greeting line and used the extra ones behind the food tables.

1987—The backdrop we made for Meilyn and Rob's wedding reception. The girls' dresses were sewed by Fay.

- The second item I built was an octagon gazebo. Seven of the eight sections were covered half way up from the bottom with wooden trellis. The last section was a doorway. The top half of each section was open so you could look into the gazebo and see the gifts, etc. I drilled a hole in the center of the gazebo roof so we could hang a light there.
- I also built five, eight-foot long sections of fencing. There were stair-case latticed boards between the three foot high ends about two or three inches apart.
- We also bought three cast iron London lights. I built them each a base and ran electric wire from the base to the top of the post so we could install light bulbs on each arm. After the light was in place, round light covers could be placed on each arm.
- We had three cast iron horse heads on a five foot post with a base. These could be used to direct traffic by hanging rope, strings of light, or ivy.
- We had two cast iron seats and one cast iron bench (a two-seater) along with two cast iron flower planters.
- Fay made table cloths for the round church tables. They went all the way to the floor, then she put different toppers on for the different weddings.

Everything was painted gloss white. We used the decorations for most of our girls' wedding receptions and several of the boys' receptions. We also rented it out, which paid for most of the mission expenses for four of our children.

We originally kept all of the wedding decorations in a shed. When we rented it out, we loaded it all in a big trailer and unloaded it upon delivery. Then after the reception, we loaded it in the trailer and then unloaded it into the shed. We eventually bought two different enclosed trailers to store it all, and the loading and unloading work was cut in half.

Reception items at Meilyn & Rob's reception

The gazebo at Rob & Meilyn's reception

1991—Reception items at Becky & Bill's wedding

12. Total Knee Replacement

By Dick:

My first of three total double knee replacements was on Halloween night in 1987. Between jogging and tree trimming, I abused my knees and wore them out.

I used to do lots of jogging, consistently five to ten miles at 4:30 a.m, to keep in shape. I figured that the farther you jogged, the better. It was too late before I realized that when you jog, six times your bodyweight crosses your knees.

I also trimmed palm trees to earn extra money. I bought a set of pole climbing spurs, strapped them on my feet and legs, and straddled the trees to climb 15 to 60 feet in the air with all my tools attached to my belt. If you can picture what I looked like, you will realize that most of the stress was on my knees as I trimmed. It usually took five or six swings of the axe on each limb, with five or six branches every eight to ten inches ascending the tree, so some tall trees took as long as three or four hours to trim. This placed lots of stress and abuse on each knee.

I had initially gone to Dr. Dennis Armstrong, the "Chevrolet doctor," to have my knees evaluated for pain and recommendations. He x-rayed and suggested the replacement surgery, but sent me to the "Cadillac doctor" in Phoenix for a second opinion. He also felt that my knees needed to be replaced after numerous tests. He then sent us into his nurse's office to schedule the surgery, explain his procedures, and tell us the cost. The kicker was the price. He wanted $7,000 per knee. I explained that I needed to check with my insurance to determine what they would pay. The nurse explained that they would not approve nearly that much, but they just didn't know what this doctor was worth!

Needless to say, I went back to Dr. Armstrong, the "Chevrolet doctor," whose price was $1,500 per knee, and if he did both at the same time he would only charge half the price for the second knee. I asked him when it really needed to be done. He said, "You will come to me when you feel it's time." A few months later, I reached my pain tolerance and arranged to have them replaced.

I chose the replacement option that would hopefully last longer than 15 years, even though I had to use a wheelchair for several weeks to give the process time to work. I also was given a spinal block for anesthesia and it shut down my bowels and other organs, so I had to remain in the hospital for a few extra days.

About ten years later, because the plastic knee pad didn't show up on the x-ray, the doctor went in again to replace the pads or the whole knee apparatus if necessary. He ended up only replacing the knee pad with teflon pads, so I got by for another ten years.

In 2007, I had both knees totally replaced—my third double knee operation.

13. Family Accomplishments

By Dick:

Missions and Military Service

We have two flag semi circles. Each circle has fifty holes, but so far we have spaced the flags in every other hole. Each flag represents a state or a country where each person in our family has served a mission. At the present time we have seventy missionary flags. We also have six flags representative of the branch of the military service where family members have served or are now serving.

OUR FAMILY MISSIONARIES

1974 - Mike Hale - Mexico • 1975 - Dale Garner - Argentina
1976 - Rick Wheeler - South Africa • 1978 - Dale Wheeler - Portugal
1981 - Rob Bushman - Puerto Rico • 1984 - Larry Wheeler - Japan • 1986 - Kevin Earlywine - Hong Kong
1988 - Bill Cox - California • 1989 - Bill Gregory - Korea • 1989 - Laura Gregory - Canada • 1992 - Mike Eagar - Taiwan
1993 - Bryan Wheeler - Japan • 1996 - Aaron Hale - Argentina • 1996 - Nathan Schlink - Florida • 1997 - Becky Hale - Canada
1998 Jon Spahr - England • 1998 - Cory Theobald - Philippines • 1999 - Tara Garner - Venezuela • 1999 - Nathan Garner - Brazil
2000 - Summer Schlink - Germany • 2002 - Mandi Acedo - Chili • 2002 - Jason Crawford - Taiwan • 2002 - Kyle Freebairn - Taiwan
2002 - Tanner Garner - Oregon • 2004 - Benson Garner - Pennsylvania • 2004 - Kristen Wheeler - Texas • 2004 - Justin Wheeler - Ecuador
2004 - Mom & Dad Wheeler - Philippines • 2006 - Hunter Garner - Brazil • 2006 - Sarah Wheeler - New Jersey • 2007 - Mom & Dad Wheeler - Kiribati

MISSIONARIES

1993 - Clint Acedo - Spain • 2002 - Ian Barnett - Brazil
2002 - Chris Boynton - Chile • 2006 - Kenny Allred - Thailand • 2008 - Chase Wheeler - Illinois
2008 - Brandon Christensen - Taiwan • 2010 - Jon Bushman - Italy • 2013 - Zac Bushman - California
2013 - Kianna Gregory - Colorado • 2013 - Kourtney Garner - Brazil • 2013 - Brookley Garner - Costa Rica

MILITARY

Ty Reber - Marines • Jordan Wheeler - Marines • Evan Earlywine - Marines • Ty Reber - Army

These are being updated to include Baily, Andrew, & Jonathan in the military & many family members who have since served missions.

Young Woman's Recognitions

We have a Young Woman's Recognition plaque which represents the highest honors that young women can achieve. We have a higher number of Young Woman's Recognition achievers than we do Eagle Scouts, forty-two to be exact.

Scouting

I have been very involved in Scouting since I was twelve years old. I am impressed with the goals and objectives of the Boy Scout program. It teaches traits that coincide with church objectives. The Scout oath, law, motto, and slogan are good examples.

The Church was the second largest sponsor of the Scouting program. Every ward and branch enrolled every boy between eight and eighteen in Scouting. The youngest boys were Cub Scouts, the deacons were regular Scouts, the teacher aged boys were Varsity Scouts, and the priests were Explorer Scouts. Scouting taught vital skills, provided advancement opportunities for the regular and Varsity Scouts, and encouraged regular outings and uplifting activities for all. Scouting taught boys about the outdoors and gave them the opportunity to experience it regularly.

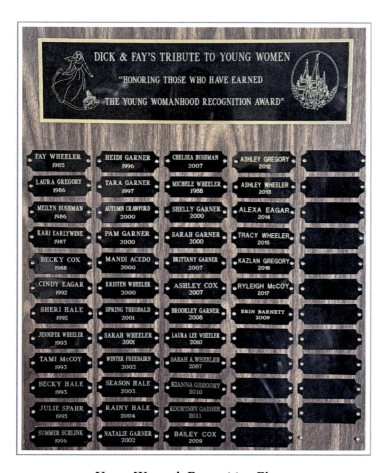

Young Woman's Recognition Plaque

Eagle Scout Recognition Plaque

With changes at the national level in the Scouting program in the spring of 2018, the Church made the wise choice to drop Scouting. When our church leaders were not present, the Boy Scout headquarters approved changes, including gay leaders and girls in the program. I'm sorry to see the program go and hope the Church develops something in its place that will teach the principles and offer the outdoor experience that young men and young women need!

Oath: On my honor (my word, my bond) I will do my best (high goal) to do my duty (responsibility) to God and my country, to obey the Scout law; to help other people at all times; to keep myself physically strong, mentally awake, and morally straight.

Law: A Scout is trustworthy, loyal, helpful, friendly, courteous, kind, obedient, cheerful, thrifty, brave, clean, and reverent.

Motto: Be prepared.

Slogan: Do a good turn daily (in a year, that equals 365 good turns).

Back: Larry, Dale, Michael, Rick
Front: Bryan, Dick, Joshua

Dick's Scouting Awards

Scout Shadowbox

Scout Awards

I have served six times as Scoutmaster or Explorer leader, served on the roundtable staff, and served as assistant Mesa District Scout Executive. I have had a lot of training.

In our own family, I received the Eagle Scout Award as a teenager, and all seven of our sons (which included our placement student, Davis Tsosie) received the Eagle Scout Award. We have made a plaque in our home for honoring the Eagle Scouts in the family, our own "Eagle's Nest," with the date they received this badge. It hangs on the wall in the family room under a picture of me and my sons who all received the Eagle Scout Award. The count of Eagle Scouts in the "Wheagar" Family (which includes spouses) is 36. That is as much as, or more than, a lot of wards have. I have been awarded the Silver Beaver Award, the highest award presented to Scouters in the state.

Eagle Scout Badge   *Wood Badge Beads*   *Silver Beaver Award*   *Scouting pins*

I earned my Wood Badge beads for Scout leader training. This involved going on two campouts, as a leader and with other leaders, to receive extensive leadership training. While there, each leader sets a goal to help him or her improve as a Scout Leader. This was called "working your ticket." My ticket was to read and study every page of the Scout Handbook and know and understand each possible requirement and badge. The goal usually takes a good year to complete. The leaders who complete Wood Badge training are divided into patrols and given an animal name to represent their patrol. We use our patrol name from then on when singing the Wood Badge song, "Back to Gilwell." This song is sung at Scouting events and at roundtable. Those who are Wood Badge trained join in the chorus with others who share their patrols name. I was an Eagle, so I stood and sang with the Eagles. The "Back to Gilwell" song goes like this:

Back to Gilwell

1. I   used   to   be   a   *Bea-ver*   and   a   good   old   *Bea-ver*   too.   But

now I've fin-ished *Beaver-ing*   I   don't know what to do, I'm grow-ing   old   and fee-ble, and

I   can   *Beaver*   no   more,   so   I'm   going   to   work   my   tick-et   if   I   can.

Chorus: Back   to   Gil - well,   hap - py   land;   I'm going   to   work my   tick-et   if   I   can.

Insert each patrol name in order:

1. Beaver - Beavering
2. Bobwhite - Bobwhiting
3. Eagle - Eagling
4. Fox - Foxing
5. Owl - Owling
6. Bear - Bearing
7. Buffalo - Buffaloing
8. Antelope - Anteloping
9. Staffer - Staffing

Part 3: Family Travels

14. Motor Home Adventures

By Dick:

Early in the blending of the Wheeler/Eagar families, we bought a 31-foot Dodge motor home. The vehicle had an international engine and chassis. It got four miles per gallon of gas, but at that time gas was not very expensive.

The front of the motor home had a driver's seat on the left looking out the front window and an engine in the middle that was mostly underneath a 12 to 15 inch cover. The engine was well insulated and not loud or noisy. The passenger side of the vehicle had a bench seat that seated three people and actually sat up over the wheel. This caused some anxiety at times, especially with Fay, because the person on that bench was right by the side of the road. Sometimes we were fairly close to a steep drop off, especially as we traveled Highway 1 along the Pacific Coast of California, and the people on the bench felt like they might go overboard.

Grandpa and Grandma Coombs always traveled with us since they and I worked for the schools and had the month of July off. For many

Motor Home

1981—Grand Canyon Trip
Dick, Fay, Michael, Meilyn holding Julie, Laura holding Tami, Bryan, Josh, Kari, Dude

years, we left Mesa on the first of July and traveled until the last day of July. The whole family went with us. Over the years, we were able to travel throughout all of North America.

We bought a membership in two travel organizations, which gave us privileges to over 6,000 RV parks across the United States. All we had to do was buy cards for $2 per night, and we were guaranteed access to all of the member facilities including a hookup in the park upon arrival for our electricity, water, and sewer. We were also granted the same price for guest vehicles traveling with us, so Grandpa and Grandma only paid the $2 fee as well. We chose this program because we found that most attractions had RV parks located nearby, and we didn't have to make arrangements in advance. It was kind of like a timeshare without worrying about reservations. Occasionally, we stayed in a state park. They were not usually very crowded. They had no hookups, but usually had picnic tables, water, and outdoor toilets. Sometimes they had showers.

We traded our first motor home for a newer 33-foot motor home with a Chevrolet chassis that usually got 10 miles per gallon. It was a little more comfortable and just had a single arm chair on the passengers side which was not nearly so close to the windows and the side of the road.

These are some of the benefits we saw of having a motor home:

1. The most important benefit was that the motor home was a great uniter for the family, especially as we worked to merge the two families. Everyone was within view of each other and could easily communicate, point out things of interest, and even sing together. After the kids had spent one month together with their brothers and sisters, they were slow to re-unite with their friends when we got home.

2. We had our own food available all of the time. If someone got hungry, they could fix a sandwich or eat some fruit or vegetables. It was possible to buy most of our groceries and carry them with us. We had a 10-cubic-foot refrigerator, so we could carry enough meat and frozen goods to last for the month. We had a four burner stove and large oven, so we could prepare meals almost as easily as at home.

3. We had a five gallon water jug for drinking and everyone knew how to use it.

4. We used mostly paper goods so that eliminated lots of dish washing.

5. We had our own flush toilet, so if anyone needed to go potty, it was always available.

6. Everyone had a bed assignment, so they were all happy.

7. Each family member had his or her own area for clothes, either a suitcase or closet space. This meant everyone was responsible for their own things. When we stopped at a laundromat, we washed and dried everything in about two hours, then everyone took their own clothes and put them away. Wow, we wished we had a laundromat at home!

8. If someone wanted to play games, there was a table and benches for easy access.

9. If someone got tired and wanted some quiet time, there was a bed in the back with a door that shut.

10. We had CB's (Citizen's Band radio) between us and Grandpa's truck, so we could keep in touch and make decisions as we traveled. Often Fay and Grandma were in the truck. Grandpa liked riding with us in the motor home.

11. We had dually's, or two wheels, on each side of the rear axle. When we were on toll roads, our cost was less than Grandpa's because he was pulling a tent trailer.

12. When we were finished with an amusement park, we fixed supper, ate, and then got ready to leave. When the traffic jam to exit was over, we were on our way.

15. Our First Big Motor Home Trip

By Dick:

I will try to relate some of our motor home travels, but they will be disjointed. I can't remember what we saw trip by trip or summer to summer.

The first trip we took after we got the motor home was up the California coast to a family reunion in Oregon in July of 1982. We took Highway 10 to Redlands, California, where we stopped to get gas. The cost of gas for the motor home was around $60. It cost Grandpa Coombs around $10 to fill up his truck. He came to me immediately and said, "Dick, we can turn back. We don't need to take this trip."

I said, "No, we have planned for this expense. We have our rooms paid for with the motor home, and we have most of the food we will need. We know that the cost of gas will be our main concern, and we are prepared for it."

We had a wonderful time and made many memories. The following stories include some of our stops along the way.

Disneyland

Grandpa Coombs had never been to Disneyland. He thought it was just like a big state fair, and he had seen lots of them. State fairs were big and dirty, and he wasn't interested. Because of that, he didn't want to go to Disneyland. Well he had a change of mind after two days at Disneyland. He was totally shocked and blown away. We lost him there once. The last time anyone remembered seeing him was when we went to "Bear Country," so we went back there. He was so enthralled with the singing and talking animals that each time they cleared the auditorium, he got in line and went again. We figured he must have seen it three or four times in a row.

When we first got to Disneyland, Grandma Coombs had a sprained ankle and was having a hard time walking on it. We said that she would be fine if she just came in, found a shady spot to sit, and watched the people and the cartoon characters as they walked by entertaining everyone. Well guess what? She was so impressed that she didn't sit once, and by the end of the day, she hardly had a limp. Both Grandpa and Grandma had a new perspective on Disneyland and were sorry they hadn't gone sooner in life.

Hearst Castle

We traveled on up Highway 1 and came to San Luis Obispo, California, where Hearst Castle is located on the hill. The menfolk weren't very interested, so Fay, Grandma, and some of the girls went for a tour. I have since visited Hearst Castle several times with Fay and some of the kids. I have learned a lot about it and been very impressed.

Randolph Hearst, a newspaper icon, inherited from his father 250,000 acres of mountainous land along the California coast in San Simeon and inland. Randolph built his three- or four-story high castle with hundreds of rooms on the property. As a young man, Randolph traveled a lot and was fascinated with art. He traveled to countries in the aftermath of wars and bought beautiful doors, whole ceilings, and lights; then he had his builder (Julia Morgan) design a room around the items. She built a room to use a ceiling Randolph purchased. If the room needed two doors and he only had one, he had that one duplicated. One art hanging was sixty to eighty feet long, so the room was built that long.

Each weekend Hearst invited nearly 100 people over for the weekend, had the staff prepare meals for the group, and they ate together at his 100-person dining room table. He seated the people he most wanted to ask questions nearest him so he could pick their brains. He had two swimming pools. Guests did not have to bring suits because he had ample for all. There were waterways coming from some of the room locations so that guests could leave their room, swim to the main pool, and then swim back to their rooms. When the castle was in full use, the last mile or two leading to the castle had a median between roads and contained a full zoo.

1980s—Dude at Mission Beach in San Diego. She wrote "I luv Grandpa" in the sand with her foot.

The taxes finally became unbearable, so the family gave the State of California the castle and much of the property in a settlement. The state has seven tours through the castle and say that it is the only state operated facility that pays its own way and even makes a profit. If you ever go to the area, take time to take one or two tours. You will be impressed and fascinated.

The Redwood Forest

The majority of the family continued thirty or forty miles on up the coast on Highway 1 while some of the girls toured the castle. We stopped because we saw a backpack on the side of the road. We were a short distance from a campsite in the redwoods, so we were going to turn it in there anyway. While we were stopped, a car pulled up behind us. The driver got out, approached me, and offered to be of help. I explained that I was okay. He pointed to the AA sticker on my bumper, which meant someone was a recovering alcoholic and signaled other recovering alcoholics to stop and see how they were doing and if they needed help. I removed the sticker from my bumper once we got checked into the Big Sur Redwood Campground and got settled. It was a really nice campground with bathrooms, showers, and camping areas.

The womenfolk arrived a couple of hours later. They had really been impressed with the castle and tour. The redwood forests of California are fascinating. The trees are huge, often over 100 feet tall. They often grow in clusters and are hundreds of years old. It sometimes takes five or six people fingertip-to-fingertip to reach around them. They grow so close together and are so thick that the sun seldom reaches the ground, so often the only growth under them is ferns. They are beautiful and almost unbelievable.

We have visited a number of these redwood forests and stayed the night in several of them. People pay years in advance to camp there and to visit them. They do not refund the fees, so when all sites have been paid for, the campground is full as far as the park is concerned. You have to beg them to let you find an open spot and pay since they have already collected for the space.

If you haven't been to the Redwood Forest, you can't imagine the size of those trees. Not only were they big around, they grew several hundred feet tall. They were beautiful, beautiful trees. As we were going through the Redwood Forest, I said to the kids, "Hey guys, look outside and see these beautiful trees."

"We've seen a tree before, Dad," was their response. They were busy playing Rook or something, and they wouldn't even look at them.

I said, "This is my first time seeing them, and I'm a lot older than you are. You've seen trees before, but nothing like these." And that's about where it ended.

We did come to one tree that you could drive a car through. We couldn't drive the motor home through it, so we pulled over and walked through it. Later on, it fell, but there was no evidence that it made any noise when it fell, because nobody heard it fall. That's the story I've been told.

Oregon/Idaho

Highway 1 follows the Pacific Coastline north, and at times you can look over the edge of the road and see the surf splashing against the cliffs. Occasionally in a bad rainstorm, a large section of the mountain will fall off and even take out a portion of the highway. On one trip back from Canada, we actually had to detour where the road was being rebuilt.

From Big Sur, we went on up the coast of California and into Oregon. We stopped for a tour of the Sea Lion Caves in Florence, Oregon. It was really a huge underground cave with numerous sea lions in it. I think they actually swim under the cliff to get into the cave.

We then went to the Coombs's (Grandpa Coombs's sisters, Aunt Belva[1] and Aunt Audrey[2]). We stayed at Audrey's home in Springfield, Oregon. At one time Great-grandpa Coombs[3] lived there in a nursing home until he died. While we were on this trip, we went by the Bonneville Dam on the Columbia River to see the locks where the salmon could jump from level to level to continue to go upstream to spawn.

After visiting Oregon, we went down through Idaho along the Snake River. We always saw lots of deer and elk, but on this trip we saw a medium sized black bear near the highway. It was a memorable first trip in the motor home!

---

[1] Belva Coombs Rogers (1923–1999)

[2] Audrey Coombs Luke (1931–Year 2006)

[3] Edward Burton "Burt" Coombs (1885–1970)

16. Church History Motor Home Trips

By Dick:

We were able to take our children to visit the Midwest in our motor home quite a few times. Each time was a unique experience, but the most important part to us was the opportunity to let our children have spiritual experiences at the church history sites.

Missouri, Mississippi, Iowa, Illinois

In about 1984, we briefly toured Tom Sawyer and Becky Thatcher's famous setting[4]. We didn't see the whitewashed fence or the famous cave where Tom Sawyer confronted "Injun Joe," nor did we float down the Mississippi on a raft, but we did cross a bridge over the Mississippi near their area.

We also saw the Lincoln Home National Historic Site in Springfield, Illinois. I missed out on the tour because it was late in the day and I needed to change a tire on the motor home. The family saw the home of Mark Twain (Samuel Clemens).

We drove through Iowa on our way to Nauvoo, Illinois. The highlight there was to see the fireflies at night when we camped. We were fascinated by them.

Nauvoo, Illinois

We have visited Nauvoo on two occasions. It is a very "must see" stop when traveling in the area. We have visited many church sites, and the amazing thing is that you always have a spiritual experience. The presentations always touch your heart as you view and participate.

There are a number of elders and sisters called to proselyte in the Nauvoo mission. I think one of their prerequisite talents is the ability to sing. The missionaries and couple missionaries perform several evenings a week in the theater there. Kenyon Udall, our former stake president and a Gilbert/Thatcher resident, was called as the mission president in the Nauvoo area[5]. He called our good friends, Kenneth and Marie

1984—Dude Coombs at the model of the Nauvoo Temple

---

[4] *The Adventures of Tom Sawyer* by Mark Twain

[5] Illinois Peoria Mission President 1992–1995

Noble, to be senior missionaries there and they were part of the performing group in the evenings. In fact, Ken Noble sang a solo of *A Poor Wayfaring Man of Grief* at the Carthage Jail rededication.

We also visited Far West and Adam-ondi-Ahman. We had a little devotional, and Dad asked us to sing, "I Heard Him Come." I will never forget that feeling, thinking about the words of that song and knowing that Christ would be coming there again!
—Meilyn

We have not been back since the Nauvoo Illinois Temple has been rebuilt and completed. The Nauvoo Historical Society was founded in 1953, and consists of families of Nauvoo Saints and other volunteers. They have purchased some of the land there and have restored the homes and buildings, turning them into museums or historic sites you can visit for free. Several of the homes, stores, businesses, and buildings have been rebuilt at the expense of the Society. In fact, if I'm not mistaken, the temple was rebuilt totally with funds from the Nauvoo Society. One member in our stake who was in the carpet business donated and installed all of the carpet in the temple. Fay would really like to go back to visit and to attend the temple there.

The Church has restored some of the historic buildings, and when you visit, the guides tell about and even demonstrate how things were in the blossoming days of Nauvoo.

- At the bakery you viewed the old brick ovens, then the presenter gave everyone a cookie. We knew the sister missionary, and she said she had to get up at 2 a.m., go to the missionary building, and bake several hundred cookies to give out each day.
- At the candle shop, they demonstrated candle making, and if you were interested you were allowed to participate.
- At the brick making area, they made you a small brick and put your name and the date on it. You had to return after it had been fired to pick it up.
- There was a welders shop where they made rings out of cut nails and gave them to some of the visitors. They also told about the building of the covered wagons and showed samples of the unfinished wood that families took home each evening to carve and shape into the spokes for the wheels.
- We toured the gun shop.
- There is a Women's Statue Garden recognizing the role of women in the Church.
- We rode in a multi-horse-drawn wagon and were able to ride past the Brigham Young and Smith homes, and even rode down to the Mississippi River where the pioneers crossed as they fled Nauvoo from the mobs. It is hard to picture Nauvoo in its prime with over 8,000 Saints living there and then being driven away. Near the crossing, they showed us where many people were baptized for deceased relatives before the baptismal font was completed in the temple.
- The Reorganized Church also has a facility there and even gives tours of the Joseph and Emma Smith home. We asked the tour guide some questions that she didn't know the answers to. She said, "I'm not a member of the church. I am just a school student hired as a tour guide."

We even attended sacrament meeting in Nauvoo the second time we visited. We spent two days in Nauvoo and at Carthage Jail on both visits. The Church sites were well organized, and we always left feeling the Spirit. But at the other sites owned by the Reorganized Church, like the Smith family home, the Kirtland Temple, etc., the presentations did not have the same spirit. They were just factual but conveyed no emotion. Overall, going to Nauvoo was a very inspiring and uplifting experience.

Carthage Jail

Carthage Jail is fairly close to Nauvoo. It is now owned by the Church and is very much as it was when the Prophet Joseph and his party of five or six were incarcerated there. The tour took us through the events of the few days they were there.

We were taken up the stairs into the upper room where audio recording was played depicting the final hours and minutes of their lives. On the recording, someone representing Elder Taylor sang *A Poor Wayfaring Man of Grief* before the overrunning of the jail by the angry mob. Then the shots rang out, and the Prophet, standing near the window, was shot and fell to the ground. His brother, Hyrum, received a fatal shot fired through the door. The Prophet and his brother were later taken by wagon to Nauvoo where they were buried near the Prophet's home. The bodies have been removed and buried in another place to avoid removal and desecration by Governor Boggs or some other vandals. It is hard to believe that citizens of a civilized country could carry out such cowardly, out of control acts, and actually get away with it and not be punished in some fashion.

1984—Michael at Carthage Jail

17. Other Motor Home Trips

By Dick:

I am going to write about some of the other sites and places we visited in the United States. We were able to travel all around the country, and show the children different cultural sites and give them unique experiences while still spending time together.

Mount Rushmore National Memorial

I'll begin with Mount Rushmore in South Dakota. The face of Presidents Washington, Jefferson, Roosevelt, and Lincoln look out over the Black Hills of South Dakota. It was an amazing site, and the lectures and tours were very enlightening. This was one of Fay's favorite sites.

Nearby, another project was in progress: the Crazy Horse Memorial. It is also being blasted out of the granite mountain and when completed, this monumental sculpture will make the four presidents' heads on Mount Rushmore look tiny[6]. It is located southwest of Rapid City, just east of Highway 385, and will depict the Oglala Lakota warrior, Crazy Horse, riding a horse and pointing. When we were there, only the face was nearly completed[7].

1984 Summer Road Trip

On our first trip to Nauvoo, our destination was a Wheeler Reunion at Uncle Doug and Aunt Lee's[8] place in Nederland, Texas. Sheri and Mike Hale and their family were traveling with us along with Grandpa and Grandma Coombs. The people that worked with Doug provided a freezer full of nearly unending buckets of the most delicious ice cream ever. They also brought over a table full of pails of crawdads—something we had never had before. It was a real adventure for us!

1983—Back: Laura, Kari, Meilyn, Michael, Larry
Front: Becky, Josh, Bryan, Tami, Julie

---

[6] The head of each president on Mount Rushmore is 60 feet tall and 1 mile above the ground, while the face of Crazy Horse is 87 feet 6 inches tall and 563 feet (0.1 miles) above the ground.

[7] The face and head of Crazy Horse were completed and dedicated in 1998, but as of 2023 the memorial is still in progress.

[8] Douglas Wayne Wallace (1947–2011) m. Lee Kocherhans

Nashville, Tennessee

Our next stop after Nauvoo was Nashville, Tennessee. We were going to go to the Dolly Parton amusement park (Dollywood), but it was raining cats and dogs when we got to the parking lot, and we realized we were scheduled to be at Fay's cousin's house in just an hour or so. So we called Grandpa on the CB radio[9] to tell him that there was no need to stay; it was too wet, and we didn't have enough time.

Fay's Cousin's House

We went on to Alabama to see Fay's cousin, Wes White. They had a city home and a lake home. They welcomed us with open arms, and then suggested that we go to their cabin home on the lake. They had a nice double-wide modular home on the bank of the lake. We had a great "get to know each other" visit, and Fay's cousin cooked up a delicious, huge rack of ribs for supper. The next day was Sunday, so we contacted the Church to find the closest ward building. After a great evening getting acquainted with them, we went to bed.

The next morning, we drove about thirty minutes to the church. They were meeting in a rented home located across the street from the Talladega Speedway, which is a race track. When we got there, we were welcomed with outstretched arms. It was a small branch, and we numbered 22, so we almost doubled their attendance that day. We offered to teach the kids' classes, but they insisted on doing it. They were very anxious to have us move there and be a part of their branch. They had to pull manuals out of the closet and unwrap them so everyone could have one. The older girls had to attend Relief Society since there were no other young women. We then spent the rest of Sunday with Fay's cousins.

Florida

From there, we drove to Florida. The kids said, "How far are we going into Florida?"

I replied, "Only as far as it takes to turn this motor home around." That was our first visit to Florida.

1984 World's Fair—New Orleans, Louisiana

We then headed for New Orleans. We were excited to attend the 1984 World's Fair there that year[10]. The theme of the World's Fair was "The World of Rivers — Fresh Waters as a Source of Life." Wow, the things you can do with water! The prices were high, so the kids only got to ride one $12 ride. There were sites to see like "high divers" exhibits from many countries, and movies depicting the ways water was used in the various countries. There were exhibits and high-priced mementos for sale. They even had a paddle-wheel boat ride on the Mississippi that cost $20 or so. On top of the fair and exhibits, the humidity was near 100% and the temperature in the 90s, so it was a miserable

---

[9] Citizen Band Radio, what we used to communicate between cars before we had cell phones.

[10] The 1984 World's Fair was the last World's Fair held in the United States to date. It was also the only World's Fair that went bankrupt while operating. Despite the high ticket prices, the seven million visitors did not recuperate the $350 million that it cost to host.

experience. The only good thing was that we were able to stay in the parking lot for the night and not have to find an RV park.

However, Grandma Coombs and Grandpa Coombs were in a tent trailer with no air conditioning. Grandma Coombs had a miserable night. She counted 17 lights through her tent trailer, so it was an extra long night. Sheri's little girl, Autumn, was a screamer. She couldn't sleep that night either, so she screamed a lot through the night. Grandma Coombs just yelled, "Go, go, Autumn! I'm with you!" Sheri was so embarrassed in the morning, but Grandma said, "She was acting like I wish I could."

El Paso, Texas

The weather was miserable—hot and humid. On the way home, we drove through the night. About five hours east of El Paso on a Sunday morning, I pulled off the highway into a small town, and at about 8 a.m., we found the church and dressed for Sunday.

The services started at 9 a.m. The speakers were from El Paso, and it was high council Sunday. We visited with the members and were told that it was the only ward east of El Paso. We were also told that the military facility was one hour south of the building, so that meant a two hour drive each week to

1984—Wheeler, TX
Dick, Kristen, Tami, Bryan, Aaron Hale, Michael, Meilyn
Front: Summer Hale, Julie

attend Sunday meetings for those members plus another two-hour drive to mutual each week as well. We learned that when you are prepared for Sunday, that you can most often find an organized ward or branch to attend even when you are traveling. It always feels good to go to church each week.

Alamogordo, NM

On another trip, we went to Alamogordo, New Mexico, where the space program was being developed.

Then we drove to Carlsbad Caverns. The cavern is a must see. It is classified as a "dead" underground cavern because it is exposed to the outside environment and even though it is full of stalagmites and stalactites, they are mostly not growing. The trail takes you down several hundred feet into a large room where you can see huge, tall, colorful stalagmites and stalactites. The lighting really brings out the size and colors. Bats live in part of the cavern and at certain times of the year in the evening, they all leave each night to go get insects etc. When they do, there are so many leaving that the sky is dark for a period of time. There are food and drink concessions in the big room as well as gift shops. When you are ready to leave, you ride the elevators to the surface.

Then we visited Kartchner Caverns, near Sierra Vista, Arizona. This is classified as a "living" cave because the outside air has not penetrated the cavern, so it continues to grow. When we entered this cavern we went into a chamber, the door behind us closed, and then after a minute or two the door ahead of us opened. This was how they maintained a living status. There were two sections to the cavern, one section was only open when the bats were on the move. It was also worth the visit.

Fay & Dude at Yellowstone

Yellowstone National Park and The Grand Tetons

We went to Yellowstone National Park many times, but I will attempt to tell about a few of our different trips together.

Old Faithful Lodge

I will start at the Old Faithful Lodge, a beautiful, stately, huge log cabin built next to the Old Faithful geyser. The whole park is built over an enormous thermal pot that may someday erupt like a huge volcano. The thermal pot fuels the 200+ geysers, but this famous geyser is called Old Faithful because it erupts about every 68 minutes. During peak season, the summertime crowds gather by it to watch it erupt. The Old Faithful lodge has 100 rooms for rent for the night, and it fills up at peak time of the year, but there are other lodges and rooms you can rent nearby. There is a museum in the immediate area and several souvenir shops as well.

It gets very cold in the winter, and the park is closed for vehicle travel. However, Uncle Marvin[11] told me that he and Aunt Lovel went there in the winter. They rented snowmobiles, snow clothing, etc., and went into the park from the west entrance to the Old Faithful Lodge. We have been in the

Yellowstone
Back: Julie, Tami, Bryan
Kristen

Julie, Dude, Jay at Yellowstone

---

[11] Marvin Ladell Blacker (1936–2021) m. to Lovel Louise Wheeler Blacker (1937–2019)

97

northern half of the park in June, and there are sometimes snow banks along the road that are six to ten feet in height left over from the cold winter months.

Yellowstone Campground/Yellowstone Lodge

One year we camped in the Yellowstone campground. We all had to sleep in the motor home that night because a bear had been seen near the area. We got up early and drove to the Old Faithful Lodge to see where the church services were that day (this was before you could look online for sacrament meeting times). It was at the Yellowstone Lodge, so we drove there.

Bryan & Kristen at Yellowstone

We arrived a little early, so the boys (Mike, Bryan, and Josh) got to help set up chairs and prepare the sacrament. Two elders and a high councilor came to conduct the services from Jackson Hole, Wyoming, which was about an hour away. There were 35–50 people in attendance, and our boys got to help administer the sacrament. The high councilor and one elder spoke, and the other elder played a special musical number on the piano. He was totally blind, but his musical number was very good. He was as good as a professional. When we talked with his companion after the meeting, the boys found out that the blind elder had just heard the song he played the night before. It really impressed the boys that someone could hear a song once and play it back the next day.

In all of our travels, we only missed attending a church meeting once. We held our own Sunday School that time, but missed the sacrament.

Tami at Yellowstone

Yellowstone in 2013

When we went to Yellowstone with Kristen, Ty, and family in 2013, we saw a minimal number of Yellowstone animals until we passed a roadside collection of them near Rexburg, Idaho. Yellowstone is a fascinating place, but I don't want to be anywhere in the vicinity when it decides to blow its lid. It will be quite a big "firework."

June 2020 Trip

In June of 2020, we went with Josh, Kristie, and Kylie to Uncle Marvin's and then to Yellowstone. We were planning to go to the west entrance (Idaho/Montana), but it was still closed, so we went to Jackson Hole, Wyoming, because they had opened that entrance the day before.

From Jackson Hole, you go north past the Grand Tetons National Park. The Tetons is a huge, rugged, tall, snow-covered mountain range that borders Yellowstone National Park. The roads in the park take you past the Yellowstone River and Falls, many geysers and steam pots, and to the mineral pools. During the drive and walking tours of the geysers, you see lots of animals. There are some deer, more elk, a few bears, and lots of buffalo.

In fact, on our way back to Jackson Hole in June of 2020, we were stopped by a herd of 200+ buffalo bulls, cows, and calves. They were sauntering across the road at their own very slow pace. We even saw two bull buffalo butting heads together as if they were vying for "Bull of the Herd." They weren't charging as male rams do for the kingship, but they were banging heads pretty hard.

San Francisco, California

Two of my cousins live on the east end of San Francisco Bay and we were able to visit with them, stay overnight, and challenge their minds as they tried to prepare meals for our large family.

My dad's sister, my Aunt Nettie[12], has a daughter who lives in San José, California. Just a few miles from San José is a town named Los Gatos where my Aunt Murnie's[13] (another of my Dad's sisters) son Freddie Abraham[14] and his family live. Fred's home is on a 10 or 12 acre hill at the end of a street lined with million dollar homes. Fred works for IBM, and he is a researcher. He was elated to see us and insisted that we park our motor home and go into San Francisco in his van, which we did. Parking a big vehicle, especially overnight, is a challenge.

When we returned to their home in the evening, his wife had cooked a large roaster pan full of spaghetti made with macaroni noodles. It was several gallons. We hardly made a dent in it. They had numerous loaves of bread and three gallons of milk. Fred also bought three half gallons of ice cream (malted chocolate and malted walnut) and a two-pound bag of wrapped candy, which he gave the kids to divide. It was also Julie's birthday, so he bought her a Barbie doll. In the morning, I came into the kitchen, and Fred's wife had a puzzled look on her face. She had all of the fixings for breakfast, but didn't know where to start. She was very relieved when I offered to help.

Fred also took us on a trail through a redwood forest near his home. Fred said to me later that he really enjoyed coming to our home each week as kids, but he couldn't believe we had so many lethal toys to play on. He was referring to our zip line from the windmill to a tree in the field several hundred yards away, two tree houses, citrus trees that you could climb high into, a large fig tree over

---

[12] Nettie Cutler Wheeler Dettman (1909–2004)

[13] Murnie Cutler Wheeler Abraham (1905–1989)

[14] Fredrick "Freddie" Fadlow Abraham (About 1937–present)

an open ditch for climbing, a rifle shooting range, and a car front axle with one end cemented into the ground for a merry-go-round. Luckily, no one got seriously hurt.

Another Trip to Disneyland

One evening at 9:30 or 10 p.m., we all got in the motor home. Everyone found a bed and went to sleep except me. I drove in peace and quiet to Disneyland. We arrived as it was opening. Everyone went to Disneyland except me. I stayed in the motor home and slept. When the park closed, everyone came back to the motor home. We ate, then everyone except me went to bed. I drove home.

A Special Memory

One summer we left home about 7 p.m. and drove the motor home towards Winslow to meet Grandpa and Grandma Coombs near Holbrook. The idea was to drive up on the rim where it was cool, spend the night, get up an hour or two early, and have a short drive to our meeting point. We topped out above Strawberry at about 9 p.m. Fay and I were awake and all of the others were sleeping. It was a moonlit night and the elk were out feeding. We saw fifty or more along the road and in the road. We finally woke the kids up so they could enjoy the scenery. Their comment was, "Wow, this is really neat." A short time later we stopped, parked, and slept until daylight.

Our Last Motor Home Trip

For our very last motor home trip. We went to Washington, D.C.; New York; and DisneyWorld in Florida.

1994—Niagara Falls on our last motor home trip
Julie & Kristen

1994—Fay at Niagara Falls

100

18. The Kids' First Airline Flight

By Dick:

I n about 1985, I woke up at 4:40 a.m. to go jogging. I took a minute to look at the morning newspaper. On the front page was an advertisement for round trip airfare to Orange County from Phoenix for $9.95 apiece. I woke Fay up and showed her the ad. Our kids had never flown on an airplane before, so we decided to call and arrange for a flight. They had one that morning, so we scheduled it for 7 a.m. We woke the kids up and went to Sky Harbor Airport for the adventure.

That was the first time our kids had flown on an airplane. It was also when the airlines gave you a can of pop and some peanuts and maybe even a cookie. Kristen was thrilled and flapped her wings most of the way there (her arms, that is) while standing on her daddy's knee. It was interesting to look out the window and see the toy cars going down the roads. The farm fields and mountains and everything gave us a different perspective of the earth we live on.

Forty or fifty minutes later, we landed in Orange County—what would have been an eight hour trip by car. When we got off the plane, we caught a shuttle bus to the nearest restaurant, Love's. There we ate breakfast and caught a shuttle back to the airport. We then got on the first airplane going back to Phoenix. We got home at about 10 a.m., and the kids went to school.

When the older kids got to Mesa High School and checked into the attendance office, the lady wouldn't accept their excuse for being late. She called Fay and said, "You won't believe the excuse your kids are trying to use for their tardies. They are telling me that they flew to Los Angeles, ate breakfast, and flew back."

Fay said, "That is the truth, and if you don't believe me, I will bring you the airline ticket stubs."

The lady persisted and wanted to see the stubs, so Fay took them to the Mesa High attendance office. After seeing them, she still commented, "I can't believe anyone would do that." But the kids will always remember their first commercial airplane experience!

Love's

19. Free Flights with Southwest

By Dick:

Becky worked for Southwest Airlines from 1996 to 2002. Southwest has a policy that the parents of their employees can fly free on any flight that is not full of paying passengers. They call the unfilled seats "standby." While Becky worked for Southwest Airlines, if we desired to go somewhere, we checked with her and she figured out how many standby seats were available a day or two before the flight.

Southwest Airlines

The Southwest Airline policy was that the first ones in line for standby were admitted first. We went to the airport two or three hours early and got in line first. We always took books with us to read as we waited, but since the flights were free, we didn't mind.

We really enjoyed this privilege and took advantage of it often. We liked flying with Southwest Airlines because they didn't assign seats and they still served cookies, peanuts, and drinks for free.

Anniversary Trip

One day on our anniversary, we caught the 6 a.m flight to San Francisco and arrived around 7:30 a.m. We took no luggage because we were only going for the day. When we got off the plane, we caught a bus to downtown San Francisco and bought a daily ticket on the trolley/street car for each of us.

We spent the day going to our favorite places in town. We went to Pier 19, walked the boardwalk from the Pier to Ghirardelli Chocolate factory, saw all of the fishing boats, and stopped at numerous shops along the way. Fay got some clam chowder, and we bought some sourdough bread. We went to Chinatown, the crookedest street in the world, downtown, the malls, and the trolley station. We also saw the San Francisco bridge.

It was a fun day. In the evening, we caught the bus back to the airport to board the 9 p.m. flight to Phoenix. We were tired but had really enjoyed the day. When the flight attendant came by our seats, she said, "Weren't you on the flight from Phoenix to San Francisco this morning?"

We said, "Yes."

Then she asked, "You only came to San Francisco for the day?"

We answered, "Yes, we just wanted to come here for the day for our anniversary and get a loaf of sourdough bread." FUN! FUN!

Salt Lake Trip

On another occasion, Fay saw some nativity sets advertised at the Deseret Book outlet store by the Salt Lake City, Utah, airport, so we caught an early flight to Salt Lake. We took a taxi to the store, bought ten Nativity sets, caught a taxi back to the airport, and flew home on the next available flight that had standby seats.

SeaWorld/Disneyland Season Passes

Becky and Bill bought family season passes one year to SeaWorld in San Diego, California, and the next year to Disneyland in Anaheim, California. Fay and I did the same. We went with them to SeaWorld several times during the year and then went to Disneyland several times the next year. We really enjoyed both of the amusement parks and never tired of going to them.

San Francisco

On another occasion, Fay and I went to San Francisco for a few days. Our flight was scheduled to stop in Monterey, California, to pick up additional passengers on the way to the Oakland airport. Unfortunately, the flight was delayed because of the 60 mph winds in Monterey. After a long delay, we were sent hiking about 1/4 mile to the other plane that was going to Oakland, but when we got to the second plane, we were sent back to the first plane. In the end, we were two of the eight passengers to fly directly to Oakland in an empty plane, and we actually arrived there earlier than the original flight was scheduled. We picked up our rental car and enjoyed our stay in San Francisco.

We used to enjoy seeing the sights in San Francisco, but it has become so scary there that we don't feel comfortable going there anymore. When we visited San Francisco there were many places we liked to visit. Muir Woods was one of our favorites. It is a forest of redwood trees where you can walk along several different trails with small creeks. There was a museum and visitors' center there, and it was an inspiring site. We usually went across the Golden Gate Bridge into Sausalito, a hillside community of people who mostly like to boat and sail. It was fun to go there and just watch the boats in the San Francisco Bay.

On several occasions, we have gone to the Science Museum which is located on the San Francisco side of the Golden Gate Bridge. The museum was part of the World's Fair when it was held there. The next area we usually visit is the Golden Gate Park. Roads wind in and about. There are numerous sites to see, areas for picnics, a Japanese tea garden, Japanese houses, museums, and aquariums. You can easily spend half a day just viewing everything there.

Another favorite site is the Winchester House located south of the east end of the Bay. The heir of the Winchester Rifle fortune was psychic and believed that the spirits of the people killed by the rifles would haunt her unless she had construction workers working 24 hours per day, seven days a week. So she continued to build around the clock year round. I will say that the experience is very worthwhile if you are in the area.

20. Flying Free with Alaska Airlines

By Dick:

In about 1999, Josh worked for Alaska Airlines for about a year while he and his family lived in Anchorage Alaska. Like Southwest, the airlines also gave parents free flight privileges on standby seats. The only difference between the two airlines was that the standby seats were available according to the seniority of the employee instead of when you signed up for them. Josh was the last one hired, so any person, even if they arrived at the gate at the last minute, could bump us from a flight. Alaska Airlines flies to different airports than Los Angeles and San Francisco.

Alaska Airlines

Fay flew Alaska Airlines to Anchorage one time and got bumped from every flight from Seattle, Washington. At the end of the day, she was in tears and in a panic because she had never had to find a hotel room, the airport was closing soon, and everyone would be locked out. A kind check-in lady finally let her get on a flight and told two latecomers that the flight was full.

One time Fay and I flew on the red eye flight from Anchorage to Seattle. It left Alaska at midnight, and there were only five passengers on the flight plus three stewardesses. We were told to pick any seat we wanted. We just sat down in two seats, and the other couple then got on the plane. They came up to us and stated that we were in their seats and insisted that we move, which we did. There is no service on red eye flights. The flight attendants go to the back of the plane, sack out on three seats, and sleep all the way to Seattle, which was fine because we didn't need anything anyway.

Part 4: More Family Fun

21. Our Cabin in Pinedale

By Fay:

Dick bought property in Pinedale and built a cabin there in the 1970s. The cabin was really just "in the rough" for most of the time we had it, but it provided shelter, a safe haven, and lots of work for Dick until it burned down in 2002.

It wasn't like we were going up to Pinedale and camping in a little pod. We had lots of space and everything we needed to be comfortable. It was a 20-foot by 40-foot, two-story cabin with a big 10-foot wide front porch and steps everywhere. Dick bought the materials to make the cabin for a really good price, and they were all new and in good shape. He tiled the floor with lots of different tiles, so it looked like a patchwork quilt. We had electricity and lights. When they renovated one of the home economic rooms at Mesa Junior High, Dick got a sink and several cupboards for the cabin. We kept our food and dishes in those cupboards. We had a nice electric stove. Dick hooked up that sink and made the water run outside through the floor; we could do the dishes, and the dirty water would run down the hill. We had a jillion milk cartons that we filled up with water. The loft was full of beds. We probably had eight or ten beds up there where everybody slept. At first we climbed up a ladder to get there, but eventually Dick built stairs. The week before it burned down, Dick got the sheetrock and insulation installed, and it finally felt finished.

Our cabin in Pinedale

Our Honeymoon

The first time I went to the cabin was on our honeymoon in 1981. After we spent our first night at a hotel, Dick said, "I've got a little cabin, and I think you'd enjoy it. If you don't, we'll just go to Show Low and get a place there." I agreed to go. I could tell he wasn't sure how I was going to react, but I loved it from the beginning.

When I first saw the cabin, I thought, "This is beautiful." I had never had a place like that. I remember saying, "This is perfect." I thought it was a perfect place for kids—and we had a lot. I could see that they could run and play and I wouldn't have to worry about them. I really was excited. He said, "Well, we have to go down to the rangers to get water."

I said, "That's okay."

He said, "And there's a toilet, but it's behind the house. It's just an outhouse."

I said, "Okay, that sounds good." He was kind of surprised. When he showed me the little bathtub, I said, "Yeah, I'm not getting in that." But then he showed me the shower, and I said, "This is perfect." I was excited!

He seemed surprised and said, "You like it?"

I said, "I do like it."

He asked, "Do you think we'll be okay here for a few nights?"

I said, "Yes, I think we will." And we were.

After Dick gave me the tour, we built a fire in the outside pit, cooked some hot dogs we had brought with us, and talked a lot. Dick started to make plans for our new life together. Eventually, I came around and participated in planning with him.

Every day we were there Dick asked, "Are you sure you're okay being here?"

And I said, "Yes, I am." I didn't realize at the time, but Joan didn't really like the cabin. Every once in a while, Dick packed up the kids and took them to the cabin for a week, and she had a week at home by herself. There came a point when I wanted him to take the kids to the cabin for a week. Since I had told Dick so many times that I enjoyed the cabin, he didn't understand why I wanted him to take the kids without me. I said, "You let your other wife stay home, so why won't you let me have a week off?"

He responded, "Because you like it, and she didn't like it." So I'd pack up and go with them.

July 1981 Family Trip

We took the kids up for the whole month of July after we got married. We had nothing to distract us. No telephone, no television, no radio; just a tape recorder with different cassette tapes we could listen to. We had a fire pit outside with cut logs so we could sit around the fire pit and sing.

That summer, Josh was six and he absolutely loved *The Empire Strikes Back*. It was his favorite thing. We had a little cassette tape that had the whole story. He put a cape on and carried his lightsaber around listening to the tape over and over again. He knew every word of it. He turned it on, and you couldn't stop him. After about 50 times, the kids said, "Mom, make him quit! Tell him to stop!" We just had to let it go because he loved it so much.

One night Dick came upstairs wearing hideous polyester pants pulled clear up under his arms. I absolutely hated them. I yelled, "Stop it! Pull them down! I'm gonna rip them off of you!"

At the cabin in about 1981—Standing: Fay & Julie
Front: Kari, Michael, Becky, Meilyn, Larry, Josh, Tami, Bryan, Laura

The kids started chanting, "Mom, do it! Do it!"

He laughed and kept walking, but I finally just had it. He teased, "Well, this is the way I wore my pants when I went to school."

I responded, "Oh, no you didn't!" I chased him around the cabin with everyone laughing so hard. I finally caught him, pushed him on the bed, and started grabbing those pants to get them off. I said, "Who's got scissors!?" I cut one pant leg off, and I cut the other pant leg all the way up. As soon as I got the pants off, I threw them as far as I could. I was so upset that I threw them farther than I normally could, and they ended up out on the rafters. And that's where they stayed for months. People came over and didn't even notice the pants dangling from the rafters until I pointed them out. He had another pair of the same kind of pants at home, and when we got home, I cut them up and threw them in the garbage. The kids just laughed and laughed. They thought it was the funniest thing.

On that first trip, we decided to take some books so we could read to the kids at night. They didn't think it was a good idea to begin with, but once we got started, they really enjoyed it. We had *The Babysitters Club* series, the *Nancy Drew* series, and Louis L'Amour books. The little kids quickly ended up sound asleep. The older kids were just getting into the story. They said, "Just read one more chapter!"

1985—Dick & Kristen at the cabin

Jun. 1996—At the school near the cabin where the kids played.

Jun. 1996—At the school near the cabin where the kids played.

I told them, "But too many are asleep, so we've got to save it." It was a good way to get everybody down, and it gave us time together to bond and share our thoughts. It was a really fun tradition for us.

I always had a fun time at the cabin. It was always fun because the kids were happy. There really was less stress and less arguing. The kids knew they didn't have their friends, and they had to rely on each other to have their fun time. It was an easy place to take the kids because they just were so happy there.

The Spider Fighters and Rats

Our cabin was not winterized, so when we went up at the beginning of the summer, we had to sweep it out, clean out the cobwebs, and drive away the pests. Pam was always willing to go through the cabin first, because nobody else wanted to. She sang a song while she cleaned the cabin. It went like this: "We are the spider fighters. We use our flash-a-lighters. We stomp them to the ground. We squish their guts around. We sweep them in a bunch. They make a dandy lunch, crunch, crunch, crunch."

They hated cleaning the cabin when we got there, but once the spiders were gone, everyone—except Tami—brought in all the food. We always brought as much food as we could. There was food everywhere. All of the cabinets were full, and we stuffed all the space above and below the cabinets with more food. The refrigerator was packed.

Once the suitcases were inside and everyone decided which bed they were using, then the kids could go play or we would go to town. When we told the kids we were going to town, Tami yelled, "I want to go!"

And we asked, "Why?"

She immediately answered, "I've got to go to the bathroom!" Going into town was Tami's priority because she wouldn't use the outhouse behind the cabin. The first thing the rest of the kids wanted to do was start lining rocks up so that they had paths leading everywhere they wanted to go. They just loved doing that. They also always made a king and a queen throne out of rocks by digging into the dirt walls of the creek.

The other pests we had to deal with were the rats in the loft. I wouldn't open my eyes, but the kids said, "There they go again! Get them out!" The rats never got on the beds while we were there, but at night they ran back and forth, and the kids hated that. Meilyn would beg to differ with this statement. She says that the rats ran across the beds with the kids in them!

Water

We didn't have running water for most of the time we had the cabin, so we had to go get water from the ranger's station in jugs. We took showers using a milk jug with a spigot on the bottom, so you could control how much was running on you. With a gallon or a gallon and a half, you could get a decent shower and feel pretty clean.

Dick really did not like to be dirty, so it didn't matter if he had time to warm the water up or if it was cold. He took cold showers all the time, but he'd make this, "Oooh-hooo-hooo" noise and squeal. One time it was raining, so the rain water was coming down through the rain gutter. He said, "Oh, I could go out there and have a shower!" It was dark, but there were people all around in their cabins. He didn't care. He said, "They can't see us!" He went out there, stripped down, and took a rain shower. When he came back in, he told us, "That was a really good shower!"

The rest of us liked to warm up the water for our baths and to do dishes. Running water was an amazing addition when we finally got it up to the cabin.

As the kids got older, they brought their children and introduced them to all of the same experiences. It was a wonderful place for them to get to know their cousins better and become best friends. Sheri, Pam, and Laura used it a ton. One year Sheri came up to join us with her girls on a

Saturday night, so we were trying to get everyone bathed. She put pure cold water in the big bath and made those girls stand in there. I almost had the water warmed up for their bath, but she said, "Well, this is the way my mother bathed me." That was the last time that happened. After that, we always made sure that if the little kids were bathing in the big metal trough, there was warm water for them.

Food

We had a few foods that we always ate when we went to the cabin. The girls remember that we always took Uckumpucky (UCK-um-puh-key), a delicious snack made by mixing peanut butter and honey together, then spreading it on saltines.

Before we went to the cabin, I always made a lot of caramel corn—at least two big garbage bags full. No matter how much I made, we always went through it immediately. It's really good caramel corn and doesn't stick to your teeth. The kids all loved it.

We usually cooked on electric skillets and electric fry pans since we were cooking for so many people. We could make eight or ten pancakes at a time that way, so it went a lot faster.

The first year we were married when we went up for the summer, Dick fixed biscuits and gravy. My kids would not touch it. I had eaten biscuits and gravy, but they never had. I thought it tasted really good. Eventually my kids tried it, and it ended up being a family favorite. A lot of the kids requested biscuits and gravy for breakfast on their birthdays.

We made benches from logs, so we all had somewhere to sit around the fire outside. For dinner, we often made hamburgers over the fire pit. We could cook five or six hamburgers at a time. Then we made s'mores. It was a lot of fun to spend time together around the campfire at night.

Crazy Corn

1½ C. sugar
1 C. butter or margarine (2 cubes)
½ C. white Karo

Stir continually until it comes to a boil. Cook to hard crack stage + pour over salted pop corn.

111

Church

One time we were at the cabin, and Heidi (Karen's daughter, our niece) was there with us. She wanted to go to church with us but didn't have a dress, so we looked around to see what she could wear. Nobody had an extra dress. All the girls had only brought one. Finally, Pam looked at the curtains and said, "I bet we could.... Does somebody have a long shoelace?" We found a really long shoelace and took the curtain down. We pinned down the side of the curtain and put the shoelace through the hole. It looked just like a skirt. She had a little white top, and she wore the curtain as a skirt. It was so cute!

Family Home Evenings

We always had family home evening when we were at the cabin. Often, it was on the front porch, and sometimes we had it around the campfire. We told stories or taught a lesson. We also challenged the kids to memorize certain scriptures. Some of the most notable were D&C 130:22, Mosiah 4:14–15, and Moses 1:39. To this day, most of them remember those scriptures, or when they hear them in conference, they think, "Oh yeah, that's the one we had to learn."

One time we had a lesson about when a third of the host of heaven was kicked out with Satan, and Dick said to the kids, "Look around. Who would you be willing to say goodbye to?" It opened all of our minds, because we didn't want anybody to not be with us. We talked about that for quite a while. They were really good about participating in the conversations we had.

We usually ended up taking the kids into town to see a movie if we were up there for more than a week. It was just something we typically did. One year, we went to Show Low to see *The Jazz Singer.* Before we went, we had a family home evening lesson about how important it is to stay faithful to your spouse. It was fun to go watch the show, but we were glad that we had a discussion with the kids before taking them.

Laundry

One of the really fun things we did at least once a week at the cabin was go to Show Low to do laundry. I typically took the older girls: Meilyn, Laura, Kari, and Becky. Meilyn and Laura sang while they folded clothes, and the people in the laundromat absolutely loved it. The other patrons told them, "You have beautiful voices!" Then, the others kept folding, unfolding, and rearranging their laundry until we left.

They were also in awe at how much laundry we had. We had SO much laundry. When we were home, I did three loads of laundry every weekday, six or seven loads on Saturday, and no laundry on Sunday. When we were in Pinedale, we only did laundry once a week, so we had all of those loads at once. People asked, "Do these girls make this much laundry?"

I'd say, "Oh no!"

They'd respond, "How many kids do you have?"

That year we had 10 kids at the cabin, so I told them, "We have 10 out here, and four still down in the Valley." That always surprised everyone. It was so fun to go, and going together made a horrible job much more fun than just having to sit there and fold clothes by myself.

Activities

We always had a lot of things for the kids to do while we were at the cabin. We found that every summer, the first few days were kind of rough, but after a while they realized that we were all we had. Then they felt happier and did everything together. It made everything so fun.

When one of the kids was having a hard time, I often said, "Let's play a game." They picked out a game for us to play, and it cheered them up. We had lots of card games, and we played a lot of Rook, Chicken Foot, Rummikub, Knock Poker, Skip-bo, Rack-O, and Scum.

1985—Dick showing Kristen a horned lizard (aka a horny toad) at the cabin)

We were close enough to the Pinedale school for the kids to walk to it. Dick got them started playing a baseball game. Sometimes they wanted to walk home, and sometimes we just loaded them all up and drove them back. They really loved playing at the school.

Another tradition we had was that Dick and the kids liked to catch horny toads. When Kristen got her first one with her dad, she had the biggest smile, and her eyes were huge. Every time we went up after that, Dick had to find her a horny toad as soon as we got there because she wanted her own.

The kids also loved the trolley. That's what we called the zip line from the top of the mountain down the hill. Everybody liked the zip line. I went on it too, and I liked it. If the kids were being naughty, the other kids would grab the rope hanging from the zip line and stop it in the middle of the run, right above the "creek" (it was more of a wash and was usually dry unless it had just rained). Because of the way the terrain dropped there, it was way too high off the ground for them to safely jump down, and without momentum, they were stuck. The stranded kids pitched a fit and begged to be pulled back to the end. Our biggest problem was that the kids became daredevils. They wanted to have two or four people on the zip line at a time. Some of them could hang on, but some of them couldn't. Then they'd fall and

Fay's Fish Face

113

get hurt. It was scary sometimes. Chris Coombs, Steve's little boy, got knocked off the platform and broke an arm when Grandma and Grandpa Coombs took all the kids to the cabin. Other than that, I don't remember any other trips to the emergency room. I'm sure we took other kids at some point, but I don't remember exactly who or when.

Chopping Wood

After seeing Dick chop wood for the fire pits, the kids all wanted to chop the wood. Dick finally roped off a space for them to practice. He told them, "If somebody's in here, nobody else can go in there. Otherwise somebody's going to get hurt." We were all worried about somebody getting hurt.

One time we had a nephew up there who got hit because he would not stay out of the area. Mike was cutting wood at the time, and had to keep explaining that there was a line to wait in. Well, the nephew slipped under the rope and his ear got nicked. His parents weren't very happy, but Mike had warned him, Dick had warned him, and I had warned him. They went to the hospital, but it didn't end up being very bad. That was the only injury someone got from chopping wood.

Dick enjoyed working with the kids and teaching them how to do all sorts of things, and they liked to spend time with him. He tried to make everything that he was teaching the kids easier and safe. He taught them how to skin a tree, and he worked with them on a lot of different projects. It provided lots of bonding experiences for them.

2002 Rodeo–Chediski Fire

Our cabin burned to the ground in 2002, when two fires started at the same time, the Rodeo fire and the Chediski fire. These fires merged together and swept across the mountains. The Rodeo fire started on the Indian reservation when a part-time firefighter who needed work started the fire and ran away thinking it would give him some work. It was so dry that he couldn't control it, and then it started moving toward us.

Laura's family was at our cabin right before the fires. They went home to wash clothes, and when they came back up it was all on fire. We had lots of people coming up that summer, but luckily nobody was there the week that the fire started. The day it started was the day we were all planning to go up.

The Chediski fire started when a lady got lost and started a little fire to signal search and rescue. Search and rescue finally found her close to Heber and picked her up in the helicopter. They said, "We're so glad we found you. We've been looking for you for so long."

And she said, "I know. Do you have any water?" She got a drink of water, and then said, "You need to take the rest of this and put the fire out."

They said, "Oh no, the forest rangers will be here, and they'll put it out," but they never came.

The two fires merged together to form the worst forest fire in Arizona's recorded history until June 14, 2011. The firefighters and rangers were given instructions to allow structures to burn down so that they could get federal aid. For example, we had 11 structures in our family, and they only foamed the two permanent residences in the 17 hours they had to foam our area. Everything else burned to the ground.

Alan Wilkins was up there. He was beside himself because he just wanted to go in and do something, but they wouldn't let him in. It was terrible. It wasn't right of them to not let the firefighters do their jobs in order to get federal aid. Some of them were going to lose their jobs if they went in to fight the fire, but they said, "I don't care. That's my home. I might lose my job, but I'm going to save my house."

When they finally let us in, we saw that the cabin had burned to the ground. Our insurance gave us $30,000 and three trees, but we missed our cabin and were sad to lose it. Over the years, we had collected a lot of petrified wood on hikes in the big wash by the fire roads and brought it to our cabin, so there was a huge pile of it. After the fire, it was nothing. We found a couple little metal things that went on the old-fashioned stove that we never used. The only thing that survived was one big cast iron bathtub out in the backyard. It was kind of like a war zone. It was a sad day when it all burned.

The Cabin Now

We didn't rebuild the cabin, but eventually we asked who wanted the cabin lot, and nobody wanted it. Finally Rick said, "Well, I'll take it," so it's in his name now. He hasn't built anything but a septic tank. One day he might get a permit and build up there again. It doesn't feel private anymore though.

About 1983—Birthday party at Pinedale
Back: Meilyn, Larry, Laura
Middle: Becky, Mike, Kari, Kelly Coombs
Front: Tami, Dustin Coombs, Josh, Bryan, Chris Coombs, Kaci Coombs, Julie

You used to only hear cars going by once in a while, but now you can see them. It's not the same, but they still enjoy going up there. They stay in a little 10 foot x 10 foot tough shed with a porch. They bought it to use as a tiny home, and they put bunks inside. The government required them to install a septic tank in order to get power again, so they got electricity, but they don't actually have any plumbing in their cabin yet. They have a bunch of hammocks and a little grill outside. Laura and Bill bought 116 acres near Heber and built a lodge, so we go up there and use their place when we want to go to the mountains.

22. "The Tales of Ole Beck"

By Dick:

I told tall tales about Ole Beck and a fictitious Grandpa Wheeler around the campfire. As with all tall tales, there are some historical facts mixed in—but not very many! My kids say that the stories got more elaborate every time I told them. Here are some of my favorites.

When Grandpa moved to Arizona, he homesteaded a place near the Grand Canyon. Grandpa and his wife came to the area with their mule, "Ole Beck," and began to build a cabin of logs.

My grandpa had built up the reputation of being a "mule skinner," which means that he could say, "Gee - Haw - Whoa - Jump, etc.," and Ole Beck obeyed the commands. But, because of the time that was spent building the log cabin and setting up the homestead, unfortunately his skills had been set aside for a short while.

As the cabin neared completion, Grandpa realized that winter was upon them and he didn't have any meat in his cool shed, so he saddled up Ole Beck and went on an elk hunt. He soon saw a bull elk, but it was on the move. Grandpa didn't get off Ole Beck, but just shot that bull elk right from Ole Beck's back. It startled the mule, and he pitched Grandpa right off of his back and then took off running for home.

Grandpa did not have time to go after Ole Beck because a blizzard was kicking up, so he cut off the head of the elk and gutted it out. By the time he got all of that done, the winds and the snow began to increase, and Grandpa thought over his possibilities. With no real shelter in sight, he decided that the only smart thing to do was to crawl into the elk's stomach cavity and wait out the storm.

Near dawn, Grandpa awoke to the sound of a lot of howling and yipping. He peeped out of the neck hole of the elk carcass and saw several big wolves going at each other. Grandpa was stranded there because the elk's stomach wall had frozen together during the night, and he wondered what he was going to do. He decided that he would try to wiggle his arms free and to see if he could reach out the neck hole and grab onto the tails of two of the wolves. He was successful in grabbing the two biggest wolves, and they began to run. The elk carcass moved with them and glided easily across the frozen ground. It slid through the fresh snow like a bobsled.

My grandpa got another idea. He tried yanking a little harder on the tail of the wolf on the right. When he did this, the wolf ran faster, turning the elk carcass with grandpa inside, to the left. He tried again, this time pulling harder on the tail of the wolf on the left. The wolf on the left ran faster, pulling grandpa and the carcass to the right. By yanking alternately on the tails of the wolves, my grandpa was able to steer himself and the carcass right up to the front porch of the cabin.

The wolves were completely exhausted and stopped right there. Grandpa started hollering as loud as he could, still frozen inside the carcass. Grandma heard the commotion and came running to the front porch. She saw the wolves and went back into the cabin for a gun. She took a rifle from the wall and shot both of those wolves right where they lay.

Grandpa kept hollering, trying to get grandma's attention. She finally took a closer look at the elk carcass lying there at the front porch. As she looked closer, she saw Grandpa frozen inside the elk's stomach. Back she went into the house and returned with an axe. She used that axe to break the ice free and helped Grandpa crawl safely out of the elk.

After Grandpa dressed out the elk and hung it in the meat room of the cool shed, he skinned out those two big wolves. He tanned those wolf hides and took them into Flagstaff the following summer, where he got $10 apiece for them. Some folks say this isn't a true story because they've never heard of a wolf hide selling for more than $5 apiece.

Grandpa continued to work with and train Ole Beck, and he became a very obedient, trusted animal and friend. He had him trained up so well that if he took him into town, he could ride up to a stop sign and holler, "Whoa, Beck," and he stopped on a dime. His obedience and precision were legendary!

The following summer, grandpa wanted some deer venison, so he went in closer to the canyon to hunt. If you have ever been to the Grand Canyon, you will remember seeing deer running through the park and the campgrounds. Anyway, he was following a deer when he looked behind him and realized that some Indians were in hot pursuit. His thoughts were, "Do I want to die with an arrow in my back, or from a mile high fall from the canyon wall?" Grandpa chose the canyon and ran Ole Beck straight for the edge and then yelled, "Jump Beck!"

Ole Beck obeyed, and over the edge they went. As grandpa looked a mile down into the canyon, he could see that rocks had fallen from the cliff and accumulated in a v-shaped pile at the bottom. With his quick thinking, Grandpa hollered, "Whoa Beck!" just as they reached the canyon floor. Ole Beck drew up tight and skidded straight into the rock pile and stopped. Ole Beck's rear end pretty well looked like hamburger, but both Grandpa and Ole Beck lived. Grandpa said to Ole Beck, "Today you have become my angel. You saved my life and even your own. From now on, you are no longer Ole Beck, but you will be called 'Angel' instead."

Grandpa was so relieved, but this did not last for long. When he looked up, he realized that he and Ole Beck (Angel), were surrounded by the Indians that lived in the canyon. These Indians believed that if they saw something miraculous happen, all they had to do was kill the animal with those powers, eat it raw, and they would possess the same characteristics. So they killed Ole Beck (Angel), right in front of Grandpa, which about broke his heart. Then those Indians each cut off a big piece of raw meat and shoved it in their mouths and began to chew it. About this time, Grandpa got another idea. Just as the Indians swallowed the hunks of meat in their mouths, Grandpa hollered, "Whoa, Beck!" Ole Beck drew up tight, and his meat choked all ten of those Indians to death.

As soon as Grandpa got his wits about him, he went over to Angel (Ole Beck) and said, "In the deepest and lowest point of my life, you came through and brightened my day. You are not only my Angel, but I will forever remember you as my 'Bright Angel!' Life is still worth living, and I will never forget you and my love for you."

Grandpa never liked seeing buzzards eat dead things like roadkill, etc. So he dragged the remains of Bright Angel and the ten Indians to a flat spot, took his shovel from the saddle, and buried those bodies. I'm sure he didn't dig six-foot graves, but he did get them into the ground, and as the scriptures say, he dunged the area well so the soil became very fertile.

After completing the job, Grandpa still had time to climb out of the Grand Canyon. But as you know, you can't just go straight up, because it is too steep. So he went slowly to the left and upwards a way, then switched slowly to the right. The procedure is called switchbacks, so he switchbacked right then left until he finally reached the top. By that time, it was starting to get dark and cold, so Grandpa gathered up pine needles and pine boughs and built himself a sort of shelter under a low hanging tree. There he slept until morning. Then he got up and walked home to Grandma.

Bright Angel Lodge

A man named, I think, George Babbitt was into real estate and had bought a couple of old Mexican Land Grants near the canyon for a "song," or for very little. When Arizona was part of Mexico, the Mexican Government gave these grants to generals and other high-uppity people. Anyway, Babbitt acquired some land grants near the Grand Canyon.

One time when Grandpa was talking to Mr. Babbitt, he happened to mention the story of his mule, Ole Beck, now "Bright Angel" to him. Some years later, the United States Government decided to designate certain areas of the Country as National Parks, for example Yellowstone, etc. This was to set the land aside, not to be sold and developed for tourism.

Well they named the Grand Canyon as a National Park. Shortly thereafter, it was named one of the Seven Wonders of the World. So Mr. Babbitt invested money in the Grand Canyon. He built a large hotel on the rim of the canyon and decided to name it the "Bright Angel Lodge." He also has a large general store called Babbitts and several large pens adjoining the lodge where he keeps his mules. They take daily trips into the Canyon, to the river, and the Phantom Ranch, which is a motel resort at the bottom of the canyon on the north side of the river.

The government parks department maintains a trail crew, and the trail from the Bright Angel Lodge to the river—switchbacks and all—is called the Bright Angel Trail. When you finish the switchbacks from the lodge, you come to a fertile spot called "Indian Gardens."

Grandpa got tired of meat, etc., and left the area and went into partnership with another family in a farming venture in Gilbert, Arizona. After two years he gave that up and became a welder.

23. Visiting Grandparents and Singing

Fay's Perspective:

Dick and I felt it was very important to try to visit grandparents every Sunday if possible. When we married, we had five sets of grandparents: my parents, Evan's parents, my grandparents (who were still alive), Dick's parents, and Joan's parents. We had a big challenge on our plate to try to get to see all of them, because some were living in the valley, and some were at the opposite end of the city (my grandparents lived in Payson). If we were on the early church meeting schedule, it often worked well. When we were on the later schedule, we sometimes were only able to visit every other week.

Traveling with 11 kids in a 15-passenger van could be a little challenging at times, but I came up with a good idea that really helped. We sang songs as we traveled between grandparents' homes. We often carried the idea over to the motor home travel. The youngest got to choose the first song, then we moved up the row by ages. That way, everyone got to pick a favorite song.

We sang Primary songs, church hymns, fun songs, and often favorite songs of the season. Around Thanksgiving, for instance, we sang *There's a Great Big Turkey on Grandpa's Farm*. At Christmas, we sang *Over the River and Through the Woods*. One real favorite was *Grandma's Feather Bed*. We often included actions. Usually we sang one or more at each grandparents' home.

The benefit of singing while we traveled was that it eliminated the fussing and quarreling. The other benefit was that we always were prepared when called upon at family reunions.

The most important benefit was that our kids know and can relate to lots of experiences with all their grandparents as their memories are full of personal and choice experiences with all of them.

Fall 1984—Edith, Josh, Lincoln Eagar

Julie with Paul Eagar

Late 1980s
Back: Paul & Edith Eagar (Evan's parents)
Front: Josh Eagar & Bryan Wheeler

Dick's Perspective:

I was never really turned on to music. In fact, when we sang "Happy Birthday," those who sang parts and recognized that notes went up and down really laughed out loud and chuckled at my singing. Later in life, I had a hearing test done and the results were that I don't hear the high notes (whatever they are). When someone sings in church, I have to ask, "Was that pretty?" I can't really tell. I do remember words to songs and sing them to myself. I occasionally sing out loud—but very quietly. I know many of the familiar church songs and sing them quietly when traveling. Many, if not all of our family, can carry a tune—all but me—and a number of them sing in choirs.

Dad read this paragraph on the left about singing quietly to us and couldn't keep from laughing, because we all know he did NOT sing quietly—whether he knew the tune or not!
—Laura and Pam

My dancing skills are equal to my singing skills. I don't feel the beat and my feet don't either, so I have never really enjoyed dancing. Way back when I was a kid, maybe 14, my mother thought I needed to take dance lessons, so she signed me up. To this day, I don't have any feeling of the rhythm of music, and after the second dance lesson, the teacher said, "Sorry, no more. You've worn out my shoes stepping on my toes." So that's where my dancing ended. I almost never danced after that.

But back to singing. Here are some songs we loved singing as a family:

I Used To Play On My Banjo
Where Is Heaven?
One Bottle of Pop/Fish-n-Chips-n-Vinegar/Don't Put Your Dust In My Dustpan
Flee Fly
Julie, Julie, Julie, Do You Love Me?
Tami's in Love
Please Don't Talk To the Lifeguard
Today
A Child's Prayer
A Young Boy Prayed
I Pray in Faith
I Love to See the Temple
Five branches of the Military medley
Fried Ham
I Heard Him Come

We include some of our very favorite songs here. The "Big One" was *Grandma's Feather Bed.* We substituted "Aunt Lou" for Aunt Linda or Aunt Judy, depending on whose house we were visiting. Our kids acted it out while we sang it, and Fay's kids performed it in a talent show one time.

Grandma's Feather Bed

1. When I was a li - tle li - tle boy, just up off the
2. Af - ter supper we'd sit a - round the fire, the old folks'd spit and
3. Well, I love my Ma, I love my Pa, I love Granny and Grandpa

floor, We used to go down to Grand - ma's house
chew, Pa would talk a - bout the farm and the war, and
too, I've been fishin' with my uncle, I ras - sled with my

ev - 'ry month - end or so, We'd have chick - en pie and
Granny'd sing a ballad or two. I'd sit and listen and watch
cousin, I even kissed Aunt Lou ew! But if I ever had

coun - try ham, 'n' home- made but - ter on the bread, But the
the fire till the cob - webs filled my head. Next thing I'd know
to make a choice, I guess it ought - a be said. That I'd

best darn thing a - bout Grand- ma's house was her great big feath- er
I'd wake up in the morn - in' in the middle of the old feath- er
trade 'em all plus the gal down the road for Grand- ma's feath- er

Grandma's Feather Bed (cont.)

bed.
bed. *Chorus:* It was nine feet tall and six feet wide, soft as a down-y
bed.

chick. It was made from the feath-ers of four-ty 'lev-en geese, took a

whole bolt of cloth for the tick. It-'d hold eight kids and four

__ hound dogs and a pig-gy we stole from the shed. We did-n't

get much sleep but we had a lot of fun on Grand-ma's feath-er bed.

We always loved to sing *Mr. Johnny McBeck.* Our version went like this:

Mr. Johnny McBeck

1. There was a lit - tle Dutch - man. His name was John-ny Mc - Beck. He
2. One day a lit - tle fat boy, came run- ing in the store. He
3. One day Mr. John-ny Mc - Beck was feel- ing aw - ful mean. He
4. One day the ma-chine bust - ed, - and it would-n't go. John-

used to deal in sau - sa-ges and sau - er-krout and speck. He made the fin - est
bought a pound of sau - sa-ges, and laid them on the floor. And then he be - gan
acc - i - dent - ally backed in-to his sage - mak-ing ma - chine. Now Mis - ter Mist-ter
ny McBeck stuck in his neck, to see what made it so. His wife was hav-ing

sau - sa - ges there ev - er were to be seen. Until one day he in - vent - ed a
to whist-le, and whist-led up a tune. And all those li - ttle saus - a - ges
John - ny Mc - Beck, why are you such a jerk? Now you've got a lit -
night - mares, and walk-ing in her sleep. She gave the crank a big old yank,

hor - ri - ble saus-age ma - chine.
went dan-cing a - round the room. BANG! Oh, Mis - ter, mis - ter John-ny Mc-Beck, how
tle be - hind in you - r work.
and John - ny Mc-Beck was meat!

could you be so mean. We told you you'd be sorr - y for in - vent - ing that ma -

chine. Now all the neigh-bors cats and dogs will ne-ver no more be seen. They'll

all be ground to sau - sa-ges, in John-ny Mc-Beck's ma - chine. BANG!

124

Another fun song we sang with the kids was *I Stuck My Head in a Little Skunk's Hole.*

I Stuck My Head in a Little Skunk's Hole

1. Oh, I stuck my head in the lit - tle skunk's hole. And the
2. Well, I didn't take it out and the lit - tle skunk said, "If you

lit - tle skunk said, "Well, bless my soul! Take it out! Take it out!
don't take it out, You'll wish you had! Take it out! Take it out!

Take it out! Take it out! Re - move it!" *Pshhhh! I re - moved*
Take it out! Take it out! Re - move it!

*it! Too late!** *plug nose while singing*

125

Oh the Bear Sat Around with His Foot on the Ground was a fun song that Aunt Lovel Blacker taught us.

In between verses, you chant, "1, 2, 3, 4, let's sing this (opera, baby, fish, billy goat) song once more." Then everyone sings the song in that style.

Before the last verse, the person who is sick of singing says, "Let's sing this backwards song once more."

At the very end, everyone chants, "1, 2, 3, 4, let's sing this crazy song no more."

Oh the Bear Sat Around with His Foot on the Ground

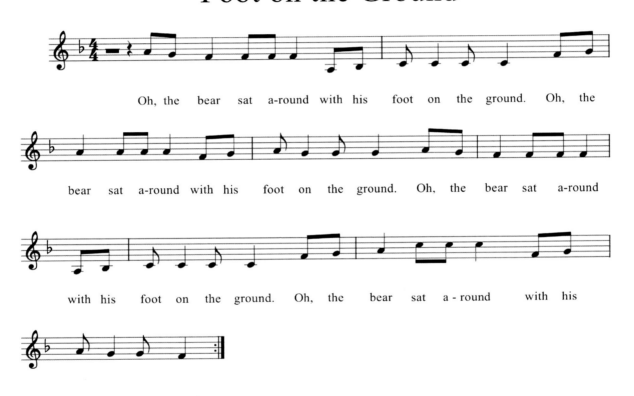

A song I (Dick) remember singing as a child was *Catalina Magdalena.* It goes like this:

Catalina Magdalena

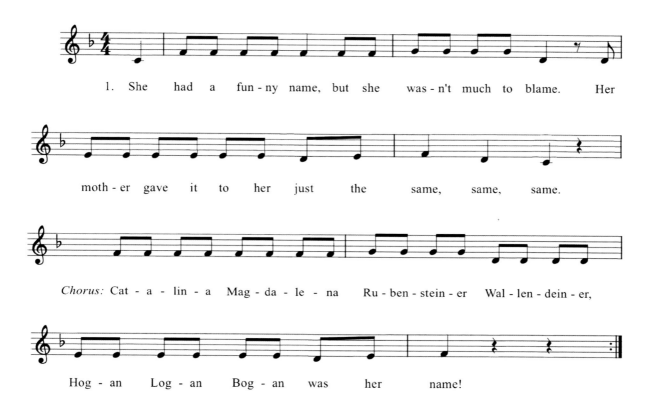

1. She had a fun - ny name, but she was - n't much to blame. Her

moth - er gave it to her just the same, same, same.

Chorus: Cat - a - lin - a Mag - da - le - na Ru - ben - stein - er Wal - len - dein - er,

Hog - an Log - an Bog - an was her name!

2. Well, she had two peculiar hairs on her head;
   One was black and one was red.

3. She had two eyes that were quite a sight;
   One looked left and the other looked right.

4. She had two arms that flopped all around;
   When she walked, they would drag on the ground.

5. She had two feet that were wide and flat –
   Each one bigger than a bathroom mat.

6. She had two holes in the bottom of her nose –
   One for her fingers ….and one for her toes.

7. She had two teeth inside her mouth;
   One went north and the other south.

8. Some folks say her breath smells sweet;
   But as for me, I'd rather smell her feet.

9. If rain makes flowers smell clean sweet,
   It ought to take a downpour for Magdaleen!

And here's one last family favorite:

Flea Fly Flo

An echo song, chanted/sung while clapping the beat

*Repeat as many times as wanted, going faster each time.

24. Wheeler Family Reunions

By Dick:

I am going to tell of some of the Ben and Lovel Wheeler extended family reunions we have had and been a part of. There have been numerous, and I probably will miss one or two because my memory is not that keen. These reunions gave us the opportunity to get to know each other better and to have fun activities as a family. Lovel's family lived in Idaho, so we didn't see them as much except at the reunions, but we were pretty close to the whole Wheeler family because we got together a lot.

2009—Back: Dick, Diane, Karen, Bill, Lovel, Doug, John
Front: Benny & Lovel

129

Lovel & Marvin hosting a family reunion

Family Reunion at Blacker Farm
Dick & Bill

Nederland, TX

We had a great time at Doug and Lee's. They were on a six-acre lot. The back four acres were a horse pasture with a race track around the edge. His girls were into performance riding, so they had some beautiful horses.

Doug also had a rack of six canoes. One day we took them to a swampy bayou to ride in and through. The waterway was laced with bamboo and other swampy tall grass (six or seven feet high). There were lily pads throughout the swamp. At the road where we launched the boats, there were six alligators with their heads out of the water. Doug's son Bryan and Matt Wheeler got in one canoe. Nobody would get in with them, so I volunteered. I got seated on the floor in the middle of the canoe and then started tipping the boat from left to right. They hollered and promised to behave on the boat ride. We had absolutely no problems paddling around the bayou, but they still remember the experience and mention it when they see me.

Uncle Doug's doctor friends were aware of the reunion and furnished 30 or 40 half gallons of fancy ice cream so we would not run short. Uncle Doug and Aunt Lee also arranged for a food wagon to come to their home and prepare one of the meals. His specialty was delicious steaks and lemonade, and we were impressed.

Doug and Lee had a pool at the back of the house and a very large, shallow bathtub in one of the bathrooms. The little kids really enjoyed taking baths together.

Blacker Farm - Burley, ID

We went to four or five reunions at Marvin and Lovel Blacker's home in Burley, Idaho. Again, this was a time to bond and get to know relatives. They lived way out in the country, so it was a fun and unfamiliar environment for our kids. The kids did woodworking and ceramics, swam in a hot spring that was a public pool, went to rodeos, went rapelling, and had a lot of other unique experiences.

Marvin and Lovel had a pond on their property. The kids thought it would be fun to make cardboard boats and see whose would stay up the longest. There was a lot of moss and stuff in the pond, so I got in and cleaned it out so the kids could float their boats and swim. In the process, it must have stirred something up in the water, but the kids all had a great time playing with their boats and swimming.

When they got out, we sprayed them down, but they all started itching. I mean, they were itching! Soon they were covered in hives and just dying. We told them not to scratch, but they couldn't hold still. We put them in the bathtub with baking soda and oatmeal. We tried everything we could think of, but we couldn't find anything that worked. We put on a movie, and the kids sat on their hands. Pretty soon they were going scratch, scratch. Finally, around midnight, we gave them some Benadryl hoping that it would help them sleep. They slept, but had little convulsions all night long. Anyway, the pond became known as The Itch Ditch. It was hysterical.

One time we had a family rodeo. They had about 10 little piglets, and the kids were supposed to go in and grab the pig by the leg. The other kids knew how to do it. They grabbed the piglets and

Late 1990s—Family Reunion at the Blackers'

held on to them. All of our kids looked at the piglets and heard them squeal and didn't want to touch them. They had a roping contest, and our down syndrome grandson won. They also had a sheep race where the little kids rode on the sheep. The only ones that liked it were the Idaho kids.

Marvin hired someone to slaughter one of their cows at his house. The man came to do the job right after the rodeo. Pam's kids wanted to stay and watch. The man slaughtering the cow said it was okay, and explained the whole process to the kids as he did it. He said he hoped he didn't ruin them, but they loved every minute of it. The rest of us went to the Snake River where someone had put up a slide. You could go down the slide on a gunny sack and splash into the river. Everyone loved that.

My little sister, Lovel, and her husband used to square dance. They went to an auction and bought two big racks of square dance dresses and all of the slips that go with them. The girls enjoyed dressing up all frilly.

I did a doll walk one year. Before the reunion, I got about 20 or 30 stuffed animals from home. I had the kids walk in a circle, like a cake walk, and when it was their turn, they got to pick a stuffed animal. When we were done, the mothers all came to me and asked, "Why didn't you tell us you were going to do that? We would have brought the stuffed animals!" We just wanted to get rid of them, and that was one way to do it.

Port Arthur, TX

In addition to the the reunion in Nederland, Texas, we attended two reunions at Doug and Lee Wheeler's home in Port Arthur, Texas.

Mesa, AZ

We hosted a reunion in Mesa where we held a carnival at our ward building and picnics at Papago Park and Freestone Park. Each of them hold special memories for those present.

2008—Lovel Unroe Phillips Wheeler, Frieda (Lovel's sister), & Dick at a family reunion

25. Coombs Family Reunions

By Fay:

We were able to attend many Coombs family reunions. All of the reunions helped our family become better acquainted with their relatives, even though we saw them so seldom and for such a short time. The kids got to know their cousins pretty well, because we gathered quite often with the extended family.

The reunions were important to me for many reasons, but the main one was that I wanted the kids to have relationships with their extended family members. There are times in your life when you can't talk to your parents, or you think you can't, and you need some love. You need to be able to talk to someone and know that they will just love you and give you the answers you need. That's one of the reasons that I loved all my aunts so much. I was very close to them. They could tell when I was having a hard time, and would take me on a walk and make me feel good again. They were so important to me. I didn't want to disappoint my parents with little things or big things or anything else, but it didn't matter to my aunts. They just loved me.

I wanted our kids to have those feelings toward their aunts and uncles and to know that there are people out there that they can go to if

> I don't think we've ever been to a reunion where Mom or Dad didn't call on us to sing or perform something. They'd say, "And now the daughters will sing. And now the family's going to sing *Grandma's Feather Bed.*" We knew it was going to happen, so after a while we'd make sure to have something prepared.
> —Laura

they need something. They can show up at their aunt or uncle's house, and they will just love them to pieces. That's one of the reasons we went to all of the reunions—to make those connections so the kids always felt that they had someone to talk to and had someone else who would always love them.

We've always felt like the biggest thing we needed to assure our kids about is that we love them and that there are other people in this world that love them other than just us.

1981–Fairgrounds - Flagstaff, AZ

After Dick and I got married and started making plans after our honeymoon, one of the first things that came up was a Coombs family reunion. At first I didn't know how we would make it work. My extended family didn't know all of the kids, and the kids didn't know everyone at the reunion. How would everyone handle that?

We thought about not going, but it was my Aunt Fay[15] who was planning the reunion, and I loved her so much. She was my dad's older sister, and they were very close—so close that he named me after her. I loved her, and I wanted all my kids to love her because she is such a special lady.

---

[15] Fay Coombs Langston (1916–2015)

133

We sat the kids down and said, "We're going to go to the Coombs family reunion at the fairgrounds in Flagstaff. There will probably be 100–150 people there, so there will be lots of cousins and lots of people." My dad was one of 15 children (three of them had passed away before he got married). He had 12 living siblings who almost all showed up to all the family reunions and had some kind of representation, so there were always a lot of people.

The fairgrounds in Flagstaff weren't very far away from Pinedale, so we drove over and talked with the kids about what to expect at the reunion on the drive. They were kind of negative and quite apprehensive. They didn't really want to meet so many people. They told us, "We're already freaks. There are so many of us." But we went, and honestly the first couple of days were rough. The kids didn't want to be introduced. They got tired of being reduced to just part of our new big family and people always asking, "Now, which one are you?" Luckily, sometime on the second day, their cousins wanted to get to know them, so they started playing together. That's when the kids decided it was pretty good and started having a good time.

The whole experience turned out to be really good for our family. The fairgrounds were in the forests of Flagstaff, and it was beautiful. My Aunt Fay was a good cook, so the food was delicious. Everything worked out well. It taught our new family to get in and do new things and meet new people. Everyone was so sweet. When we introduced another relative to one of our kids, they turned around and said, "This is our new niece/nephew." All our Coombs relatives, including their kids, were so welcoming, and the kids really enjoyed it. When it was time to go, our kids even said, "Can't we stay for another day?"

We said, "No, we've got to go." But it made us glad that we took everyone—even though it was rough at the beginning. That was their first introduction to their new Coombs relatives.

> The Coombs family was so welcoming to all of us. We were immediately part of their family.
> —Laura

1983 - Aunt Edith's Ranch - Hooper, CO

The reunions were normally every other year. Our next reunion was at Aunt Edith[16] and Uncle Curt's house in Hooper, Colorado. Aunt Edith was so sweet, happy, and good with everybody. Her home was really clean. Uncle Curt was known for the fact that if he borrowed equipment, he always took it back in better shape than when he got it. For example, people were glad to loan him a hay baler to bale 30 or 40 acres of hay because they knew that if anything went wrong, he would fix it even better than it was before.

Aunt Edith and Uncle Curt were really country folks. They lived out away from most people. Probably the closest neighbor was a quarter of a mile away. They had sheep skins and cow hides hanging over the fence and a used car lot with some antique cars that were priceless. They were poor, but they had everything they really needed.

---

[16] Edith Coombs White (1913–1997) m. Wesley Curtis White (1907–1987)

It was a different world for us, but it taught the kids that there are a lot of good ways to live. As a family, we talked a lot about that and helped the kids learn to appreciate differences in other people's way of life. They learned to love better and quicker and not judge as much.

Our kids also knew they had to help. They regularly asked, "What can we do to help? Can we help you do that?"

Most of the time my aunts told them, "No, just go play. We're fine. But thank you for offering," but the kids made that gesture, which everyone was grateful for.

We ended up having two reunions in Colorado that I remember. The first reunion was at the ranch, where they had a big sheep farm. It wasn't glorious there. Everything smelled awful all the time—like rotten eggs—because the water had sulfur in it. The water was so horrible that we wouldn't even take a shower in it. It was stinky, stinky, stinky. We went into town sometimes and got good water so we had something to drink. Eventually, one of the uncles brought a Bondel water purifier that took all the impurities and smell out of the water. We could drink that water. In fact, it was so good.

For some reason, the unfiltered sulfur water made the best pickles. Aunt Edith made dill pickles that were to die for. The kids kept asking, "Can I have another one? Can I have another one?" The pickles were so good that I kept asking the same thing. Aunt Edith gave us all her recipe. We tried to make the dill pickles at home in Arizona, but they didn't taste right. The only thing we could figure was that the awful sulfur water was what made them so wonderful. My mom tried making them once. My Aunt Fay tried several times, even carrying the water back from Colorado. Apparently all the sulfur stuff settled to the bottom and she just dipped it out instead of pouring it.

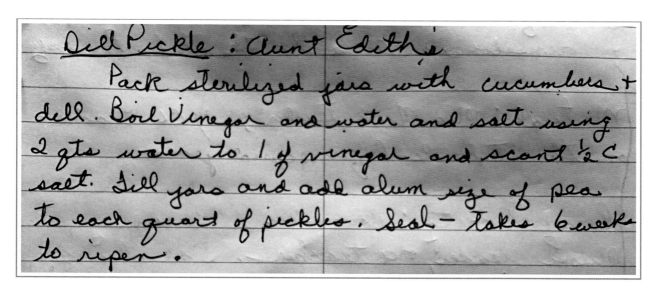

Aunt Edith's Dill Pickle Recipe

One day during the reunion, we went to the sand dunes for the day. The kids spent hours hiking up the long hills and rolling all the way down in the sand. They had a lot of fun and got to know their cousins well. There was almost always somebody that could be their friend while they were there.

135

The other reunion we had in Colorado was at a ranch that Aunt Edith and Uncle Curt bought up on a hill. Their last name was White, and the mountain was named White Mountain. The place used to be a mill, and it still had some of the machinery there to cut and process the logs. There were also a few cabins, and they were building more.

After Edith died, they buried her on that mountain by her husband. They dug a huge hole for her with a backhoe. After the services, they told the kids (her grandchildren) they could help shovel some dirt in, and they started throwing these rocks down on her casket. They were denting it! My dad lost it and said, "Get back right now! This is my sister!" The kids all ran off, and he took care of burying her by himself.

To give you more of an idea of how the family lived, the son, who kind of was taking charge of things up there, showed up with a goat and a pig to roast for dinner. He butchered and cooked them right there in front of everybody. It was a crazy and different experience. The kids had never experienced anything like that, so it was very memorable for them. We felt really glad we got to go.

Stake Camp - Beaver Dam, UT

Uncle Paul[17] and Aunt Bonnie hosted a reunion at a stake camp in Beaver Dam, Utah. The stake camp area was near a creek, and it was so green and beautiful. We loved that camp! The kids could play in the creek all day, and they did. They were constantly muddy and wet, but it was fun. Most of our Coombs family reunions didn't have a big reason to happen or a set program; we just visited, had a good time, played games, and had talent shows.

One of the nice things about having reunions in new places and planned by different people was that it helped our kids interact with people who were not the same as us. They learned that we could still love them, pray for them, and worry about them. They were our family. Our kids learned about some of the differences that came from people's upbringing and the decisions they made.

Uncle Paul and Aunt Bonnie had a daughter who fell in love and was soon married. They spent their whole honeymoon going to every temple session they possibly could for two weeks. She felt like her new marriage was very spiritual and she had married the best person on earth. After two weeks, he told her he had a surprise. He loaded her up and took her to a remote location in the mountains somewhere—I'm not even sure where it was. She couldn't tell where they were or exactly how they got there. There were homes and people and buggies, but she could see right away that it wasn't like a normal town. She soon figured out that her husband had been sent to find a bride that could go into the temple so he could learn the ceremony and bring it back to the group. She told her husband, "I didn't get married for this."

But he said, "Well, you are married to it now."

She tried to get away, but there was no phone and no way out. Somebody followed her all the time. Her parents didn't hear from her for months. They had people looking for her, but they had no idea where she was. She got pregnant and had a child. Since she couldn't go anywhere without the child, they gave her a little more freedom. She eventually had seven children. She never did leave, because they wouldn't let her kids go. My aunt and my uncle just sorrowed.

---

17 Paul Woodrow Coombs (1917–1994) m. Bonnie Cornum Coombs (1919–2009)

Her dad finally found out where she was, and he and his wife were allowed to see her. They were blindfolded, so they couldn't tell where they were taken. They took some food and some of her clothing she had left behind. They met three or four of their grandkids that they had never seen. They were only allowed to stay for one day and had to be gone before dark.

She still believed in God and had a testimony of the Church. She and her husband and some of their kids came to the reunion in Beaver. He wouldn't let her talk with anyone unless he was by her. Her clothes went to her wrists and ankles, and she was covered all the time. She didn't wear make-up, but she was beautiful with long, braided red hair. She was hoping her kids would go to church and realize the Church was true and the cult was wrong.

Her husband wanted to get another wife. She fought him and fought him. I don't know what happened with all that. I honestly have no idea if she's still alive.

It was scary. She was a beautiful young woman and a very good daughter, but she fell for someone without really knowing him. I think that seeing what happened to her made my kids really alert to things like that. I think they were a little bit more careful. I hope all my posterity will be aware that strange things can happen. Get to know the parents and family before committing to someone. And know that you can do hard things and still keep your testimony.

White Water Rafting - Snake River, UT

Uncle Paul and Aunt Bonnie hosted the next reunion at the Snake River in Utah. After going to enough of these reunions, our kids were friends with all of the other kids. As soon as we arrived, they found their cousins and went off to play.

The big activity was white water rafting down the Snake River. The old ladies, like me and some other people who didn't want to go white water rafting, just spent about an hour and a half relaxing by the water on a calm stretch of the Snake River. It was beautiful and fun.

The only problem that we had was that every afternoon it rained and rained and rained, so nobody could do anything. Finally we got everybody's tarps and tied them all together so we could at least meet together and visit during the daily rainstorms.

On the day that the river guides took the kids white water rafting, there were at least four rafts full of kids. The raft that Becky was on tipped, and under they went! The guides were scrambling to try and get all of those kids out of the freezing cold water. They were scared, but nobody was hurt. When we heard they had flipped, all of us parents were in a panic down at the river. But when they came back, they were laughing and saying, "It was so funny, Mom! It was so funny!" It was a little scary for all the parents, but it was a good bonding moment for the kids.

Ranch - Eagar, AZ

Grandma and Grandpa Coombs hosted one reunion on a ranch west of Eagar.

Whiting Ranch - Eagar, AZ

The Ron White (the son of Fay's dad's sister, Edith) family was in charge of one reunion on the Whiting Ranch between Eagar and Show Low. There was a big building, and a big hill. The kids liked to roll down the hill in tires. We were not too happy about that, but they loved it. The kids also really loved swinging on the swing they set up.

Pinedale, AZ

One summer, we had a reunion in Pinedale. Everyone else stayed about three or four miles away from our cabin. We went over for breakfast, stayed all day, and then went back to sleep at our cabin since it was so close.

This reunion was memorable because of an experience we had with my Uncle Raymond[18]. Uncle Raymond was my dad's youngest brother. He was in the Air Force when they were just beginning to make jets, and he was amazing. He learned faster than anybody else. He trained people faster than anybody else. One day he was in a car accident and was in a coma for three months. They thought he wouldn't make it; and if he did, his brain wouldn't work properly. But he woke up, and his brain was recovering. By the time his brain development matched a 20-year-old, they put him back in a jet because they thought it might help. He was so good. He remembered everything about flying and jets, and everyone realized he was going to be okay. Later on, he was driving when a car came out of nowhere and hit him again. He was in a coma for another three months, and when he woke up, he was never the same again. His brain development never grew past age 12, and from that point on, he was just a funny man. He always had ice cream or cake or some other dessert for supper.

Before his first accident, Uncle Raymond was married, but after his accident she left him in a motel, and gave the owners two weeks of rent money and a phone number to call when the last day came. One day my Aunt Elsie[19] got a call saying, "Your brother's here, and he's been here for two weeks. His wife's not coming back for him, so you need to come get him." He lived with Aunt Elsie for the longest time, and then he lived with my Aunt Fay. Our kids learned a lot about charity watching his sisters take care of him. It was incredible to see. The sisters were always ready to pick him up again when he fell down.

Uncle Raymond loved walking. He wandered for hours and hours all over Mesa wearing really big earphones because he didn't like the traffic sounds. When he got thirsty, he drank out of people's water hose. We were worried people would get mad at him for doing that, but they knew him and knew he just liked to walk. He needed to be moving, but he always came home.

At our reunion in Pinedale, he went out for a walk. He was told he could walk along the fence, but instead of coming back when he got to the corner, he turned the corner and kept following the fence. After a few hours, everyone realized he was gone and started to panic. We searched for him for a couple of hours, but nobody could find him. We even got in our cars and drove around trying to find him. We stopped and had a prayer that he would be okay and we would find him. Later, the kids asked, "Can we say another prayer?"

We told them, "Of course. You can say as many as you want." The rescue people finally found him around 10 p.m., still walking along the fence. They told him they needed to take him back, but he

---

[18] Raymond Dick Coombs (1932–2005)

[19] Elsie Coombs Pankratz (1919–2017)

wanted to walk back, so they just drove right behind him. He waved to us as he walked right by us. He wasn't concerned at all. My aunts were so worried, but he was okay.

It might not seem like it would be an impactful experience, but for our family it was. Our kids learned one very important thing, which is that if they are lost, they will be found. Everybody in the family will go out, try to find them, and pray for them. Prayer truly is a miracle that the Lord gave us. When we use it right, it gives us peace. It gives our children peace. It gives everybody peace. And then we can move forward.

26. Wheagar Family Reunions

By Fay:

Our extended family reunions are a big part of our family memories and traditions. As our kids have grown, gotten married, and had children and grandchildren of their own, we have continued the tradition with the next generations. I'll call these the Wheagar family reunions.

Sometimes we plan the reunions out with games and activities. Other times we just go hang out together, and that's usually everyone's favorite. We may plan a couple things, but mostly we just let people do what they want. They visit and get to know each other and relax. We usually have two families in charge of each meal. Everyone does their part so all the responsibility isn't on the host. It's nice because everyone pitches in to help clean up even if it's not their meal. It always works out really well.

We always plan to be in church on Sunday no matter what. When we were at places like Pinetop or Lakeside where they had plenty of churches, we always went to the building. If we were there on July 4th or Labor Day, the chapel that usually had 50 people had 300 people. It took them 30 minutes to pass the sacrament. When we went to Heber, we knew that their chapel would be full, so we got permission to hold our own sacrament and testimony meeting at the lodge. It was really good.

Dick likes to tell the stories about Ole Beck, and all the grandkids love it. He also plans a service project, and he makes a point of praising whoever is working really hard. Service is a value of his. It's fun to see the different grandkids step up because they want Grandpa to notice.

Grandkids born in 1999–2000
Bethany, Jacob, Kassidy, Kinley, AJ, Cole, Kallen, Paityn

We have watched a couple of kids really grow at family reunions. One of the grandsons was a little grouchy sometimes about helping. When we were at Aaron's, there was a tree that needed to be cut down. We decided that would be our service, and that little grandson stuck with us the whole time. He chopped and piled up the wood, then he put it in the truck. He got it out of the truck and put it where it belonged, and he did it all with a smile. I thought, "Hallelujah, finally!" He loved that reunion. Lots of the kids are that way sometimes. They don't want to do a service project, but it always brings us closer, and is always a good experience. We have so many people that we can accomplish a lot really fast.

Bill and Laura bought 116 acres between Forest Lakes and Heber, Arizona. It is about 7,000 feet in elevation. They are off the grid, which means they have solar electricity, their own wells for water, and large propane tanks for gas. The property had two cabins, two modular homes, and some trailer hookups for electricity and sewer when they bought it. Bill and Laura built a large lodge that accommodates many people comfortably. We've had three reunions there so far with up to 120 people. There's plenty of room for everyone to spread out. People can bring a tent or trailer if they want to.

One year for our service project there, 50 of us cleaned up the weeds and rocks in an area and made a fire pit and bench. Now we use it every time. When we were up at LoMia, we had the kids walk around and pick up all the trash. They said, "This isn't our trash."

We told them, "That's okay. We will still pick it up. We want to leave the place cleaner than we found it." They griped sometimes, but they always got happy as they did it.

We love the reunions because all the cousins don't live close to each other, but when we get together, they become best friends.

Camp LoMia

The church used to allow families to rent Camp LoMia when it was not being used by the stakes for girls' camp. Camp LoMia is about five to seven miles east of the LDS Church building in Pine, Arizona. I think we were able to rent it on Labor Day weekends for three years in a row. On two of the occasions, we rented a camp and ramada. We called it the "Upper Camp." It was used during girls' camp by the fourth year or older girls, and they were involved in high adventure type activities.

The upper camp had a large open but covered ramada with folding tables and chairs that could accommodate 60 to 80 people at a time. In the north end of the ramada was a large kitchen with a huge gas stove, oven, and large grills. There was also an outdoor ramada for the performing arts.

Across the road to the west of the ramada was a huge bathroom facility. It was divided in half by a wall, so it required two separate doors. When the camp had only girls there, they used both sides, but when men were present, the men used one side and the women used the other. On each side there were six shower booths, seven or eight toilets, and about 12 basins or sinks for washing and looking in the mirror. There were eight or 10 separate cabins that had a full porch and two sleeping rooms that accommodated six or eight people.

For the family reunion one year, we had an Olympics theme with all kinds of fun competitions. One of the families organized a parade, and many people came dressed to represent different countries. Everyone brought craft items to be put together, painted, etc. There were lots of games

141

shared by all. One of the fathers organized a nature hike where the group walked through the forest identifying trees, bushes, flowers, rocks, animals, etc.

On Sunday, we went to the Pine Ward. The attendance tripled their regular weekly meeting and the Sacrament had to be administered an extra time or two. Because it was fast Sunday, it limited the number of testimonies born. Most of us also stayed for Priesthood, Relief Society and then Sunday School. That evening, we held our own testimony meeting in the camp chapel.

The reunion was a great opportunity for the family to get to know each other and to share our lives with each other and for cousins to play with cousins. We also held a talent night and many of the family members shared their talents with everyone. We rented the upper ramada or camp twice, and the second year was very much like the first.

The third year we rented the Orchard Camp, which accommodated one hundred-plus people. That camp was located in a flat area with lots of space for games like softball, volleyball, etc. The cabins and restrooms were much larger and nicer. The covered ramada was larger and had a raised stage on one end. The kitchen was larger with two cabins for staff and the camp nurse at the ramada end.

Sep. 2011—Parade of Countries, LoMia Reunion
(Skipping people whose faces you can't see)
Natalie Garner, Aaron & Becky Hale & daughters, Bryan Wheeler, Josh Eagar, Kassidy Wheeler, AJ Hale, Abby Theobald, Nathan Schlink, Ethan Schlink, Aceson Hale, Gunner Spahr, Kutler Gregory, Aro Hale

Sep. 2011—Parade of Countries part 2, LoMia Reunion
Summer Schlink holding Faith, with Belle & Liberty Schlink in front & Kaden Gregory behind. Heidi Garner holding Mikah. Nate Garner, Hunter Garner, Jacob Garner, Kazlan Gregory, Maesyn Garner

The whole west side of the ramada was covered with permanent picnic tables and benches. In the main ramada, we had two large outdoor heaters, which made it more comfortable to visit and share experiences in the evening. There was also a zip line in the camp. We followed the agenda as explained above. We always had between 75 and 125 family members present.

2013—Playing games in the Ramada at LoMia Orchard Camp
Back: Liberty Schlink, Griffin Spahr, Abby Theobald, Mary Freebairn
Front: Maggie & Spring Theobald, Mandi Acedo

Pinetop, AZ

We held the next two family reunions at Aaron and Becky Hale's cabin in Pinetop, Arizona, which is South of Lakeside and North of the Honda Casino on the White Mountain Indian Reservations. The cabin is about 5,000–6,000 square feet with a five-car garage and many rooms and bathrooms. There are beds for 70 people, several self-contained rooms for couples, a large kitchen, and a large living room with a fireplace. The home is built on a double lot. The back yard is enclosed with a ten-foot chain link fence. In the back yard, there is a large covered ramada with five picnic tables under it. This area is usually occupied with people eating, snacking, and playing games. There is also an outdoor fire pit that is enclosed with a circular brick wall. The brick wall is about three feet tall and is just the right height for sitting.

We usually have a fireside, sing, tell stories, roast marshmallows, and make s'mores. There is also a zip line in the backyard, a large slide, swings, a horseshoe pit, lots of grass, and large pine and blue spruce trees. Behind Aaron's place, there are two or three vacant lots, and Aaron owns them so there is plenty of room for other activities there.

One year for a service project, we cut down a large dead pine tree, cut it into pieces, split it into firewood, and hauled it into a covered storage area next to the house. We had several pickup loads and ended up with enough firewood for a year or two. It was an enjoyable experience.

Pinetop is at about 7,000 feet in elevation, so it is much cooler there in the summer. In the winter, there is always snow and rain, but the cabin is comfortable and gets lots of use year round.

Part 5: Church Callings (1981–Present)

27. Fay's Callings

By Fay:

I have had the opportunity to serve in many different callings in our wards, missions, and temples. These callings have been a blessing in my life as I have served with some amazing youth and leaders.

Primary Presidency - Mesa South Stake

While I served in Primary, I was a ward Primary presidency counselor, a teacher, a music leader, and a counselor in the Mesa South Stake Primary presidency at different times.

When I was called to serve in the stake Primary presidency, I thought they were going to put me in charge of the music because that's what I had been doing in my ward. Instead, they put me over the scouting program. Even though I had a bunch of little boys, I had never done any scouting because Dick was always the scout leader. Dick and I ended up falling into a routine with handling my scouting assignments. I'd ask him a million questions, then I'd go to a presidency meeting where everyone asked me questions that I had no ideas about. I wrote the questions down, then took them home and started the process of asking Dick a million questions again. It was a really hard calling for me. I really put in a lot of time and effort into it, but I never felt like I was right for the calling.

I was also in charge of coordinating all the Primary softball games in the summer while I was in the stake Primary presidency. I had to make sure that people showed up and that all the teams had coaches. I was also in charge of solving any disputes that came up. We had each Primary president form two teams from their ward. Things were going really well until one man switched around the kids in his ward so

1990s—Fay teaching the Hookieluau at girls' camp at Camp Kenyon by Prescott

that he had all the good players on his team. We were just playing for fun and didn't keep score, but he always wanted to keep score. He drove me crazy. I said, "That is not what this is for."

He responded, "Well, it is for my team."

I said, "Then you can take your team and go home, because that's not what we are doing here." Every group that they played went home thinking they were nothing because he told them they were nothing. I fought with him and fought with him, and at the end I told the counselor in the stake presidency that the coach should never be a leader again. I finally just said, "You are not to show up again, and someone will be there to escort you and your team out if you do."

He said, "You're a woman. I'll show up if I want to." That did it.

The stake president was there, and they took him out and told the boys, "We're sorry boys, but you can't play anymore."

He was really mad at me, but I just smiled at him and said, "I won't be here next year. You can fight with the next person." I was in charge of softball and scouting at the same time, so I was glad to get out of that.

YCL Leader

After serving in Primary, I was called to serve with the youth in mutual. I was a youth camp leader (YCL) at the stake level for more years than I can count. The YCLs are girls who have graduated from mutual, but they come back as camp leaders. There were generally two YCLs for each cabin, and they were really cute and fun. They made little gifts and things for the girls in their cabins every day, and it was really fun to work with them.

I got to serve with a lady who had been serving as a YCL leader for 20 years already when they called me. She was wonderful. I'd say, "What do you want me to do?"

She'd respond, "Oh, I've got all this stuff from all these years, so let's just use it." So we would. She did most of the work, but it was really fun. It was such a nice change after serving in Primary. I went to camp so many times, and I loved that.

Mia-Maid/Laurel Teacher

I was also a Mia-Maid teacher for part of the time I served as a YCL. I did not like being a Mia-Maid teacher. My daughters were in my class, which was not a good thing, because they thought all the lessons were based off them. I finally sat them down and had them read the lesson before we had it on Sunday. I explained, "This is what girls do. This is how girls act. That's why this is in the lesson, and I did not write this book." They still didn't like it, and I still didn't like it. My mom always said that Mia-Maids are like an armpit. They're not the happiest. They aren't the youngest ones. They are old enough to go to dances, but they can't date, so they are just kind of crabby.

Three years later, I was asked if I would teach the Laurel class for a few months while they kept trying to find a permanent teacher. I said, "Some of those are the same girls I had in Mia-Maids three years ago, and it didn't go well."

The bishopric member said, "Well maybe they've grown up. Let's see." So I gave it a try, and it was amazing. The girls listened—they never listened before! I had a great experience, and I really felt like that was where I needed to be.

1984—Horizons
Back: Tami, Becky, Kari, Laura
Front: Kristen, Meilyn, Julie

1984—Horizons
Meilyn, Kari, Becky, Laura, Fay

One experience that was a blessing for me and the older girls was the opportunity to go to *Horizons* in Flagstaff in 1984. It was a gathering of about 9,000 young women from Arizona and several other states. We stayed together in the dorms at NAU. We listened to spiritual talks from Hartman Rector, Jr., Elaine Cannon, general authorities, and others, and did various activities. We were definitely able to get closer as a family because we were in a special environment having spiritual experiences together. As part of the event, we all had to dress in white. I made white dresses, not only for the girls who went to *Horizons*, but for all the girls, even the little girls who didn't go.

Relief Society First Counselor - Mesa 36th Ward

At this point, most of my Church service has been in various Relief Society callings. In my patriarchal blessing at age 29, it said I would be a big part of Relief Society. I thought, "I can hardly ever go to Relief Society, because I'm always in Primary or something else." I was called as the music leader when we were first married, I served as a Relief Society teacher for a little while, and I've always been a visiting teacher/minister. I love the Relief Society.

We hadn't lived in the Mesa 36th Ward for very long when they called Sister Yamamoto to be the Relief Society president, and she called me as her first counselor. I didn't know her very well. All I knew was that she was originally from Switzerland, and she was married to a Hawaiian man. Because English wasn't her first language and her husband had an accent, the way she talked was kind of upside-down and backwards. That caused a lot of problems with people being offended by what she said. Right after they called me as the first counselor, she reached out to me and said, "I need to talk to you." I went over to her home, and when she started crying, all I could think was that she wanted to release me. I said, "Do you want to change me?"

She said, "No. I need you to understand me. I know the Lord told me to call you because you would know what I mean to say instead of what comes out of my mouth." After that, she never went to one-on-one visits without me. When we'd meet with someone, she'd say something, and I'd say, "She means this and this and this."

Then she'd say, "Yes, that's what I mean." When I was bedridden for two and a half months, I told her she probably needed to release me because I wasn't helping, and she said, "Oh no. I'm in so much trouble with so many people, and you have to fix it!" It was one of the funnest callings I've ever done because I felt really needed. She was the sweetest lady, and she loved serving the ladies in our ward.

Speaking of the illness I had while I was serving as the first counselor in the Relief Society, I kept having problems with my back. The doctors kept trying to figure it out, but we weren't making any progress until one of them finally said, "Well, maybe this has to do with your cycle. Do you have a normal cycle?"

I said, "Every 29 days." He asked if my back hurt most during my cycle, and it turned out that it did. They checked to see if I had endometriosis, but the only thing they could figure out was that my uterus was tipped enough that they could justify doing surgery.

When the doctor came in to talk to me about removing my uterus, he said, "I don't leave anything. Everything comes out, because when you leave stuff in, you just get cancer on it."

I said, "That's fine with me. I'm through." So we went forward with the surgery. I also asked him to lift my bladder at the same time even though it would make my recovery much longer.

Right before I went under for surgery, my doctor said, "Sister Wheeler, just remember that your back is still going to hurt."

When I woke up and he came into the recovery room to check on me, the nurse said, "She's already been up and walking." He couldn't believe it!

He asked me how my back felt, and I said, "It doesn't hurt at all." That was so surprising and confusing to him that he went to the lab to see if they had figured out what was wrong, and on the top of a manilla envelope in huge letters it said, "Severe Adenomyosis." It's like endometriosis, except on the inside of the uterus. He hadn't ever checked inside, so we had no clue that's what was going on.

My recovery was long and difficult. I could move and do things, but I was just in bed most of the time. I felt like my insides were floating, I was hot, and I was miserable. It just felt so odd. I finally went up to my folk's house in Eagar for a couple weeks. Dick took me up, went back to the Valley for a week, and then came back up and stayed there for a week with me. By the end of that trip, everything came together and I was fine.

Temple Workers

Dick and I served as temple workers for 12 years. For three of those years, we were coordinators in the Mesa Temple, right before the Gilbert Temple opened in 2014. During those three years, being temple coordinators was our calling because we were there every Thursday and Friday from 4:30 a.m. to 11:30 a.m.

On our mission to the Philippines, we only got to go to the temple one time. That was really hard, because we were used to going every week. So when we went on our mission to Fiji, we worked in the temple on our P-day (Saturday) because we love the temple.

For a while, we've been going to the temple together every Tuesday morning. We attend the 7 a.m. and the 9 a.m. endowment sessions when our health permits. We love it, and we love going together. It is service, but it is fun service. It's even more enjoyable now that we've been taking our own relatives' names to the temple.

Missions

We had other opportunities to serve in the church with two missions, the first to the Philippines and the second to Fiji. When we were in the Philippines, my testimony of the importance of callings grew. All the native missionaries went home and disappeared because their home branches didn't give them a job or responsibility in the branch, so they had nothing. They didn't have jobs or anything there, but if they just had callings they would still have felt the blessings of serving in the Church. I know that service, whether in an official calling or not, is what helps keep us on the right path.

My Feelings About Serving in The Church

There have been times in my life when I thought I was too busy and had too much on my plate to have a calling. One time was when Dick had both of his knee surgeries done at the same time, I was so overwhelmed and I thought about being released. I didn't ask them to release me, but they did, and then I went a long time without getting another calling. That was really hard for me, and I missed it. I felt like I wasn't worthy of having a calling because I wanted to be released when I was feeling overwhelmed about Dick's surgeries. That wasn't true.

I know that blessings come when you fulfill your calling. You do it because you've been called and set apart, and you try to do your best. There have been times when I have done that, and times when I haven't. I can tell you that when you give it your all, you receive the blessings that you need. I have learned so much about other people and how to work with different kinds of people. I am serving in Primary right now by sitting with any classes that need some extra help that week. But I feel the blessings just because I'm there, and I'm trying to help. I love that part of having a calling.

28. Dick's Callings - Mesa 36th Ward

By Dick:

I was serving in my seventh year as the first counselor in the stake presidency when we got married and moved into Fay's home. Since we lived in the same stake, I served in the stake presidency for one more year before being released in 1982.

Scoutmaster/Varsity Scout Coach

My church calling after my release from the stake presidency was Scoutmaster of the 36th Ward, and that calling lasted for three and a half or four years. Mike, Bryan, and Josh were in the troop, so I was able to see them receive their Eagle Scout rank. There were 30 boys from our ward in the troop, and we also incorporated the 55th Ward boys, which averaged about eight boys per year. They furnished an assistant Scoutmaster, so I got to work closely with Ed Guthrie for several years.

When Rick was a Varsity Scout, I was the Varsity Scout coach. As a varsity team, we decided to go on a 50-mile hike on the Black River that turned into more than we were able to handle. Before going, we made arrangements with Falcon Field Airport to take our Scouts on a flight over the area we would later be hiking, along the Black and White River. From the aerial view, we could see that

1984—Dick (yellow shirt) leading a Scout activity

because of cliffs and steep embankments along the river, it would be necessary to cross the river about fifty different times during the hike. We packed freeze-dried food and tried to make our packs as light as possible. Our plan was to catch and eat a lot of bass on the trip, so we packed fishing poles and minimal food.

One of the boys in our team was Chris Standage. He was diabetic, and his mother worried that the hike would be too difficult for him. She sent him with old clothing so that he could burn his dirty clothes each day and not have to pack them out, so each day his pack became a little lighter. She also sent his older brother to come along and help him, which proved to be a blessing!

We thought we were going to wade the river, but the river was running too full and we couldn't wade it in most places, so we had to stay on the same side of the river bank. Before I went, I talked to a friend of mine who knew the road, and he said, "Dick, there's a road that comes down to the black river," and he showed me the approximate location on a topographic map. I told the guys we were going to hike up on that hill and find a road and follow it down to the river. That road would then lead us back out to the town of White River. The road was not very visible, and we soon realized we had overshot the road, so we went back a couple miles.

My son (Rick), and an Indian boy that was living in our ward, and I decided to get on that road and hike it out so we could notify the people that were going to pick us up that we were not going to be where they thought we were going to be. Howard Standage was with me, and he was probably 18, so I left him with the boys.

The three of us took off early in the morning. I said, "Hey, we're not going to wear our coats because it's just extra weight. We'll get a ride in a few minutes and ride right into White River." Well, we didn't see a car, and we ended up walking the 18 miles clear into White River. I made a phone call to tell everyone where we would be, then we went back to the old Fort Apache. We decided to sleep in a wash next to the fort. We gathered up a whole bunch of firewood, built a fire, and froze to death. It was one cold night! We'd get one side warm, then turn over and get the other half warm. If we had used our heads, we could've found a garage sale and bought some old coats and stayed warm.

In the meantime, the Standage kid and the Scouts packed up and hiked back a couple of miles. We did manage to find them, and we all made it back safely, but with some huge blisters on our feet.

Area Welfare Agent - Mesa Stakes

After Scouting, President Carl Olsen called me to be the "area welfare agent" over the 10 Mesa stakes. I served in this capacity for 12 years. I worked closely with Roy Beach who had the same assignment with the Tempe stakes and another brother who was over the Phoenix stakes. We had semi-annual training meetings with a brother from Salt Lake, which usually lasted a day or two.

The welfare agents are responsible for the training of stakes in welfare matters which

Mesa Cannery

included social services, employment, bishops' storehouse, wet pack canning, dry pack canning, Deseret Industries, the humanitarian spearhead unit, and church farms.

The agents receive their work needs for the coming year from each of the above in August. We divided the work assignments up between the three areas and then made up a work assignment sheet for each stake. We asked them not only to accept the assignments, but to trade with another stake in their area if there was a problem that interfered with their calendar for the next year, and let us know of the switch so I could send out a final assignment sheet by the 1st of October. Then every month, I called the stakes to remind them about their assignments for the month.

The assignments included:

1. Farm Labor: There were two main farm labor assignments. One was a weeding assignment for the cotton farm in Stanfield near Maricopa. This assignment usually required 100-plus men and boys at 6 a.m. and included one or two weekends of two or three hours of work. The other was working at the 40-acre sweet corn field east of Queen Creek High School. Depending on the time of year, that assignment included hoeing, thinning, cultivating the weeds out, and then picking the corn.

2. Wet Pack Canning: Mesa canned all of the Church's salsa, spaghetti sauce, and catsup. It took twenty people for each four-hour shift, and there were two shifts per day. We assigned each stake ten people per shift and no more than one shift per day. Occasionally, we had to add some more shifts later in the year according to the extra needs of the Church.

3. Bishops' Storehouse: The Bishops' Storehouse was like a grocery store. We assigned ten people per shift for a four hour shift. The workers kept the shelves, vegetables, milk, and meat cooler stocked. They also assisted families to collect their food orders that had been prepared by their bishops.

4. Deseret Industries: We assigned each stake about 500 hours per year to work at Deseret Industries. The people either worked at the receiving area or they sorted the bins into categories (shoes, toys, kids clothes, adult clothes, appliances, etc.). We totaled the number of hours requested by each area, divided it by three (Mesa, Tempe, and Phoenix), and then made assignments from there. Early in the preceding month, I called each stake high counselor in Mesa to remind him of his upcoming assignment at each location.

5. Humanitarian Spearhead Units: The spearhead unit was not a unit of people; it was supplies stored on the shelves. We had stored enough bedding, cooking gear, and 48 hours worth of food for 2,400 people. If the spearhead unit was called, we also had use of the 2,500-gallon water tank on wheels, stored in Chandler, that we could use. One time we had to use the spearhead unit to help a town that they thought would be wiped out from a flood that came down the canyon. The Church was equipped to help with emergencies like that, we got the supplies out, and then the Red Cross used them at the scene of the emergency. It wasn't used much, so it ended up being sent down to South America when they had a big emergency.

One time, a stake couldn't fill the assignment. The stake member in charge told me, "Brother Wheeler, we can't ask people who make $35 an hour to take off work so they can go work at the cannery. Why don't you just go find people who are standing at Circle K waiting to be picked up for a job and bring them down to fill the cannery positions instead?"

I said, "Brother, you're missing the whole point. You were given this assignment one year ago. You're telling me that in over a year, you couldn't find 10 people in your stake that could come down here to serve? We're getting ready to dump 600 gallons of product in the garbage because you're not here. It has to be put in bottles today."

I called Milt Turley, my stake president and he said, "We're finishing up a concrete job. I'll just bring my whole crew over there." So he brought all of his workers down and we filled the assignment. He personally paid the men their regular wage for their time, because they weren't all members of the Church. He was willing to make a personal sacrifice to bless the lives of everyone who would receive that food.

Roy Beach and I alternated the monthly training session at the bishops' storehouse facility for 50–60 newly called stake presidencies, bishoprics, and Relief Society presidents. Different directors gave a presentation about each of the following topics followed by questions:

1. Counseling
2. Employment
3. Bishop's Storehouse
4. Cannery
5. Deseret Industries

Following the training, we gave them a brief tour of the church facilities. We showed them the cannery, stockroom, the bishop's storehouse, and the employment office.

High Priest Group Leader

President Olsen did not think the Area Welfare Agent assignment was too big, so he also called me to be the high priest group leader of the 36th Ward. This assignment lasted for three years while I still served as an Area Welfare Agent.

Each year as a group leadership, we visited every high priest family in their home to better know them. We held monthly personal priesthood interviews to see how their home teaching was going.

Sometime later, after President Olson was released as stake president, he was called to be the Area Welfare Agent. He came up to me later and said, "Hey, that welfare agent job is a big job and a lot of work."

Wet Pack Cannery

While I was still serving as welfare agent, Fay and I were called to work at the wet pack cannery once a week for two years. Fay was the secretary at the main desk. She answered all the calls and scheduled people for both dry pack canning and wet pack canning. She had some very interesting conversations.

My job was to orient the twenty volunteers, then assign them, rotate them as needed, and keep things flowing. This took the load off of the paid cannery employees. I then oriented the second shift and got them underway before I left. The second crew finished bottling and then cleaned up, which usually took two to three hours.

While working at the cannery, I volunteered the extended Wheeler family to can carrots for the food banks in the area. We had twenty members each for two hours of the four hours. Some worked the whole four hours and others rotated in for two hours each. My mom, Grandma Wheeler, was 90 years old, but even she worked at the cannery feeding empty cans onto the conveyor belt. One of my nephews wanted the easiest job, so he tried to convince Grandma Wheeler to switch jobs with him. I put a stop to that! As a family, we also scheduled two, four-hour sessions bagging beans into one pound packages that were donated to the food banks. All of these service opportunities were special experiences for everyone.

29. Dick's Callings - Gilbert 9th Ward

By Dick:

After my retirement from the school business in 1993, we began to look for another home with a little more land so I would have more to do. I later realized why Fay was not real anxious for me to retire. Glen Guthrie (a co-worker) said that his wife had the same reaction. After she died, he decided to read her diary. She wrote only this statement: "Today Glen retired early. Now I have twice the husband and only 1/2 the salary."

In February of 2001, we finally bought the home we now live in and became part of the Gilbert 9th Ward. Our home is on 1.4 acres, and at the time was 3,500 square feet in size. The original house had been added to in the back. The addition included a large L-shaped room that was the dining area/family room, a laundry room, and a full bath. There was a pool just north of these rooms, so another half bath was added for pool convenience. A large master bedroom was also added with a large bathroom, including a tub half the size of the pool.

Later, Fay's parents built a two-bedroom mother-in-law apartment on the back of our house that was 1,500 square feet in size. This turned out to be a blessing for them and for us also.

We were blessed to be able to pay off the mortgage. The home has served us well, and we have been able to share it with many of our kids in their time of need.

Counselor to High Priest Group Leader

I was called to be a counselor to the high priest group leader. This only lasted for a few months because there was some friction in the group leadership. Without going into detail, I want to say that when we work closely with people in any organization, even in the Church, we don't always see eye-to-eye, and that's okay. Sometimes we are asked to work or serve with people whose personalities are different from our own or who see things very differently. Sometimes it works out, and other times a change is needed. We just do the best we can with the situations we are given, and let the Lord take care of the rest.

Ward Mission Leader

I was then called to be the ward mission leader. This meant that I attended ward council weekly with the high priest group leader with whom the friction had occurred. I got another chance to practice patience and try my best to serve.

Mission - Philippines

In 2004, Fay and I received a mission call to the Philippines for 18 months, which I talk about in Chapter 30.

Priesthood/Gospel Doctrine Teacher

After our mission, I taught a monthly lesson in priesthood meeting and occasionally taught the Sunday School Gospel Doctrine lesson.

Stake Baptism Coordinators

For three years, Fay and I were the stake baptistry coordinators. That was a four-hour job each time the font had to be filled for a baptism to take place. It usually meant setting up the baptistry room for 70–80 people, filling the font with warm water, and clothing the persons involved. After the baptisms, we cleaned and then took the baptistry clothes home to launder and to fold up, then return them to the stake center in preparation for the next baptisms. Sometimes this would amount to two or three assignments per week or per day, but if it was on the same day, we didn't have to refill the font, so that took away three hours of the job.

Sunday School Presidency

At another time, I was a counselor in the ward Sunday School presidency. A few feathers were ruffled in that calling as well, but nothing of a permanent nature. We just do our best where we are asked to serve. There's always something to be learned and ways we can try to be more like the Savior. Some of these more difficult experiences end up being our best teachers.

ITEP Mission - Fiji

In 2007, we served another mission for 18 months. This time, we were called to participate in the ITEP (International Teacher Education Program) in Fiji. I discuss this in Chapter 32.

Part 6: Missionary Service (2004–2006, 2007–2009)

30. Mission to Olongapo Philippines: Dick's Perspective

By Dick:

After Kristen finished her degree at Chandler Gilbert Community College, Fay and I decided that it was the right time to go on a senior couple mission. When we talked to Kristen about our call, she had already decided to go on a mission. She submitted her papers, got her call to San Antonio, Texas, and was in the mission field before we even got to the MTC in Provo.

Getting our Mission Call

We began the process, saw the doctors and dentists, filled out all of the paperwork, and had our interview with the bishop. Somehow the bishop misplaced the paperwork, so we had to start over. After the second time, we were interviewed by the stake president, and the papers were sent in.

The very next day we got a call from an Elder Monson, a member of the senior missionary department. He wanted me to submit a resume of my experience as a teacher and principal, so I prepared it and faxed it to him the same day. He called back and said he wanted us to do an ITEP (International Teacher Education Program) mission, and he wanted me to be over the South Pacific Missions. He said the director was on a tour of the South Pacific and would get in touch with me as soon as Elder Monson could communicate with him.

In the meantime, we had plans to spend the week at Kino Bay, Mexico, with the family. We had an enjoyable week on the beach and in the surrounding towns near Kino Bay, and we attended a Spanish speaking branch in Miguel Alemán (a local town). When we got home from Mexico, our mission call was in the mailbox.

The call was to the Olongapo Philippines Mission on a leadership/activation assignment. Surprised, I called Elder Monson to ask about the ITEP assignment. He said that there were seventeen senior couple committees, and we had been selected by one of them. He said that ITEP wanted us, and that if we served a second mission, he would handle the paperwork differently. Anyway, we began to prepare to go to the Philippines where we served from July 2004 until January 2006.

Mar. 1997—On the way to Kino Bay

Going to the MTC

After the mission call came, we immediately got a call from the Philippine language department at the MTC, and we began to take lessons in Tagalog over the phone. It was too much, so we asked our mission president[20] his opinion. He advised us not to bother with the language. He said that the first language of the Philippines was English, and if we weren't proselyting and teaching daily, Tagalog would not be very helpful to us, so we discontinued the lessons and kept preparing to go.

We spent an enjoyable week in the MTC in Provo, Utah. While there, we completed the last requirement: the psychiatric test. The person interviewing us asked if we were of a sound mind. I asked, "Do you think we would accept a call to the Philippines if we were of a sound mind?"

He laughed and said, "WOW! You passed with flying colors!"

Arriving in the Philippines

We flew from Salt Lake to California. From there, we flew all night to Taiwan and then to Manila, Philippines. After a few hours in Manila, the counselor in the mission presidency drove us to the mission home in Olongapo. We arrived there late at night.

The mission office was located on a five-acre lot in a complex that included a ward building. The lot was surrounded by an eight-foot block fence with an eight foot steel gate at the entrance and a night-time security officer on duty with a gun. The windows were all covered with 1/4 inch steel screens to protect from break-ins. When I went into the office for an evening meeting or church

North part of the Philippines

council, I always took Fay with me, and she visited with the mission secretary who lived in an apartment above the mission office. I did not feel comfortable or think it was safe to leave her alone at night. We know that the Lord protects his missionaries, but we saw no reason to test Him.

We stayed in the mission home for several days while they made arrangements for a car and an apartment for us to live in. We moved to a barangay (very small town), but I can't remember the name of it. Our apartment was a tri-plex on a four-acre lot. The windows had light metal screens installed on them. It came with a broken-down wire fence around most of the property, a nice eight-foot steel double swinging entrance gate for security, and an eight-foot cement fence by the gate with broken glass cemented on top of it for safety. It was not a secure feeling at night.

---

[20] President Keith F. Kinghorn and Sister Elizabeth Kinghorn, served 2002–2005.

They let us use the front two apartments so we had a place to put our suitcases and other things, and the elders lived in the back apartment. Our apartment had a bedroom, a living room, a kitchen with a three-foot-high sink and counter, and a shower and bathroom. The living room was so narrow that when you sat on the couch and put your feet out in front of you, your feet touched the wall. We were in our apartment for about three weeks before we finally got phone service.

Water heaters were non-existent. We had a small heater unit on our shower which made bathing bearable. Some of the elders just had a bucket of water and a cup for bathing. The water in the Philippines was not drinkable for the missionaries, so the Church furnished filters for each apartment. It was a challenge to get the missionaries to change the filters regularly, and pinworms were the consequence. It was a third-world country and they were about fifty years behind the rest of the world.

Once our ward had an activity, and some Tongans brought a squealing pig. They killed it, cooked it, and we all ate it. That was quite an experience!

Bataan Branches (Mariveles and Mabayo)

While we served in the Subic Bay area, we were assigned to visit and assist six branches within twenty or thirty miles of us. Two of the branches were in Bataan, the real jungles of the Philippines. The American troops were stationed there and learned jungle warfare tactics there.

We had to go through a security checkpoint to get to and from one of the branches. It was located near the nuclear power plant and housing built by the Filipinos. However, they never fired up the power plant. They feared that it might set off another volcanic explosion like they had at Clark Air Force Base, a bomber facility about fifty miles east of Manila. The explosion spewed a sand-like, light ash over large portions of the area called "lahar." In many places, the ash was eight or more feet deep and continued to wash down the rivers when they had heavy rain storms, which they did every year.

We were assigned to visit a branch near the nuclear plant by Mariveles. It was a church constructed chapel about an hour and a half from our apartment. It had a baptismal font outside. We only visited them two or three times.

Another branch we worked with was in Mabayo, a town next to a large bay. On our first trip there I told Fay, "I think this is the road into town," but we weren't sure because there was a lake-sized pool of water spanning the road, and we thought we would sink out of sight. After backtracking, I realized that it was the way into the town, so we tried it, and guess what, we didn't sink out of sight!

When we got to the town, we took a two-car-wide paved street through the town. As we drove, we noticed everyone was staring at us. Later we realized that it was because they couldn't see in our tinted windows. Eventually we saw the sign for our Church in front of a rented building, so we knew where the branch met and at what time. Sometimes on a Sunday during church, you could look out the window to see the neighbor who had decided it was shower time in his outdoor shower!

On our drive back to Olongapo, the road looked like a jungle trail, and we got a little teary-eyed because we weren't sure whether to proceed. We saw trees overhanging the roads, monkey colonies often to the right or left, and big bats with a three-foot wingspan hanging from the trees. We even imagined Japanese snipers in the trees. But a mile or two down the road, we came upon the main road back to Olongapo. Wow, were we ever relieved!

We visited the Mabayo Branch several times and even had a picnic with them on the beach once. Fay taught the Primary kids songs for a sacrament meeting program, and the teachers all went to the Relief Society class. When she was finished with the music, she went to the Relief Society room and told the teachers they could go back to teach the kids. They said, "Oh no, we belong in here. The kids just go home. They don't stay for the third hour." They'd just go home, even the tiny ones, without parents or anyone. It was dangerous since it was right on the bay, but I guess the adults didn't worry about it. The kids knew to stay out of the water.

One of the most reverent members of the ward was a former branch president's dog. He came in early, laid down in front of the pulpit, and listened carefully through the remainder of the meeting. The only thing he didn't do was take the sacrament. I guess he hadn't been baptized yet.

Downtown Olongapo Branches

There were two branches that met in the church-constructed Olongapo building in downtown Olongapo. That building was cooled with large, noisy fans. The windows had to be left open for air. Karaoke music was often played loudly outside, and the noisy jeepneys (minibus-like vehicles used for public transportation) turned around in front of the chapel.

Mission Home Olongapo Branch

The next branch was at the mission home and office in Olongapo, and was a regular church-constructed chapel. One time we attended a baptism there. A very drunk man was approached by two elders. He said "I need help. Come back when I am sober." They did; the missionaries taught him, and he set a baptismal date. His family and friends attended, but laughed. They said that if it changed him, then they would investigate the gospel. It took! He changed, and some time later, his family and some of his friends joined the Church also.

Branch in the Barangay (can't remember the exact name)

There was a branch with a chapel in the town where we lived. I remember one night it was pitch black, there were no street lights, and we saw two sister missionaries walking home. We picked them up and took them to their apartment. Fay was beside herself. She said, "It's a good thing parents don't know all that's required of our missionary sons and daughters. They might not send them on missions." But we realized that God watches over them as much as possible.

Other Branches

There was another branch we only attended a couple of times. It was in the next town over and had a fairly large church building off the main road, several blocks into a neighborhood. We attended a district conference in this building where Elder Michael John U. Teh was the presiding area authority.

There was also another branch in a neighboring town and located one block off the main road. We were invited to attend a roadshow-type performance from the Primary. They really wanted us to attend, so we did. We arrived on time. One hour later, the first person showed up but did not have a key to the building. Within the next hour, the building was finally unlocked and the others showed up. By the time it started, we had another assignment to attend, so we got a rice cookie and excused ourselves. I don't remember ever attending a service there.

Serving as a Counselor to the Mission President

Three months into our mission, I was called to be a counselor in the mission presidency with President Kinghorn and assigned to work with the northern third of the mission (three districts and seventeen branches). We moved to Santa Cruz to be closer to the branches we worked with.

District presidents do not have the authority to sign temple recommends, so the mission presidency had to interview and sign all the temple recommends for the six districts in our mission. During the fifteen months that I was in the mission presidency, I signed approximately 150 temple recommends. I had the questions written in Tagalog and handed a copy to the person being interviewed if they didn't speak fluent English. I asked the questions in English and received their answer. In the cases where English was foreign to the member, I invited a brother or sister missionary into the interview for clarity.

Dick sharing a mango with his dinner, a roasted pig!

There were a few occasions when a missionary was unable to see the mission president on his way home from his mission, so I was authorized to interview and release them. I did that two or three times.

I had a correlation meeting every month with the district presidencies, their branch presidents, and the missionaries. First, we met with the missionaries to correlate their teachings and encourage member participation. Then we had a training session with the Filipino leaders, where I taught out of the church handbook. Customarily, Filipinos do not like to read, so this was a big help to them.

Manila Philippines Temple

The mission presidency was also responsible to conduct all district semi-annual conferences unless there was an area authority assigned and present. We set up a rotation to visit all the branches, but it was far too seldom. Because of conference interruptions and other meetings, it took approximately five months to make the rounds. If they could have been visited once a month, it would have been a great lift for the branches, which is one reason there is a real need for senior couple missionaries.

We visited a different branch for their Sunday meetings every week. Almost every week, Fay or I were asked to speak in a sacrament meeting. I tried to limit my time to ten minutes or less so I wouldn't take up the assigned speaker's time.

When we went to Santa Cruz from the mission home, we crossed a 1/4 mile bridge on the way to and from our home. The bridge was about an hour and a half from the mission home and office. Around and in the wash or river was a lot of heavy equipment to remove the lahar, and often there was evidence that they were doing it. Sometime after we left the Philippines, a flood washed the lahar over the bridge and closed the road for a year or two. The only other road into the inner cities was clear around the mountains and took 4 1/2 hours or more to get to the mission office.

We attended two conferences in Baguio City, one for the youth and one for the young adults. We went by ferry boat to Corregidor Island for a tour. Later, we took a tour of a cemetery in Manila where they had five acres or more of headstones placed for every U.S. military man or woman lost in combat there. We were able to go to the temple in Manila for an endowment session.

Attending a Sister Missionary's Mother's Funeral

We were assigned to take a Filipina sister missionary to her mother's funeral, which was a choice experience as we got to witness a Catholic funeral. The sister missionary's father was an alcoholic and had objected when she and her sister joined the Church several years before, so she finally left home. While she worked in Hong Kong, the family she worked for encouraged her to go to her church meetings, and the ward encouraged her to go on a mission. She did, and when she got word of her mother's death she was devastated. Her mother had promised to meet her at the Manila Temple when she finished her mission.

One problem she had at the time was that she and her companion had twelve baptisms scheduled for the weekend of the funeral; but arrangements were made, and we took her home. She was silent for the five hour drive to her home.

She asked us to conduct a church service at their home. I said I would if her dad approved, and he did. The missionaries and I sang a song, and one of her uncles who was a member gave a talk. This prompted the Catholics to also conduct a church service at their home, which they had not planned to do.

Her mother's friend bawled and hollered, stating that the mother wanted this sister missionary to stay home and care for the father. It became a continuous chant, and the sister missionary asked me if I would cast out the evil spirit from the mother's friend by the priesthood. I consented. When she told the lady what I was about to do, the screaming and chanting stopped immediately. I have not seen the priesthood work so fast before.

When things were over, Fay and I told the sister missionary we were going to the car and would wait for her as long as she needed. Within five minutes, several members of the family walked her to the car. She was ready to go back to her mission. As soon as we went around the corner and her home was out of sight, she breathed a deep sigh and then talked non-stop for the next five hours. A big load had been lifted from her shoulders.

Christmas

They had a funny Christmas tradition in the Philippines. Any month that ended in "ber" was considered a Christmas month. In other words, it was Christmas from September through December. The kids (and sometimes the adults) came to our gate and sang, "We wish you a merry Christmas," and then held out their hands. They wouldn't leave. We couldn't figure it out at first, but finally learned that we were supposed to give them a penny. We were told that if the kids came with an instrument, we were to give them a nickel. I was confused because I hadn't ever seen them with instruments, but it was explained to me that rocks and sticks counted as instruments. It was so funny, and we really enjoyed it. Sometimes it went on and on, and one time someone told us, "Tell them to have a good day, lock the gate, and go into the house." Sometimes we had to do that, otherwise, we were just there forever.

My Key Takeaways

By the end of our mission, I felt that many of the saints and leaders were really beginning to understand and apply gospel principles in their lives and in the lives of the saints. We were able to attend their stake conferences, and we were really impressed. Many of the leaders we worked with were faithful members who were developing into strong leaders. The Church is still growing in the Philippines. They have seven or eight temples there now. There were only three when we were there.

It is hard to leave family and serve a full-time mission, but it is truly worth it. Memories of the experiences there come to mind almost every day even now. The hardest part for Fay was that eight new grand babies were born while we served in the Philippines. In fact, Kylie was born the day we entered the MTC. She was 18 months old before we saw her in person and held her. Yes, there is sacrifice, but we always need to be ready to magnify our callings and honor our membership in the Lord's Church.

31. Mission to Olongapo Philippines: Fay's Perspective

By Fay:

Serving a mission was an experience that I wouldn't trade for anything. I was so grateful for the opportunity to serve the people of the Philippines with Dick.

Deciding to Serve a Mission

I didn't receive my patriarchal blessing until I was 29. At that time, I heard Joan give a talk on patriarchal blessings. When I talked to her after her talk, I told her, "I've always felt cheated because I didn't get a patriarchal blessing."

She asked, "Well, why don't you get one now?" I explained that I thought you had to get it when you were young, and I was always gone in the summer when they did them.

She said, "Oh no! How do you think converts receive their patriarchal blessings when they are older?" I had never thought about that.

When I received my patriarchal blessing, one of the only things it said was that I would go on missions with my husband, and I decided I would do that. At the time, I thought my blessing was talking about my first husband, but it turns out it was my second husband, and we went on two missions.

I got in real trouble one time. I was close to 40, and Dick was in his 50s, and the stake asked us to talk about serving a senior mission. I talked about how wonderful missions were and how I was looking forward to it. Afterwards some women, mostly older women, kind of berated me, saying, "You don't know what you're talking about! You don't have any grandchildren. You're too young to know how it will feel to leave your grandchildren, your home, and everything you are used to."

I just listened to them, then I said, "They asked me to give a talk on how I felt about going on missions. This is how I feel, and I will go on missions."

I went to two third-world, foreign countries, and I loved them both. Eight of our grand babies were born while we were on our first mission, and there were three weddings and one grand baby born while we were on our second mission. I missed all of that, but I lived through it. I came home, and I loved the kids that I hadn't been there for. You just have to make up your mind to serve. I am grateful that now there are so many service missions for people who don't want to leave home so that they can serve and be comfortable.

Experiencing Culture Shock

I experienced some culture shock when we arrived in the Philippines. The first three weeks we were there, Dick asked, "What should we do today?"

And I'd respond, "Go home."

He'd say, "We can't do that honey."

So I'd sigh and say, "Oh, okay."

When we arrived in the Philippines, I realized that I had never been farther away from my parents than four hours; all of a sudden, I was halfway around the world. I had always been able to go see my parents and children, and I couldn't stop thinking about what I would do if something happened and they needed me. When we were set apart for both of our missions, we were told our families would be healthy, nobody would die, and we'd be able to see all of our family when we came home. We believed that, and it was true.

When we left for the Philippines, our daughter-in-law was having a lot of complications with her pregnancy. They kept sending her to the hospital and fixing problems, but we were all still worried. She came with us when we were set apart, and heard the promises they made about everyone being okay. She's a convert, and she really grabbed onto that. The day we left for Provo, she went into labor, and that time they couldn't stop it. The baby was six weeks early, very small, had a hole in her heart, and had an extra vertebrae. When we heard that, we thought, "What should we do?" We talked about the blessing we'd been given and decided to stay on our mission. I called her and said, "Do you need us to come home?"

She said, "No. I need you to stay out so that your blessing will come true." We stayed out on our mission, and before we left Provo to go to the Philippines, our son called to tell us that there was no hole in the baby's heart anymore. The doctor said, "I saw that hole in an x-ray! Now where is it?" She was safe and healthy while we were on our mission. We saw so many blessings on our missions, but this was a special experience. It was difficult to be on the other side of the world, but we felt the Lord bless our family for our service.

Training Primary, Young Women, and Relief Society Leaders

When Dick went to district correlation and training meetings, I was supposed to teach any sisters who came from Primary, Young Women, or Relief Society. I always had trainings prepared knowing full-well that nobody would come. The problem was that Filipinos are so poor that the women couldn't afford to travel to the church for extra meetings. If they came to the meetings during the week, they couldn't go to church on Sunday, and that wasn't worth it. I felt bad for the sisters because the brothers could get money from the Church to travel for meetings if they needed it, but the sisters didn't have that option. So I sat out in the car with the air conditioning running because it was so hot, and I read a book or cross stitched my kids' Christmas presents. Every year, I made a different cross stitch for each of our 15 children with different quotes like "Love One Another" or "Families Are Forever" in the colors they decorated with in their house.

One time I finally got to teach about Primary in a district meeting. I was getting frustrated because it seemed like they didn't know anything about Primary. I asked, "What are you doing for singing time or sharing time?"

They said, "We don't know what that is."

I turned my back to them for a minute, took a deep breath, and silently prayed, "Heavenly Father, help me. I don't know what's going on." All of a sudden a question came to my mind, and I turned around and asked, "Could I see the hands of the people here that were in Primary when they were young?" Not one hand went up. I thought, "Okay, now I know where to go." They really had no idea how Primary was supposed to function, and nobody ever thought about that—including me—until that meeting. So we started training them from the very beginning.

During the next district meeting, Sister Cabrito asked me, "What could we do to help these people learn?"

I said, "If we had a video in Tagalog that they could watch about how to do different things like teach a lesson, lead music, and plan and lead singing and sharing time, I think it would help them more than anything." They worked with members in Manila and came out with videos that explained how each class in the priesthood worked, how Primary worked, etc. They were beautifully done. The only problem was getting the members to watch the videos on their own. We watched them during our trainings, and it made a big difference in how much everyone understood what was going on. As the trainings got better and better, the work really started progressing. They just needed the chance to learn how the Church worked.

Teaching Members About Music

I had the opportunity to serve as a music director. I also taught members about music in church. Those trainings usually occurred after a district meeting in the afternoon or early evening. When we first got there, the choristers were just randomly waving their hands in the air. Most areas didn't have anyone who could play the piano. I gave them CDs with the hymns and taught them how to pick a song and play it from the CD. I taught them how to lead the music for the songs they sang most of the time, and they really enjoyed it. One area had a choir and a man who played the organ. He learned it by ear, and did such a good job. He was the dad of half the choir. He was really good.

Feeding the Missionaries

I spent most of the rest of my time baking rolls, baking cookies, or finding some type of cheap food that we could buy to give people. One time we found lots of "chippies," which was what the Filipinos called bags of chips, for cheap. Everyone there loved all kinds of chippies. When we saw the sisters or the elders, we gave them some chippies, and they were delighted because they didn't get fed by the people there. The Filipinos were just too poor and could hardly feed themselves, so they couldn't feed the missionaries. The missionaries had to use their own money to feed themselves. Honestly, many of them ate a baggy full of cooked rice that they carried with them for lunch. That was all. Then at night, they put some vegetables in the rice and had that for dinner.

I always made way too much food. At first it was not on purpose, but then I did it on purpose because we always had some elders or sisters come by when they were in our area, especially when we were up in Santa Cruz. We'd ask, "Are you hungry?" Of course they were always hungry, and we'd sit them down, feed them, and give them a root beer float. They loved it, and we loved it.

32. Filipino Culture

By Dick:

One of the most interesting things about serving a mission was integrating ourselves in the Filipino culture. Here are some of my favorite memories of cultural experiences we had.

Nani and Tati

Fay and I had a "Nani" and "Tati," a couple from the branch who looked after us. They were super people. She did the laundry, cleaned the floors, and other jobs that we asked of her. He went to the market for us because he knew the quality of the products and got the native prices. He also took our electric and phone bills in and paid them. They checked on our house when we were gone and even checked on Fay regularly when I was out on assignment. We paid him and his wife a little extra each month for their services. He told me that in a regular ten-hour day he made, after paying for his gas, about 200 pesos (about $4 USD). The average family probably lived on less than 2,000 pesos per month (about $40 USD).

Our first Christmas in the Philippines, we bought them a five-gallon bucket of paint that they used to paint the inside and outside of their house. They actually watered it down a lot, and their son, nephew, and niece were also able to paint the outside of their homes. The next year, we got them another five gallons. They had the prettiest house in the neighborhood and were so proud. She grew beautiful flowers, including orchids, and she often brought Fay a bouquet. I gave him an eagle carved out of mahogany wood from Baguio City, and he was thrilled. They were very kind, loving, and thoughtful people. They were much younger than us, however both of them are dead now. We love them and miss them a lot.

Transportation

Almost no one owned a car. There were two main types of public transportation in the cities. The first was the "trikie." It was usually a 125 hp scooter with a skinny two passenger side car. If you asked anyone, "How many people can a trikie hold," the answer was always, "One more." We saw as many as 10 passengers in one vehicle, usually kids. The cost was two to five pesos for a short ride and more for longer rides, so the missionaries were told not to proselyte beyond a five peso distance, otherwise many families could not afford to go to the church meetings because of the cost of transportation.

The other mode of transportation in the city was the "jeepney." It was an extended jeep with bus-like sides, bench seats along each side, and a seat in the middle. Again, the capacity was always, "One more." Often there were twenty or more people in a jeepney. The jeepneys in the city were painted different colors depending on the neighborhood, so you needed to know the color for your area of the town.

As far as transportation outside of town, most people traveled by bus. There were some modern buses with storage, which is what the missionaries rode for transfers. They cost more, but they stopped in each large town instead of picking up passengers on the side of the road. The other buses were Japanese surplus and World War II buses that were pretty worn out. Those buses stopped wherever there were passengers on the side of the road, so it took hours to get places on them.

Making Ends Meet and a Testimony of Tithing

We found that in the Philippines the grandparents often raised the kids from generation to generation while the parents worked. Parents did all they could to make sure the oldest daughter had a good education and a good profession so she could take care of her siblings and parents when they got old. Often the responsibilities were so great that the oldest girl never had the opportunity to marry and have a family and life of her own.

One of the branch presidents we worked with had a wife and several daughters, a small ten to fifteen acre farm with animals, and a small rice mill. His wife was a nurse and often went abroad for three years at a time to work, so the daughters had to raise themselves the best they could.

One time, their thirteen year old daughter talked to Fay about how she really needed her mother around, and asked Fay to pray with her that her mother wouldn't find work abroad. When the mother came home, Fay told her about her daughter's prayers and talked to her about trying to find a way to stay at home and earn money. The branch president's wife told Fay that if she would give her $30,000 pesos ($600 USD), she could set up a tindahan[21]. Fay told her that she could not give her the money, but that her husband (the branch president) could build the small store and she could begin selling things. Above all Fay told her that she should pay a full tithing and the Lord would bless her. She set up the store and began selling things and soon found herself with money to meet the family needs. When her husband said, "We need money for this," she said, "Well I just happen to have it right here."

She told Fay, "When I go to church, I tell the sisters that I used to pay a token tithing and I got token blessings. But now I pay a full tithing and get full blessings. I am so happy! Sisters, you need to be full tithe payers and let the windows of heaven be open to you." Needless to say, the daughter was so grateful to have her mother there as a friend and companion.

Weather

The temperature in the Philippines was very predictable. April through September was the wet season. The average rainfall during the wet season was 144 inches. Sometimes we got 10 inches of rain in one day. That is a lot of water!

The second six months, October through March, were the dry months with not a drop of moisture. The temperature remained the same day and night, 80 to 90 degrees with at least 85% humidity. That meant that when you stepped outside day or night, you began to sweat. We were lucky because we had two air conditioners in our house, and our car also had air conditioning. The elders and sisters had fans if they were lucky.

---

[21] A small store built in a front yard that sells eggs, chickens, pigs, goats, rice, etc.

Cock Arenas

The most prominent structure in each town was the cock arena. It was a circular stadium made of blocks with a roof, and usually sat 150 people or more. They did a lot of gambling in the Philippines, and cock-fighting was a big thing. It was illegal, but it happened in every single town where we lived. Everyone raised fighting cocks. When it was time for the contest, the two birds were tossed into the ring, each outfitted with razors on each toe. They immediately went for the jugular, and within seconds, one of the birds was dead and thrown into the stew pot that evening. The winner had the razor removed and awaited the next fight.

The cocks were actually really beautiful animals. I have often asked Fay why people paint chickens for house decorations with so many colors. These cocks came already painted in many beautiful colors.

Food

Rice was a big crop in the Philippines. Most farm work in the Philippines was still done by caribou-pulled single-blade plows. Very few people had tractors. They used a machete to cut the grass along the highways and planted a few blades of rice at a time by hand.

When rice was harvested, it needed to be laid out in the sun and turned three times a day for at least three days to dry it enough to send to the mill. Guess what? There were not enough places to dry it. Every cement basketball court was used. The main roads were two lanes wide, so they spread rice on half of the road for several miles, and then they'd go for a mile on the other side. We referred to the process as "Rice-a-Roady." The family drying the rice sat there with the rice to watch it. They stirred it several times a day by running a wooden rake through it so that the rice underneath got some sunlight and dried out. When there was no oncoming traffic, you drove on the wrong side of the road, but when a car approached you had to drive over the drying rice, because there was nowhere else to go. Most of the time we didn't have to drive on the rice, but I hated it when we did have to. It was quite a sight to see half of the road covered with rice for as far as you could see. From there, they sent the rice through the mill. There was a whole cleaning process, so it wasn't dirty from the road.

The Philippines grew the best carabao mangoes in the world. They were delicious, and we ate them often. One mango tree owner climbed up a wooden ladder and wrapped each mango in newspaper. I cannot even imagine what a challenge that would be.

Another fruit we enjoyed from the Philippines was the pomelo. It was almost like a grapefruit, but the skin was much thicker and the membrane between each slice was thicker and tougher. I ate at least half of one every day. They were very good.

Sacrament Meeting Clean-up

Everyone in the Philippines thought that if they didn't eat something every 15 minutes, they were going to die. They ate during the meetings, and then the wrappers got thrown on the floor. Even the district presidents had candy in their pockets and put something in their mouths every 15 minutes. It didn't matter if it was fast Sunday or otherwise.

One time the area authority asked, "Brother Wheeler, what did you think about the meeting?"

I said, "Well, this is the Lord's house, and He wants us to respect it and take care of it because 'cleanliness is next to Godliness.' If you look around, you'll notice that the whole floor is covered with candy wrappers and chippy bags." Sister Teh overheard that, and I was surprised when she didn't stay inside for the whole meeting. When we went outside, she had two huge garbage cans stuffed solid with trash that she had gathered from the chapel and the Relief Society and Primary rooms.

I'm not sure how smart this was, but when I was a bishop, after a sacrament meeting I had the deacons collect all of the trash that was left in the chapel and put it in a cellophane bag. The next week in sacrament meeting, I dumped it out onto the floor and said, "This is what we picked up from the building last week after you all left the chapel. I wonder how the Lord feels knowing we treat His building this way. We need to clean up after ourselves and not expect someone else to clean up after us. This is the Lord's house, and it needs to be clean."

33. Mission to Fiji

By Dick:

In 2007, we decided that it was time for another mission. When we were submitting our mission papers for our mission to the Philippines, they recommended an ITEP (International Teacher Education Program) teaching mission, so we wanted to serve an ITEP mission this time. We got in contact with a senior missionary brother who knew what to do, and he processed the paperwork so we could get a call for an ITEP mission.

Getting Our Mission Call

We submitted all the paperwork, did the doctor and dental exams, and received a call to serve an ITEP mission in a small island called Kiribati near the equator in the South Pacific. It was a very small island, but they had a high school there with 300–500 students. The language of the people was Bislamic or Pidgeon English. God is "Big Daddy," and Christ is "Daddy," etc.

We had received our call and were preparing to go to Kiribati when two doctors on the missionary committee turned me down because of a reported heart murmur. The medical facilities in Kiribati were limited, so anyone sent there had to be very physically fit. I went back to my doctors and they both stated that I was physically fit and if I lived to be a hundred, I might have to have a pacemaker. With new doctor recommendations from home, the missionary department approved for us to go to Fiji because the medical facilities were more modern and acceptable. We served there from September of 2007 until March of 2009.

MTC

And so the mission began. We went to Provo, Utah, to attend a Philippines Mission reunion. While we were there, the senior missionary office called our home, and Kristen relayed the message to us. When we were originally called, the ITEP was an entity unto itself, but the message was that the Church Education System (CES) had incorporated the ITEP into its system. They called to tell us that they wanted us to come to the CES office in Salt Lake for two or three days of training. Because we were already in Utah, we arranged to go to the training immediately. We received the indoctrination for the next two or three days.

We then reported to the MTC in Provo on the appointed date. On Thursday, we received our flight plans for our assignment in Fiji. On Friday we were called in and instructed that the flight plans were being changed because we needed to receive CES training the next week. When we told them that we had already received the training, they verified it with CES and our flight plans were not changed. We left on Saturday morning and flew to Hawaii for the first week of our journey.

Hawaii

When we arrived in Hawaii, we were treated like royalty. They gave us a car to drive for the week, and they entertained, instructed, and housed us in a beach resort called Turtle Bay. We visited the

Polynesian Cultural Center, ate the Luau meal, and attended the Polynesian program in the stadium with the mountain backdrop and natives doing all of their dances, etc. We also had two or three days to just drive around the island visiting whatever we desired. It was a grand tour of Hawaii for free.

The Salvesons, who were the couple over the school's ITEP program, spent time orienting us on the goals they wanted us to achieve in Fiji. Brother Mike Salveson was the head of the Logan University Education Administration department before his mission call, and he said that they wanted us to teach education administration courses at the elementary school and college in Fiji using the same Logan University Model courses, textbooks, etc.

While we were being taught and receiving instruction, the Salvesons explained that ours was an ITEP mission. They said that the native people would try to get us to fill local assignments, but that was not why we were there, so we should not accept local callings from church leaders.

Traveling to Fiji

After leaving Hawaii, we flew to New Zealand where we had a six hour layover. The area authorities picked us up at the airport, and we went to their offices, met their staff, and received a brief orientation. Then we flew to Nadi[22], Fiji, where we were met by the missionary couple who we were replacing.

They took us to dinner and began a non-stop orientation through the meal, through the evening in our room, through breakfast, and through the three-hour car trip to Suva. They had literally planned out their different orientations, and as soon as one stopped, the other one took over. They wanted us to continue their mission.

As we later learned, they had accepted every church calling they were asked to do in the local area. They had also decided on ten goals for the self study for the following year. They realized that ten goals were unreachable, so they had narrowed it to three goals and expected us to carry them out. On top of all that, the brother was not even an educator. Thank goodness for the advice from the Salvesons. Needless to say, we failed the missionary couple that was leaving. We did not complete their mission for them.

Map of Fiji

Arriving in Fiji

The Salvesons had given us a warning about the native people asking us to fill local callings, and it was well taken! Our first Sunday in Fiji, I was asked to be a counselor in the high priest group leadership, to teach Sunday School, and to be a

---

[22] Pronounced "Nahn-di"

home teacher. I accepted the home teaching assignment. Our landlord volunteered to be my companion, so we home taught his four assigned families along with mine. I declined the other two callings as instructed by the Salvesons, and it was good that I did!

The high priest group leader went abroad with his wife and left their five children with a family member. They planned to be gone for six months. They had still not returned nine months later when we moved into another apartment and ward. Then the landlord went abroad for eight months or more, so I had eight families to home teach. Thank goodness Joseph, our little car washer, volunteered to go with me and teach some lessons. He was the most faithful person there. He even washed our car in the rain. Wow, I liked him!

Visits from Family Members

While we were in Fiji, we had a couple visits from our family members. Fay's sister, Shannon Thomas, came in August 2008. She was quite nervous traveling by herself to somewhere she had never been.

The first thing we took her to see was the mountain where the local cannibals killed people and ate them. It was quite a long and winding hike up there, and Shannon had just got off the plane and was just in flip flops so it was extra hard, but worth seeing. She also wondered why there were SO many bright colored houses everywhere—pink, orange, red, purple, yellow—the Fijians just loved those bright colors! She was able to see more of them everywhere we went.

When she had been there a few days, Joseph, a young man who helped us out, came over to wash our car. It was pouring rain but he just kept washing the car so he could earn his $5 for his mission.

Shannon was nervous going to church, wondering if it would be like it is here in the U.S. During the sacrament, a paper airplane flew right into her leg, and then she knew the Church was just like it is at home.

At Christmas time, some of our granddaughters came to see us. Tara Garner, her friend Sharon, Season Hale, and Sarah Wheeler made the trip. We were able to trade our car for a big van and saw lots of the Island of Viti Luva with them. We even shared a few days in the Salveson's timeshare just outside of Nadi in a a big resort. It really enjoyed sharing our Fiji experience with our sweet family visitors.

ITEP

Our call to Fiji was to teach administration and education courses to teachers in the elementary and the high school/college (grades 9–13). We were given the title of adjunct professors. The reasoning behind the ITEP program was that the instructors were not paid, and the sponsor (in this case, the Church) furnished the textbooks—one per every four or five teachers—to be shared and then remain as a resource for the school. The courses cost the teacher $5 per semester hour, and since

Church College in Fiji

the courses were linked to either BYU–Hawaii or BYU–Provo, the credit hours went toward each teacher's transcripts through those schools. For example, for $15, a teacher could take a 3-hour bachelor's or master's degree course and it counted toward their college graduation.

Brother Salveson selected the texts for each class, sent us enough copies of the texts so that every three teachers could share one, and sent a thumb drive to each member of the class highlighting the important concepts and ideas. He did this for every teacher in the Pacific: Tonga, Samoa, American Samoa, and Kiribati. Then on the night of class, he Skyped each of the schools and the CES directors in Salt Lake for two hours. In the administration class, we had 32 teachers enrolled. It was a great experience for Fay and me!

During the eighteen months we were serving there, the teachers we taught were able to earn over 150 university credit hours, with most of them being 500-level courses (master's degree). Some accomplishments our students achieved were:

- Eight of the teachers we taught earned 14–18 hours of credit.
- One teacher received her education certification[23].
- Three teachers were short one course in English, titled "Research Paper." We helped them complete the course, and all three earned their Bachelor of Arts degrees from BYU–Hawaii.

The Church CES department changed their name three or four times while we were serving, so we kept getting new name tags. At first it was ITEP, then CES/ITEP, then CES–Provo CES–Idaho, then CES Hawaii and CES–Church Education, then CES–S & I.

One missionary couple from Logan, Utah, was sent to each school in the Pacific with the assignment to go through the library, discard the old unusable books, restock the library, and set the program up on the Dewey Decimal system. She also taught a one credit hour course on library skills, and eight or ten teachers completed it. Her husband was a weather science instructor at Logan University. He taught three or four teachers a one hour science class and provided them with microscopes at the completion of the class.

Working with a Local Administrator

A certain brother (who will remain unnamed) was the Seminary/Institute country director in Fiji, the principal of the elementary school (grades K–6) with one assistant, the principal of the college (grades 7–13) with two assistants, and was one of the stake presidents. He had a bachelor's degree in business and a master's degree in computers. When we arrived, he had never taken even one education course.

As part of his employment package, he received a two-story house next to the school and a 15 passenger van for his use. The van was helpful with his seven or eight kids, but he walked to school every day since it was next door. When the Church (CES) decided to separate schools, they gave him the choice to either be the country director or be the college principal. At first he chose to be the country director, but when he learned that he would be on the road a lot and wouldn't be able to keep his house, he decided to stay on as the college principal.

---

[23] A person with a degree in any field (in this case business) but with no education courses could complete 26 credit hours of education courses and become a fully certified teacher.

Whenever I wanted to speak to him, I visited him in his office where he was looking busy at the computer. The school had a dress code, but he never once enforced it. He never visited a classroom nor evaluated a teacher, nor did he know how. He also never noticed one thing wrong at the school building even though it was 30+ years old and in need of lots of repairs and work. He felt that was the responsibility of the maintenance men. He reminded me of a horse wearing blinders. He never looked to the right or the left.

Repairs/Maintenance

Since the school buildings were so old, there were several glaring problems that should have been addressed and repaired years before we got there. A few of the problems I addressed included:

1. One of the classrooms was built like a Fijian hut with bamboo, windows, and carpet. It was a beautiful building, but the thatched roof leaked. One of the leaders hired a relative to replace the thatched roof a few years before, they didn't fix it. By the time we arrived, the room stunk because of the wet carpet. When I went to the area authority, he told me that nobody knew how to fix it. I reminded him of three things: (1) They had huts all over the Philippines. They could hire a Filipino to come and fix the Fiji hut! (2) There were people in the Church that would contribute to have a metal roof installed. (3) At the time, the University of Fiji in Suva was building a large room with a thatched roof, so we could try to hire someone working on that project to fix our thatched roof. We finally got the thatched roof replaced, and the room was used often as a meeting room and classroom.

2. There was no hot water in the home economics room, so for thirty years they had to heat water to do dishes in the foods class. Ten years prior to our assignment, another relative was paid to put in a solar hot water system, but the system never delivered any hot water. I took the maintenance man out to the shop, and we went up a ladder to the roof of the home economics department (which was totally open with no insulation or anything) and said, "Place a water heater here, hook it up to water and power, then connect the hot water to the building pipes." One week later, there was hot water in the home economics rooms for dishwashing.

3. I also brought up the men's school restroom in a meeting with the administration and maintenance. I demonstrated how you had to open the door, straddle the toilet to lock the door, and reach into the tank to flush the toilet. The next day, all of the doors in the restrooms were reversed so they opened outward instead of inward, and the mechanism to flush the toilet was fixed. During the next school break, the office was remodeled and nice bathrooms for the men and for the women faculty members were built.

Church Organization

There were three stakes in Fiji and that means several organized wards in the stakes. In an organized ward, there must be enough Melchizedek Priesthood holders to fill ward and stake positions like the bishopric, priesthood leaders, high counselors, and auxiliary leaders. The branches in Fiji struggle since many of the leaders were relatively new to the church and have not had real training in the workings of the church. A few of the leaders were returned missionaries, but they served locally, so they didn't see other examples of leadership. But the church is getting established more each year and progress is being made.

One stake center was located on the property next to the elementary school, adjacent to the genealogy facility, and just a half block from the Fiji Temple. The three temple couples and auditing couple lived very near the chapel and attended their meetings there. Those couples filled almost every position in the ward, and one even served on the high council.

The Fiji Temple

The Suva Fiji Temple was located on twenty acres of land on a prominent hill and could be seen for many miles away. When it was time for us to go home, they were about to dedicate some newly constructed facilities on the property. These included three temple workers' apartments, a home for the temple president and his family, a home for the mission president and his family, mission offices, all the church offices, a distribution center, patron housing (large enough to accommodate fifty or more), facilities for preparing meals, and a large parking lot. All of this could easily be guarded by one security guard.

We were set apart as temple workers, and we served during the Saturday mornings sessions. We were able to assist with the baptisms, confirmations, initiatory, new name, officiate sessions, assist at

Suva Fiji Temple

180

the veil and wherever else needed. Following the temple assignment, we went to lunch with the other senior couples and developed strong friendships with them.

Bao Branch

When a new mission president came to Fiji, he decided that it wasn't in the best interest of the mission to have all of the couples serving in the stake and ward positions. He assigned each couple, including us, to a small ward or a branch in the outlying areas to give them council, provide leadership, and to try to strengthen them.

During the last three months of our mission, we were assigned by the mission president to attend all of the meetings of the Bao Branch of Nausori Stake near Bao Island. The branch met in a small, rented, open-air Bush Chapel. Birds nested in the rafters, and wasps were frequent visitors' during the services. It was not uncommon to see the branch president swat at a yellow jacket flying near the speaker. There was a separate building for Primary, and the bathrooms were open-air, didn't have doors, and were usually water drenched from the rain.

Very few members have cars, and the most frequent mode of transport is hoofing it. The branch president lived about 5 kilometers (3 miles) from the chapel, and on a rainy day would walk through two or three rivers that were sometimes waist deep. He was in his 50s and a bit overweight, and it took about 15 or 20 minutes into the presidency meeting before he quit sweating.

When we started going to the Bao Branch, I asked the clerk for a branch roster so I could see how many members were in the branch. Guess what? No branch list. So, I met with the local authorities in Suva. The following week I had three branch lists (one for the clerk, the branch president, and the missionaries). The chairs in the building were old and had been replaced with newer plastic chairs, and the water supply had been improved.

Before we left Fiji we had eight or nine stake visitors, including stake presidency members, high councilors, and area authorities, visit our branch. The branch began to feel like they were members of the stake and that they were cared about again. Part of the change came about because our Area Authority reminded them that they were looking more like a district than a stake and they needed to step up, which they did.

In one of the branches, the Primary president was nine months pregnant and not able to do the Primary sacrament meeting presentation. One of the Primary teachers accepted the job of putting it together and helping the kids perform it. She had never done it before and was really worried that she would do it wrong, so she asked for advice from everyone she could and put a lot of work into it.

The primary kids were all very reverent and did a great job. After the program, the Relief Society president told her the program was poorly done. When the Primary teacher didn't come back to church, Fay and I went to visit her. We sat on the floor of the home (she was very poor and didn't even have chairs). Fay told her that the program was well done and that the Relief Society sister was out of line. I told the sister that when we left on our mission, President Hinckley had told us to tell everyone that we visited with or talked with how much he loves them and how grateful he is for their service. That really touched her. I told her that the little kids loved her and that they needed her. She was the only one who always showed up for Primary. Fay told the Primary teacher that the kids really loved her and needed her to come back.

At that time, the branch president also asked us to speak in church and told us to choose whatever topic we thought would help them best. It was shortly after General Conference, so we both chose to teach from a talk that was about strengthening your ward family. Fay said that when she talked about how important it is to support people in their callings and not be critical, she couldn't help but look at that Relief Society president. After church the sister talked to Fay and confessed that she was resentful because it had been her calling before and she hadn't received as much praise as this sister was getting that day. She felt really bad, and Fay suggested she apologize. She did apologize and admitted that she was jealous and asked the teacher to forgive her. They hugged and made up. That Primary teacher was later called as Primary president, and she was able to get her shy friends in the ward who had avoided callings to come help in primary. She did a lot of good for that branch.

When we left Nausori from a small airport that was five or six miles from the sister's home, she walked all the way there and was waiting to see us off. She stayed for an hour or two until our plane left, holding Fay's hand. Fay told her that if she got to see President Hinckley, she was going to tell him about this sister's amazing service. She gave Fay many hugs when we had to leave. She is another sister who was close to us was there. We felt blessed to have served in that small branch every Sunday for the last two or three months of our mission!

Key Takeaways

It made a great difference to have a missionary couple to be of service and assistance, especially in the Bao Branch. The people felt appreciated and cared for. The high priest group leader there stated that, "If you can make it here every week, I can too." Lots of adult missionary couples are needed throughout the world and their presence and service really makes a difference.

We finished our mission in 2009, and returned home just a week or two before my younger brother, Ben, died with Mesothelioma cancer.

34. Fijian People

By Dick:

W e enjoyed choice relationships with the people in Fiji through home teaching, serving as temple workers, and working with other senior couples and missionaries.

The Bowmans and Other Senior Couples

Richard and Connie Bowman, the office couple from Morgan, Utah, moved into the upstairs apartment next door to us, and we developed a lasting relationship with them. Our apartments were by the home of a rooster who saw the sun at 4 a.m. every morning and continued to crow until everyone was wide awake. The Bowmans were assigned to work with a branch on Sundays, so we often went with them and helped when we were able.

At least once a month, we invited all of the senior couples in Suva over for a potluck dinner and social hour or two. This was always a great time for all. We had between ten and fifteen couples, and it provided everyone a good break. We also met in smaller groups at other places for a meal, social hour, and a taste of Fijian cooking.

QaQa "Gonga" Mitchell

Working with QaQa "Gonga" Mitchell, the elementary school principal, was a choice experience. Every time we suggested something in a meeting, he immediately implemented it in his school and then reported its success. He was a true believer and implementer. He received his bachelor's degree while we were in Fiji and later became a bishop.

One day, I clipped a wanted ad seeking a school principal from the local newspaper and showed it to the administrators as an example of important qualities of a principal. A few days later, Gonga came into our office to tell me he had applied for the position, along with thirteen others, and that he had been offered the position. He wanted my opinion on the job offer, so I told him that he was a choice administrator and that the Church and kids in the Church school really needed him to stay put for a while. He chose to stay. He kept living in his house next to the elementary school, and the Church named him as the principal of the Church's elementary school soon after.

Home Teaching the Family of the Chief of Police

I had many home teaching assignments while in Fiji. I home taught the family of the Chief of Police —an outstanding family with athletically talented children. All their children received scholarships to BYU Provo for their education. The girls were talented in basketball and volleyball and were strong members of the Church. The boys were very athletic also and received scholarships.

Home Teaching the Stake President's Family

Another family we visited was the stake president's family. We usually met with him and his family in his church office at the conclusion of the meetings. He was one of three people that completed their bachelor's degree while we were there. He was also one of our teachers, and as we were leaving, he had just been designated country director, which meant he was over all of the seminaries and institutes in the Fijian islands.

Home Teaching Sister Wright's Family

I also had the opportunity to home teach Sister Wright's family. Her deceased husband was from England, and she lived with her brother and many grandchildren. She always had a full house. She was a choice lady and always welcomed us into her home. She and her brother (who was not a member of the Church) were responsible for the translation of the *Book of Mormon* in Fijian.

Sister Wright taught the adult Sunday School class, but she did not have a set of the new scriptures with all of the footnotes and cross references. When we realized this, Fay suggested that we buy her a new set and get them to her anonymously. Somehow Sister Wright found out that they had come from us.

Home Teaching Ernie's Family

I home taught Ernie's family and had some experiences with them that strengthened my testimony of the importance of home teaching. Ernie was one of our shop teachers at the Church college. His father, "Big John" as he was called by everyone, had served on the city council for 13 years, had been the Suva mayor for one year, and had been instrumental in securing the property and surrounding grounds for the temple. Over the years, Big John had not been very active in the Church. One week, I invited him to become active and then to take his wife and children to the temple to be sealed. He accepted the challenge, became active, and then was sealed to his wife and one son (Ernie).

One day, Ernie came into our office and informed us that his dad, Big John, had passed away in the night. He said, "I have a big problem." He then explained how his sister had arranged for a friend to sponsor Ernie and his family for two years to attend BYU Hawaii to complete his four year degree[24], and the family had their airfare scheduled to depart on Friday, the day before the funeral.

I first asked him the question, "What would your father want you to do?"

Ernie responded, "Go ahead with my plans and get my degree."

I then said, "You have been here for him and your mother for many years while your brother has worked in New Zealand and your sister in England. You were sealed to your parents when they received their endowment. Your mother can travel to Hawaii, and your brother and sister can go there and be sealed to your parents. You can become an eternal family, and you can stand proxy for your dad. You have been here when they needed you, and there is nothing else for you to do that would require your change of plans." Ernie wrote a nice talk for the funeral, then left for Hawaii. His talk was read by his brother at the service.

This incident was another testimony to me of the importance of fulfilling your home teaching calling. All of the children—Ernie, his brother, and his sister—thanked me for getting their father to the temple to unite their family eternally.

_____

[24] In Fiji, you only needed a two year degree to become a teacher.

35. Fijian Culture

By Dick:

Fijian Culture was very interesting. Fiji was under the leadership of a coup the whole time we served there. The military had taken over the government, but we never felt threatened or in danger.

Ethnic Tension

One problem in Fiji was that the country was 55% Fijians and 45% Hindi. The Hindi were there as indentured servants. When they finished their indenture—sort of like slavery—they tried to go home to their native land, but their native countrymen said, "You are second-rate citizens and we don't want you back." Then they had to return to Fiji where they were also treated like second-rate citizens. The Fijians declared a "No Free Hold Land" policy, which meant that only Fijians could buy property. So Hindi people had to rent property, run the stores, drive the taxis and buses, and do the farming while Fijians did very little.

Quite a few Fijians looked down their noses at the Hindi people, even the church members and church leaders, and did not welcome them with arms outstretched. Some even refused to sit in the same row in the temple with them. We saw some Hindi bishops shunned by members and treated differently at church and at work. It reminded me of people you read about in the south and how they felt about slaves. There was and still is room for improvement and growth.

Tribes

In Fiji, the social hierarchy is organized into tribes. We learned that each tribe is divided into three groups.

1. The first group is the chiefs' families. They have their own separate area and housing. They are the bosses.
2. The second group is the warriors' families. Again, they have a separate area on the island or village. They are the protectors.
3. The third group is the fishermen. They provide the food from the ocean. Again, they have separate housing in a separate part of the island or area.

At the invitation of a temple worker and a member of the Bao tribe, we visited the chief's island where Chief Cakobau's[25] tribe lived. He was the Big High Chief. At low tide, the water was no deeper than two or three feet, so it was possible to cross from land to the island on foot. But at high tide, like it was when we visited, the only way over there was by boat.

On the island, there was a large assembly room held up by large tree poles. They told us that when they installed the trees, they placed one or two captive, alive enemies at the bottom of each hole.

---

25 King of Fiji, Chief Cakobau b. 1817–d. 1883

There was a large pool of fresh spring water on the island. This is the source of drinking water and the bathtub for the tribe.

There was a fairly large Methodist church on the island. At the front of the building was a large rock where they placed the babies when they baptized them by sprinkling. They also told us that was the rock that they used to behead their enemies before they roasted them and ate them. They continued the practice ten or fifteen years after the country abandoned cannibalism. One of our teachers told me that his grandfather told Chief Cakobau, "If you kill and eat one more man or woman, you will be on my plate for dinner."

On the highest hill on the island is a large marble-like tomb in the form of a teepee. When the chief was close to death, he gave his wives a choice. They could either be buried alive with him or live and help take care of the grandkids. They told us, "Some chose to be buried alive with him." They also told us, "These stories get better with age."

Highways

There are two main highways in Viti Levu: the Queen's Highway and the King's Highway. The Queen's Highway went from Suva to Nadi. The road followed the coastline, and the waters of Fiji in that area were beautiful and clear with many colors of blue. We traveled the Queen's Highway many times for various reasons. The Queen would be upset with the road conditions. It was full of potholes, some large enough to blow a tire. The road was two lanes wide, and you could cross over the line if no other car was coming *or* if you had the biggest vehicle. But beware! Most drivers were looking for the smoothest surface.

The other highway was called the King's Highway. It went from Nadi to Suva and followed the other coast line. About 20 miles out of Suva, there was a small LDS branch building where we occasionally stopped for a few minutes to attend an activity or Primary there. We drove it twice, and that was enough. Because of so much rainfall, it was a muddy, washboard-like drive. The road was under construction, but instead of working on a five mile stretch at a time, they were working on the whole thirty or forty miles, including the bridges. Believe me, twice was too often to travel the King's Highway!

Part 7: Our Forever Family

36. Fay's Parents' Passing

By Fay:

My parents were both teachers up in Eagar, so they were always there during the school year. After they retired, they traveled down to the Valley for two weeks to be temple workers, then they went back to Eagar for two weeks. Since there wasn't a temple by Eagar back then, that was the only way they could work in the temple. They did that for several years. They loved working in the temple so much. They stayed in different places. For a few years, they found a place and switched off every two weeks with another couple from Flagstaff that worked in the temple on the opposite weeks.

My mom hated the heat down here, but I finally asked, "Why don't you just move down here?"

She said, "I can't exist in this heat."

I responded, "Yes you can, because you'll be in a home that has a cooler, you'll get in your car that has a cooler, then you'll go to a building that has a cooler. It's just like how we handle the cold when we visit in the winter."

In 1994, they looked around for a house, and after living in an apartment for a while, they found a house in a really nice area on East Vine in Mesa. There were a lot of older people and people they had known from other places. They were really happy there for a long time. Eventually, they stopped feeling safe there. The helicopters were over their roof all the time, and they often heard sirens. They were really afraid. They wouldn't actually say that, but they wouldn't go anywhere at night or anytime unless they really needed to.

For a while, my sister, two of my brothers, and I all took turns going to check on my parents. It generally ended up working out that two people a week stopped by and just made sure everything was fine. It made me feel so guilty. Some weeks it was so hard to get over there. One time, we didn't get over there for two weeks, and neither did anyone else. We tried and tried to call, but no one answered. One of my brothers went by and banged on the door, but nobody answered. When Dick and I finally made

1983—Kari, Dude, Kristen

About 1983—Kristen & Jay

1987—Retirement Time
Marlin LeSueur (Marlin was also retiring),
Jay, Dude, Mr Smith (the principal)

it over there and got in the house, we found that my parents had been very sick for about four days. They couldn't get up to get to the phone because it was in the other room. They could barely get from their bed to their bathroom. All they had to eat was some crackers in their room. It was a mess, and they were a mess. I felt so bad. They looked like they were going to just lay there and die.

One day I asked Dick, "How would you feel if we asked Mom and Dad if we could build an apartment connected to our house for them to live in?"

Dick thought it was a good idea. I knew my dad would have a fit and say, "We're not going to do that," but I went over to talk about it with them anyway.

I talked to my mom first, and she said, "Oh Fay. That would be a blessing! You don't know how bad it is here."

I said, "I do know, Mom, and that's what has me upset. It would be so much easier if I could just walk through a door and check on you every day."

I could tell as soon as I brought it up that my mom was ready. She said, "Yes!"

I said, "Well, now I have to go ask Dad. What do you think he'll say?"

She immediately responded, "I don't know, but if he says no, I'm still saying yes!"

I went outside where my dad was working on the lawn and said, "Daddy. Can you come talk with me for a minute?"

He said, "Sure."

So we sat down, and I said, "I just talked with Mom about this. Dick and I have been talking about how bad it is around here right now, and how scared we are for you and Mom. We checked, and we can build a little apartment on the end of the house, so we were thinking maybe..."

He interrupted, "Yes!" I didn't even get to

1989—Meilyn, Fay, Chelsea, Dude

About 1993—Five generations of "oldest" (except Jonathan)
Back: Meilyn, Fay
Middle: Dude, Willie Cluff
Front: Chelsea, Jonathan

189

finish my sentence. That's when I knew that he was really afraid too.

They sold their house and moved into the two-bedroom apartment that we built for them. My bedroom door goes right into their living room, so every day I could get up and go over to check on them. They could come over anytime they wanted, and whenever they heard the grandkids, they'd come and play with them. It was absolutely perfect. They could do whatever they wanted, and they felt safe. That was one of the biggest blessings for me because I was really worried about them. It was a great thing for our grandkids too because they were able to get really close to them.

Feb. 1987—Dude, Jay, Fay Coombs

My Mom - Willie Mae "Dude" Rutherford Coombs

Right after we went to the Philippines, my mom broke her hip. She was coming back from a funeral, and she tripped over a concrete parking curb at a rest stop in Prescott where they stopped to go to the restroom. An ambulance came from Cottonwood, and they took her to the hospital up there.

When she was finally discharged from the hospital, they sent her to rehab, but they never explained what she needed to do to be able to go home. It was not a happy time for her. We were in the Philippines, but when I called, my siblings said, "Mom is just not happy. She's not eating."

Then my mom emailed me and said, "I'm just miserable. I can't stand it here anymore."

Finally, I said, "Somebody go find out what she has to do to go home!"

Meilyn went over one day and asked, "What does she have to do to be able to go home?"

The rehab workers finally said, "She has to be able to walk all the way around the big hall twice." I still don't understand why it was so hard for them to tell us that.

As soon as Mom found out, she said, "Okay, can I do it now?"

They said, "If you think you can, yes." She immediately got up, and she did it. She was not going to stay there for a minute longer.

They let her go home. After that fall, a nurse came by to check how thin her blood was. Then the doctor would call her and let her know if her medication was a little high or low, but they never changed the dosage.

When we got home from the Philippines, we spent a lot of time visiting with her, and she kept saying, "When are you going to go see Kristen?" Kristen left for her mission before we did, so she got home and was at BYU by the time we got home.

We were enjoying our time with my mom, so we said, "We are going, but we want to be here for a little while and visit with you."

She urged, "I'll be here forever. Go visit your daughter. When you come back, we can have a good time."

We left one morning and got up to Provo in the late afternoon. We took Kristen to dinner. We thought everything was well and wonderful until we got a call that my mom had fallen again, hit her head, and she was brain dead. They had her on life support, but they needed me to come home as soon as I could so that they could take her off life support. I was flabbergasted! We called Kristen, and we said, "We're sorry, Honey. We'll make another trip up later, but we've got to go home now."

We packed up all our stuff and left around midnight. We drove straight to the hospital and got there close to noon. All of our kids were there for a little while, and my dad was there. He didn't understand what was going on. He had Alzheimer's disease, and he just wanted to go home. The doctors let me come in, give her a hug, and talk to her for a minute when we first got there. Then they unplugged life support while most of our kids were still there. Her heart kept beating. Just beating, beating, beating. My boys took my dad home. He kept saying, "I want to go home. I'm done. She's up. She's done. Let's go." He didn't know what was going on. The rest of the kids trickled out until Shannon was the only one still there with me and Dick. Several hours later, on January 23, 2006, she very peacefully took her last little breath, and she was gone.

It wasn't the way we had planned to lose my mom. I'm sure that the Lord said, "Dude, if you want to, we'll let you go back."

And she said, "Oh no. I'm not going that way." My dad was always her rock. With his Alzheimer's, he wasn't a rock anymore, and she didn't know how to deal with that. It was so hard for her to see him going downhill, so she left that job for us to do.

She had so many people she wanted to see up in heaven, people she loved who had gone a long time ago. She wanted to meet my dad's mother who had died when he was 10. I know she missed her grandmothers and Uncle Clyde and Aunt Pearl. They were her best friends, and she wanted to see them again. She was ready. She told me all the time, "I can't wait to go." I can so vividly picture her conversation with the Lord. I know she would have chosen that way if she had the option. She was such a special mom.

191

My Dad - Jay Ballard Coombs

After my mom passed away, my dad's Alzheimer's disease got worse and worse for years. Luckily, he didn't ever try to run away. One time, he fell and hit his head and he had to go to a specialty hospital in Scottsdale for a couple of weeks. When he was discharged from the hospital, they sent him to a rehab place that was just awful. When it was time for him to leave, we didn't know what we were going to do. My dad had told us our whole lives that he didn't want to be left at some home, but we weren't in a position to take care of him. Shannon, Dick, and I all have bad backs, and when we tried to help him up, he pulled against us in an effort to help, and made everything harder. It wasn't sustainable.

1990s—Dude & Jay

Shannon found a hospice facility that was recommended to us and looked okay, so we prepared to move him there. It was close to us. Dick's sister-in-law had worked in it for years and said it was the best one she'd ever been in, so that's where we wanted him to go. The lady who worked at the rehab center started talking to us about the hospice they were sending my dad to right before we left, and we realized it was a different hospice than we picked. I said, "We already told you that we have everything in place for hospice, and he's not going to the one you're talking about. He's going to the one we chose." She threw a fit, trying to pressure us into sending him to the hospice she picked, telling us that the ambulance was already there and how it would be a better place for my dad.

Finally, the department head heard her and asked, "What's going on?"

By that point, Scott was there, and responded, "This woman is being very hateful because we won't go to her hospice."

He asked, "Is that true?"

She just let it all out, and he said, "You're fired. I will talk to you after we get this settled." There were two ambulances there for us, one for each hospice, so we took the ambulance to the hospice we had decided on.

When we arrived at the hospice facility, they informed us that my dad would never be able to walk again. That was a relief to know because I knew if he was in a bed, then we could take care of him in the apartment.

He was at the hospice facility for about three days. The hospice team set us all up at home. They brought the beds and everything else we needed. Whenever we got low on anything, we'd let them know and they'd bring it. After he decked (hit) a nurse and a doctor at the hospice, they gave us a

192

lotion-type rub to use on him that calmed him down. They gave us two tubes a week, but told us, "If you need more, just call us, and we'll have it to you within an hour." And they always did. At night when he was fidgety and wouldn't settle down on his bed, we put on our gloves and rubbed the lotion on one of his arms. Then he'd just lay down and be calm. It really helped.

Dick went over to the apartment and fed my dad and talked with him for a while. We knew things were getting really bad when my dad started spitting food out at Dick. He got a few faces full of food. My dad was happy, I think. He never really knew where he was or what was going on. Every time I walked in, he asked, "Who are you?"

I said, "I'm your daughter. I'm Fay Ellen."

"Fay Ellen? You're not my sister Fay?"

"No, I'm named after her."

"Oh yeah, Fay Ellen. You're my daughter?"

"Yes." It happened every time I walked in or when Dick walked in.

My dad asked, "Who's he?"

"He's my husband. He's Dick."

"Dick? Okay."

My dad saw people who I couldn't see all the time, but he didn't know who they were. He said, "Who's that, Fay?"

I said, "Daddy, I don't know. I can't see them."

"You can't? They are just right there."

"Do you recognize them?"

"I think so, but I don't know who they are."

So I asked, "Is it Mom?"

"No."

"Is it your sister or your mother?"

"No."

The hospice team sent a nurse to check on him twice a week, and a different hospice worker came and bathed him twice a week. Other than that, for the most part, we took care of him. It was not hard. I took care of him at night and did most of the diapers, and my sister handled most of his needs during the day.

On the morning of July 26, 2010, the nurse who came to check his vitals said, "He's getting near the end. You need to get hold of your family if any of them are interested in seeing him before he's gone, but he won't last through the night."

When she told us that, I leaned over and said, "Daddy, if you see Mom, you grab her hand and run."

I left the room to call Steven, and Shannon left the room to call Scott. When I got off the phone, Dick said, "He's already passed." I guess he was ready to go. He didn't struggle, he just passed away peacefully. Nobody was there from our family except my sister, Dick, and I, but it was time. We missed him, but we were happy for him because he was with his mom and my mom.

I'm not afraid of dying anymore. I've seen a lot of people go. I really do believe that my mom and my dad are together, that they're happy, and they've met his mother. I'm excited to meet my grandmother one day, but not today.

37. Dick's Parents' Passing

By Dick:

My dad was a good man and always took care of his family and friends. He taught me to have stick-to-it-ive-ness and to work hard. I have a lot of great memories of working with him, making and repairing things. He also taught me how to enjoy life. He played with us and took us on hunting and fishing trips. He loved the outdoors. When the kids were grown, he bought little motorcycles for himself and my mother (nothing fancy, I think his was a little 90cc motorbike, and my mom's was a 70cc). They would take their airstream trailer out and go camping and then go riding.

About 1961—Lovel Wheeler & Diane on a family camping trip

Dad always took good care of my mom. Having nine kids took a toll on her body, and she had some health problems, so Dad retired early from APS to help her. He didn't make much at APS, so his early retirement was made possible in part by the decision to subdivide and sell off most of their five acres. They just kept a small lot in the corner to build a new home on. Dad hired a brick worker to start building the house, but he was doing a crummy job, so Dad took over and basically ended up building the whole house himself. He designed the house to have porches and low overhangs so that the sun never beat down into the house, which kept it cooler. He was always good at woodworking and made built-in custom cabinets in the walls around the house. He lined everything with real wood panels instead of drywall. He even carved a huge totem pole pillar for the back porch. He loved carving things; I still have some of the neat things he made, including bust-style statues of my mother and some of us kids.

About a week after they moved into the new house, the gas hose on the dryer broke, and the house caught on fire. The laundry room had a small staircase that led up to a big open attic. The attic ran the entire length of the house, had a floor, and was easy to walk through. They got the fire out before the whole house burned. Most of the damage was up in that attic. Dad was able to get up there and reframe it and fix everything. They were also able to scrub all of the wood paneling to repair the smoke damage, so they saved the house.

A few years after Fay and I married, my brother John decided to open a hardware store. My dad was 68 at the time, but he was happy to help John hang the True Value sign up on the building. They balanced a ladder on some scaffolding in order to reach high enough. The shop was already open for business, and a customer showed up while they were hanging the sign, so Dad sent John in to take care of the customer. After John left, the ladder shifted and Dad fell and landed on his head. The doctors spent hours operating to try and stop the bleeding, but they couldn't save him.

Mom had a hard time when dad first died; she particularly hated to be alone at night. For months, we would take one or two of the kids over at bedtime. They would sleep there, and we'd pick them up in the morning to take them to school. That seemed to help a lot.

I used to tease my mother that since she'd married for love the first time, she should find someone to marry for money the next time around. She would just chuckle, shake her head, and tell me she had everything she wanted and to quit being a pill. She never remarried, though she lived another 28 years as a widow, which gave us a lot of years to visit and serve her. The kids loved visiting Grandma on Sunday nights and playing with their cousins while the grown-ups talked. Mom always had lots of treats for the grandkids—everything from homemade popcorn and curly fries to gourmet suckers and Schwan's ice cream bars.

My mother loved painting, and in addition to collecting ceramics, she started to make her own pieces. My dad encouraged her to work on her talents and do what she loved, so he built a little workshop out back for her to work in. It was pretty rustic and wasn't fully enclosed, so it got hot and dusty. We later built a nice enclosed ceramics shop for her in the backyard. She had a kiln in the corner, and the walls were lined with shelves for her molds, statues, and paints. There were cabinets and a countertop along one wall, and there were also tables in the center to do the painting. Our kids and grandkids all have great memories, and probably some ceramic statues, that they made with her.

We worried about Mom being lonely, so we visited her regularly. She also always had a dog as a companion. She had several good widow friends as well. Her friend Norma lived down the street from her, and they used to love to watch the Phoenix Suns basketball games together. She also had a friend named Winnie, who lived a little further away and didn't have much money. Winnie loved to crochet, so mom would have her crochet baby clothes that she would then buy to give to the grandkids (or sometimes she would trade them for ceramics that Winnie wanted). One day when mom was in her 70s, she was driving to Winnie's house and got in a very serious car accident. I don't know exactly what happened, but somehow she hit a telephone pole. The accident left Mom pretty broken up. It was a long recovery and led to her suffering with a lot of arthritis pain and limited her mobility in her later years. We never let her drive again after that, so the kids took turns taking her to appointments and shopping. I feel like my youngest sister Diane did the lion's share of the driving and shopping.

Mom had some ups and downs with her health over the years, but when she was in her late 80s, she was diagnosed with diabetes and had a hard time regulating it. She was really going downhill, so my sister Karen and her husband Scott converted the ceramics shop out back into a bedroom so they could move in and help her. They got her on a good routine and helped get her diet on track. She really rallied for a while and was able to live on her own again for a time, with the help of family and friends checking on her. Eventually, she declined enough that she couldn't be alone anymore. My youngest sister, Diane, and her husband built an apartment on the back of their home and took care of Mom there until she passed at the age of 96.

By the time Mom died, my parent's posterity had passed 300 people. One of the special musical numbers at her funeral was to be sung by her grandkids, but there were so many of them that they didn't fit on the stand. The family filled the entire chapel, so we decided to just have all of the relatives stand and turn around and sing the song together. One of the grandkids thought it was crazy that there were only a few rows of non-relatives sitting behind the family, but I guess that's the difference between dying young and living so long that you've outlived all of your friends.

Wheeler family at Lovel's burial in 2010

38. Other Deaths in the Family

By Dick:

In addition to our parents, other beloved family members have passed away. We miss them deeply and wanted to honor their memory by sharing their stories here.

Season

Sheri and Mike's daughter, Season, was born in 1988. She married Ian Barnett in 2009. Season was a very organized girl. She made picture books for each of her children. When we were in Fiji, she came over and spent a week with us. She was a sharp little gal.

In 2013, Season had a teaching degree that she wanted to use to teach her toddler, so she started a little pre-school out of their home. Her husband Ian was working for Lockheed Martin. A few days after their second child was born, Season had some terrific pain. After a few trips to the ER, the doctors finally did a scan of her chest and found an aortic dissection. By the time they decided to operate, she had already gone septic and they couldn't save her. She died within a few hours, just a few days after their second child was born.

Mike Hale (Sheri's husband)

Mike's father died when he was young, so he wasn't raised with a father. He put himself through school. I taught several of the boys to trim trees, and Mike was one of those that taught me some things. He'd go through the neighborhood and knock on the doors at houses with palm trees that needed to be trimmed. If the owners weren't home, he'd leave them a note saying, "I came by here to bid on trimming your tree. Here's a bid good for 30 days, and here's my number." He got a lot of follow-ups from those notes, so he trimmed trees a lot. Mike loved swimming and racquetball.

Mike loved to travel, so they traveled a lot during the summer. They went to the Arctic Circle and all the way up the Alcan Highway. They went with us on the trip to Tennessee and Florida.

Mike's mother was a Reber, and many in the family had heart issues. Mike had some health concerns and some close calls with aneurysms. On April 29, 2018, Mike went to a self-reliance workshop. When it was over, they were having a little luncheon or party with cookies and popcorn. He got some popcorn and brought it back to the table, then he just collapsed and died right there.

Sheri

As soon as Mike died, Sheri put her house up for sale with the idea that she was going to spend a few weeks with each of her children and help them out. At the same time, Pam and Dale were in the Dominican Republic on a mission. Dale was a counselor at the MTC in the building right next to the temple. They had a big home with an extra room next to the mission office and suggested to Sheri that she live with them and be a missionary, so that's what she did. She was assigned to work with the Primary in a branch that was two or three buses away from where she lived. Sheri called me one day and said, "Dad, I'm having a hard time learning Spanish."

I said, "Well, let me teach you the words I know: taco, tamale, enchilada, frijoles."

She said, "They don't speak that language out here." She was there for about nine months and loved every minute of it.

While she was there, she had some weird episodes of not being able to find her words. Then one morning, they couldn't get her to wake up, so they took her to the hospital. They found out that she had glioblastoma cancer in her brain. They flew her home and immediately did surgery, but she died about 18 months later on September 30, 2020. She wrote her life history before she died.

When my wife, Joan, died in 1980, I bought a bunch of plots for $250 apiece next to where my grandparents are buried at the Mesa City Cemetery. I won't sell the plots, but I give them to family members when they die. Joan, my parents, Joan's parents, and some of our siblings are buried there. Now Mike, Sheri, and Season are buried there as well.

Sheri's house in Tempe, AZ
Back: Fay Ellen Coombs, Meryl Reber Hale, June Denham, Lovel, Dick
Front: AJ, Sheri, Mike

39. 40th Anniversary in 2021

Introduction Written by Fay:

For our 40th anniversary in 2021, all our kids worked together and planned a surprise party for us at Laura's house. We didn't suspect anything. Our daughter Kristen flew in from Baltimore, and we picked her up from the airport. After we picked her up, we dropped her luggage off at our house. The other kids told us to take her to Laura's house so they could see her. Unbeknownst to us, they had planned for everyone to be color coordinated for pictures, so they told Kristen to sneak my gray shirt over too. While we were at our house, she slid the gray shirt into the back of the car.

When we got to Laura's, I saw a lot of cars parked and started wondering what was going on. When we walked into the house and I saw all the kids and the table all set, I asked "Oh, is this for our anniversary?"

Dick said, "Yeah, I think you're right. Are we dressed well enough?"

Kristen handed me my shirt, pushed me into the bathroom, and said, "Change into this, Mom."

2001—Back: Josh, Meilyn, Tami, Julie, Dale, Kari, Kristen, Bryan, Becky, Laura, Pam, Mike, Rick, Larry
Front: Dick, Fay, Sheri

They had tables set up all the way down the room, filled with all of our kids and their spouses (except for Kristen's husband), and they told us to sit at the head of the table. It was wonderful. People took turns standing up and telling us how they felt about us. It brought tears to our eyes. They sang some songs that they knew we loved. They had taped a lot of the grandchildren congratulating us, so they played the video of them. I couldn't believe that they had gone to all of that trouble for us.

We had a wonderful dinner. They gave us a choice of a steak or a different kind of meat, and the food was delicious. The company was wonderful. It made us feel so special.

After dinner we were able to stand up and tell them how much we loved them, how we were so glad that we had been able to put this family together, and that we were glad we could be together and feel such a special love for each other. It was really wonderful. Just perfect!

Then they took us outside for pictures. We got some with us and our kids, and some with all the spouses. Later on, I got frames for them and hung them up in our house.

The whole party was such a surprise. It was beautiful, and we felt very loved and accepted.

Words from Fay at the Anniversary Party:

I'd like to tell you how I feel tonight. I just look at you all and my heart swells. It's just a beautiful sight. I love every one of you. I was telling some of you parents the other day that I decided I should have started hugging people more, as they came and left. I just wanted to, but I didn't know how to approach some of you, and I just finally said, "To heck with it." You know I'm just gonna give hugs. I needed to show how much I love you all and the examples that you are to us. You have no idea. We talk about you, we love you.

We have 71 grandchildren, and we're in the 100s of great-grandchildren, and we still have a ton of grandkids that aren't married. Our first great-grandchild has been married, so it's just overwhelming, but we love this posterity. We love you all. We love your babies. We love your grandchildren. I cannot tell you how much it fills our hearts when we think about all of you, because we do love you. We're so proud of all the things that you're doing and things that you're accomplishing, and we love it when you ask us to come to something like a baby blessing, baptism, or ordination. We haven't had a lot of those in the last year because of COVID, but we try to go when we're invited. We really want to be with you and just know we love you so much, because I do and I know that he does too. Thank you.

Words from Dick at the Anniversary Party:

We haven't had answers to everything we've tried to do, but we've just tried to set a goal and go to work at it, and things have worked out. It's been a great experience. It's been a great journey.

This heart condition that has slowed me down a little bit in the last year or so has been a challenge, but every time someone has questioned something, we've said to them, "Ask Heavenly Father for an answer and you'll get the right answer. You'll get the answer we got, and we know that it's the right thing to do."

I love my first wife. I'm sealed to her. We had 26 years together. Fay loved her first husband. She's sealed to him. They had 12 years together. But these last 40 years have been choice for both of us, and we'll let the Lord decide what happens afterward.

We are just grateful for the time we've had with each one of you. We love you all. We don't often tell you that. We don't see you all as much as we'd like, but we do love you and appreciate you.

It hasn't been real easy raising this many kids on one salary. It wasn't easy in the mission field because all of the couples we worked with had two incomes and lots of money, and we were kinda struggling as we went through. Dale and Pam can tell you it isn't cheap to go on a mission. It's not a $400 expense, it's more like $1,350 and even more than that probably in Fiji. But that's beside the point. It was well spent, well worth it.

I looked at the flag board in our bedroom today and there are over 60 of our direct family members who have served missions. You multiply that by a year and a half or two years and that's a lot of time in the mission field serving the Lord. And why are missions are important? When a young person serves a mission around the age 20 you figure that they've been a year and a half or two years in the mission field and they've actually done something most young people don't do at that age and that's tithe in time to the Lord. They've given a tenth of their life to the Lord in missionary service, and that's just like paying a tenth of your time. And that's just the start. There's so much you can do and so many opportunities.

The gospel is true. Heavenly Father lives. He knows every one of us by name. He loves us. His son Jesus Christ is our Savior and Redeemer and our Advocate with the Father. I can bear that testimony to you that Joseph Smith is the prophet of the restoration that the Lord called him and He restored the gospel through the prophet Joseph. The Book of Mormon is true, and if you don't believe it, read it every day, and you'll find out that it is true. We just finished it today. This is probably the first time this year. We read it somewhere between two and half and three times a year. We do that every year, and we'll start tomorrow with the first page and start over again.

We do love each one of you and want you to know that.

2023—Dick & Fay

Words From the Children (some were in person at the anniversary party, and some were recorded):

Pam and Dale Garner: Happy anniversary, Mom and Dad. We really appreciate 40 years of getting together, having home evening, your diligent efforts in keeping our family together, how much you have loved all of us and helped us to stay close as a family, and teaching us to love each other and know our brothers, sisters, and cousins. Building those relationships is a special part of our lives. We're thankful for that. We also especially appreciate the counsel that we received from you when we were asked to serve our mission. You had come over and explained to us that the Lord needed young senior missionaries and that we were called on a mission and we would be gone for just 18 months; we could always come back home, pick up where we left off, and start to earn money again. It was the greatest counsel we could have received and the best experience of our lives. We're so grateful that we went. It will change our life forever; it's shaped who we will be forever and ever. It's been fun since we've been home. It seems like nobody really wants to hear us talk about our mission because we go on and on because we had so many wonderful experiences. Sometimes we cry, but we can go over and talk with Mom and Dad. You have the same experiences, and we can talk for hours together about our wonderful missions, what we learned, how we grew, and how we felt the Spirit. It's just a really great blessing to have had your example and your encouragement to do something that was really hard and really scary. To sell our home and quit earning money for a while, when we weren't retired, and take that leap of faith. We're just so grateful that we did it and for both of you. We appreciate the fact that we now have an additional 475 or 500 kids that are starting to have kids, and so I think we're going to have well over a thousand grandkids. Even if we're only at 28, we feel like all those kids from our mission are our kids, and it's just been such a wonderful experience. So, we just want to thank you for that. We hope your anniversary is wonderful and you have a lot more years together. We love you so much. We love you, happy anniversary.

Laura Gregory: Happy anniversary. I have a clear memory of the day that Dad said he was going to get married again. I was 12, of course, and you and Mom had been on that first date, and you were in the living room, and I was really sad and really confused, and I asked you to come into my bedroom. You laughed and came right away. You came into my room and I said I was upset, and I told you how I felt and that I really wanted you to explain to me what was happening and why you would make the choice that you were making—to be dating and to be out with somebody else. Then you said Heavenly Father told you that you needed to marry her and that you needed to do what Heavenly Father told you you needed to do. I felt, at that time, the Spirit just come over my whole body, and I knew then that was exactly what Heavenly Father wanted for our family—that you were supposed to marry Fay, and that she was supposed to become our mom. From that time, I've always known that Heavenly Father wanted us to be a family. As I was thinking about what has happened because of that, like what has come into our lives as a result, there have been lots of things come to my mind that are great, but the greatest things that I could think of are Meilyn and Kari and Mike and Josh and Tami and Julie and Kristen. Those are the greatest additions to my life that I can think of. I'm so grateful for these sisters and brothers, for the relationships that we've had over the years, and for the love that has been learned, I guess, from the way that you guys have taught us by taking us on trips and having home evenings and always doing the things that we're supposed to do so that we can grow as a family. The relationship that we have with our older siblings as well, and all our siblings. I better not forget Buck and Becky. All the siblings. I love this family. I'm so grateful, Mom and Dad, that you made the sacrifice and the commitment to be a family and that you made this marriage of "convenience" for us because we are happy and we have had a wonderful life because of the sacrifices that you have made. I love you very much. Happy anniversary.

Becky and Bill Cox: Hi, Mom and Dad. Happy Anniversary. We wanted to tell you how much we love you. We are so grateful that so many years ago you decided to get married and put this family together. My life would be so different if we didn't have it. I'm grateful for our big family, the life that we've had, and the many many memories. I'm grateful for the strength and support. Thank you for being such a great example of how to continue to work hard, even through trials and challenges, to make your marriage work and to provide a really good and safe place for us to live. We love you. We appreciate everything that you've done. Happy anniversary.

Tami and Devin McCoy: Hi, Mom and Dad. We just wanted to let you know how much we love you and how much we appreciate everything you've always done for us and continue to do for us. Happy anniversary.

Mike: I happened to get baptized on the same day you guys got married, and Uncle Steve passed out. But, I am thankful for the example of ongoing family and strength. It's really cut to the forefront recently as we are in the process of blending two families and our kids are one of the most important steps, and it's all due to the example not only of you two, but to each of my siblings and your spouses, and I'm thankful for that. I'm thankful for how I was able to be raised, to have the incredible example of how to live a happy loving life, and to help others to know their family loves them.

Kristen: So, obviously, the best thing to come out of this union is me. As I was watching some of those video clips earlier, hearing Laura talk about how life would have been different—obviously my life would not have been, my children would not have been. So, I feel like I have the most to be grateful for. I love telling people about our family because they always are amazed, especially living in Maryland, when we say all 14 of my siblings live in the same county and here we are 2,000 miles away. A lot of times people ask if it was hard growing up in a family like this, and I say, "Well yeah, but not for me!" And I say, "It's because everybody loves me best!" A lot of hard stuff happened, and there were a lot of bumps in the road, but by the time I was old enough to know what was going on, you guys had done a lot of work and smoothed that out. So, I never had to deal with that blending, and even though there's Wheelers and Eagars and I'm neither of those things, I never felt that. I felt completely and totally loved and that our family was a family and not a mismatch of people thrown together. That's been an amazing blessing.

Bryan: I was the baby. I wouldn't give any of it up. I'm grateful for my extended family. When I married Christina, you know, that was a challenge, and I think I really turned to you [gestured to

Dick & Fay|, and I turned to our life growing up of how are we going to make this work because it was insane. There are a lot of things that we're glad are behind us. I just wanted to give our love and appreciation for your example, and for all of our family. We're so grateful for such a wonderful family that we have and the relationships that we have that are all unique and different, but wonderful at the same time. I just love you mom and dad. Thank you. Congratulations.

Dale: As the oldest son-in-law in the family, I just want to tell you how it was for me. I married Pam and had Joan as a mother-in-law and for about two and half years I guess, and then she was gone. Dad and I ran together in the mornings. I remember he called me up one time and he said, "I need you to run with me. I just need time to think, and I need a partner. Will you run with me?" I was not a runner. When I was in high school and college I ran to the very inch that the coach made us run, and not an inch more. I walked everywhere else, but I ran with Dad. I told him one time, "You're always welcome to come on over and talk with Pam and I if you ever need to talk." So, we got a call about midnight one night, and he said, "Can I come over and talk?" We invited him on over. When

Aug. 25, 2007 Back: Larry, Julie, Bryan, Josh, Tami, Mike, Dale, Kari, Rick
Front: Becky, Pam, Sheri, Fay, Dick, Laura, Kristen, Meilyn

Dad came over and talked with Pam and I, he told us what he was feeling and what happened with Fay. The day that they got married he said to Pam and I, "I need you." He was crying, and he said, "I need you, from the start, to call her mom. We need to pull in this family together, and it has to come from the oldest to teach the youngest." From that moment on, we always called Fay mom. On the onset, I know that it was extremely uncomfortable for Pam, and it was uncomfortable for me, but after an extremely short period of time, it was the most natural thing to call her mom—and we're pretty close in age. They have been such an incredible example for Pam and I. Raising nine children has not been easy. We have talked on occasion, and they give us a little bit of counsel here and there. It's always been information that was well received simply because we had no other choice. I just wanted to let you know that she is our mom, he is our dad, and we love you.

Julie: I feel like my experience is just like Kristen's; I don't remember any of the bumps. I don't remember not having a dad or feeling that loss. I'm so grateful for my dad and the love that you always have shown me and my kids, especially through the last couple years. He always knows when I'm having a bad day; he always calls to check on me and to tell me he loves me. I feel so, so lucky to have had you as my dad. I'm grateful that you picked my mom and that you took us all in and took on that challenge. I told my friends all the time that it was a marriage of convenience—It was just convenient that they got married. Clearly, I know now. I'm grateful for your continued love and support always, even when I make dumb choices. You've always just reached out your arms and told me you love me, both of you. I'm so so grateful for that. I'm grateful that even though we're the Wheelers and the Eagars, I know I have 14 siblings that love me, that I can call at any time, day or night, even if it's for spider killing. So, thank you.

Meilyn: There's so many funny things that are just so unique. I remember going to the grocery store and having a whole cart full of milk and bread—like, that's all that was in the cart. We did learn to put the milk on the bottom. Or a whole lot of Kotex. There are just things like that that you cannot forget. When we're going into Show Low to do laundry because we're out, we would have to wait for the laundromat to be empty so we could do all the laundry. We sang a lot when we were there. It was awesome. I also remember loading up to go visit Grandma and Grandpa's and singing in the car every Saturday's Warrior song that was on tape.

Words From the Grandchildren and Great-grandchildren:

A. J. and Sarah Hale: Hi Grandma and Grandpa, we love you so much, and we're so happy for the memories we've been able to have with you. The joy that we've felt as the two of us have come to family home evening is incredible. I'm grateful for all the memories that I was able to create throughout childhood and high school. I'm glad I was able to come to your home and feel the love in your home. Thank you so much! We love you! We love you!

Aceson Hale: Hey Papa and Grandma. I'd just like to tell you how grateful I am for both of you. I've loved coming over for family home evening all my life, getting to know all my cousins, having great lessons, and enjoying being there with all the family. I'm so grateful you've done that all my life and for knowing the importance of family. I'm so grateful for both of you, the example you've been to me in serving all the different missions you've served, for being such great members of the Church, and being so righteous. I love you guys so much, and happy anniversary.

Hannah Hale: I just wanted to take the opportunity to tell you how grateful I am for you, the opportunity I have to come to your house every first Monday of the month, for all the wonderful experiences there, and the chances I've had to grow closer to all the rest of my family on the Wheeler side. I love you so much and happy anniversary.

Haleigh, Hinzlee, Harper, and Anderson Hale: Happy anniversary! We love you!

Rainy Christensen, Summer Schlink, Winter Freebairn and family: We love you Grandma and Grandpa! We've appreciated all the years of you holding home evenings for us so we could all be together as a family and learn the gospel, and to love music, from you.

Schlink, Freebairn, and Christensen kids: Happy Anniversary Grandma and Grandpa! We love you!

Spring Theobald and family: Happy Anniversary Papa and Grandma! We love you so much!
[Off camera speaker] We love you, happy anniversary from Cory and Spring Theobald family!

Brecken, London, Watson, and Ian Barnett: Happy 40th wedding anniversary. Bye! We love you!

Tara Roland: Hi Grandma and Grandpa. I wanted to, first of all, wish you a very happy anniversary, and just wanted to share a couple of fun memories that I have over the years. Since I'm one of the older grandkids, I got to spend the night over there a lot. Every year in elementary school we'd have grandparents day; Grandma would always come and have lunch with me, and that was really fun. Also, I got to go on lots of trips to Pinedale and Magic Mountain in the motor home and all the fun memories of that. Even the time when the motor home broke down and we had to spend a couple of days at a mechanics shop, and Grandma had to go get us sweatshirts because we didn't have anything warm, and it was really cold—I just have lots of fun memories of trips. One of the most special trips was when Sarah, Season, and I got to visit you both on your mission in Fiji. That was such a fun time, and we did so many fun things. I appreciate, so much, all of the time and attention that you always give us—all of your grandkids—to make us all feel like we're special, even though you have so many of us. I greatly appreciate all of the amazing letters that I always got from Grandpa every week on my mission. I just love and appreciate both of you so much, and again, I wish you a very happy anniversary.

Nathan Garner: Hi Grandma and Grandpa. I hope you have a happy anniversary. We miss you in Northern California. We miss getting to see you all the time, but I want you to know that we love you. Thank you so much for all that you've done for our family. You guys have been great examples over the years. Happy anniversary! Hope you have a great day!

Mandi Acedo: Hi, Grandma and Grandpa. I wanted to wish you a happy anniversary and tell you how grateful I am that I got the unique experience of being one of the grandkids to hang out with Kristen. I got to go on all the family trips with you guys, well at least some of the really fun ones— Magic mountain, tons of trips up to the cabin, and up to Utah. It was always really fun to be able to travel with both of you guys and to make tons of memories. Then, when I was in high school, I got to come home to your house while I was waiting for my parents to come pick me up. I'd walk home from Mesa High after doing cross country and hang out at your house until who knows when. Sometimes it was only a few minutes, and sometimes it was many many hours. I'm also grateful that I always had a place to go and was able to spend time with you guys and get to know you better by being with you guys. I love you so much, and I hope you have a good anniversary!

Lincoln, Aubrey, and Regan Acedo: Thanks Grandma and Grandpa for letting us swim in your pool, and thank you for letting us pick all your fruit! Happy anniversary! We love you!

Tanner Garner: Happy anniversary. We love you!

Hunter Garner: Happy anniversary. We love you so much!

Brittany Boynton: Hi Grandma and Grandpa. I still wanted to get on here and tell you how much I love you both, and I wanted to tell you that I really appreciate your love and example throughout my life. I'm so grateful that you guys had relationships with our family. Not only do I think of all my cousins as my best friends, but also I have grown from the examples of my aunts and uncles. I'm so grateful to have a relationship with all of them. I feel like, because I've seen their examples in my life, all throughout my life, and seeing them go through challenges and trials and still come out on top, it's made me a better person and I'm so grateful for that. I love you both so much, and I wanted to wish you a happy anniversary.

Brookley, Nick, Graham, and Marshall Hansen: Happy anniversary Grandma and Grandpa! We love you so much! We love you! Bye!

Austin, Sarah, Brent, Laura Lee Wheeler and their families: Happy anniversary! We love you!

Kianna Gregory: Happy anniversary. I'm so grateful that I have a grandma Fay and a grandpa, or dumdrampa depending on who you ask. I'm grateful for your example of a happy, loving marriage, and I hope you have the best anniversary. I love you.

Kazlan Gregory: Happy anniversary Grandma and Grandpa. I love you so much, and I'm so grateful for all the family meetings that I got to spend at your house, for the relationships that I've grown with our family, how close our family is, and all the reunions and everything. I always brag about how close and how amazing our family is and all the support that I have. I'm so grateful for you guys. I love you!

Kutler Gregory: Happy anniversary Grandpa and Grandma. Something I really love about you is that you made your house a place for family to gather, and on your wall, you have this quote that says, "Grandparent's house is where cousins become best friends." I just feel like that's really true because I feel like your house is really where I became best friends with my cousins. Your house has always been just a place of sanctuary where I come and have fun with cousins, and I get to know my family, and it just feels safe. I love you!

Josh Ray reading for Kelton Gregory: I'm Josh Ray, Kelton's best friend. Since he can't be giving this, I'm going to be telling you his message. He said, "My favorite memories of Grandpa and Grandma are of Grandpa's stories and coming over every first Monday for family home evening. I also liked going over on Sundays and playing softball with siblings and listening to Grandpa and Grandma tell my mom and dad the gossip in the family, old stories, and things about their life. Some of the gossip is very interesting. I loved when Grandpa came up to the cabin and got his own little scooter zooming around with his hand on the switchy thingy, going as fast as he could. I loved how they show up to everything we ask them to if they are available. Another favorite memory is, every Sunday, getting the fruit by the foot when we came over. I remember always the nativity, one candy cane we got off the tree, and just being there with the whole extended family and having fun. I love you! Kelton."

Andrew, Chelsea, Molly, and Gabriel DiLello: Happy anniversary. Thanks for everything, and merging this crazy family of ours, and making it important to have family.
Molly: It's me, Molly. I love you, Grandma Fay and Grandpa! I hope I come to your house again!

Chelsea DeLello: Hi Grandma. Hi Grandpa. I hope you have a good anniversary and I just wanted to let you know how grateful I am to have been able to grow up with such an amazing family. We have an awesome support system that is always here and that's all because of you guys. Thank you. We love you.

Ashley Cox: Hi Grandma and Grandpa. I just wanted to say happy anniversary and that I love you. You guys are both such amazing people in my life and great examples to me. Love you both and hope you have a great day.

Josh and Alexa Smedley: Hi! Happy anniversary. We're in Guadalajara, Mexico where Josh served his mission. We're at the temple here just enjoying it. We wanted to wish you guys a happy anniversary and tell you that we love you so much. We love you so much! Can't wait to see you again! Happy anniversary.

Cole Eagar: Happy 40th anniversary. Love you guys.

Jason Eagar: Hi Grandma and Grandpa. Congratulations on your 40th anniversary. I love you guys.

Kylie Eagar: Hi Grandma and Grandpa. I just wanted to say happy anniversary, and thank you for all that you do.

Ryleigh McCoy: Hi Grandma. Hi Grandpa. I just wanted to wish you guys a happy anniversary. Love you lots!

Liam McCoy: Hey Grandma. Hey Grandpa. Happy anniversary. Love you guys.

Meghan McCoy: Hi Grandma and Grandpa. Just wanted to say happy anniversary. Love you.

Gavin Keppel: Happy anniversary Grandma and Grandpa. Love you guys.

Gunner Spahr: Happy anniversary Grandma and Grandpa. Love you.

Griffin Spahr: Happy anniversary Grandma and Grandpa. I love you guys.

Gage Spahr: Hi Grandma. Hi Grandpa. Happy anniversary. I love you both.

Julie and Grady Spahr: Hi Grandma and Papa. I love you Papa! I love you Grandma! Happy anniversary!

Jaxon Reber: Happy anniversary Grandma and Grandpa.

Jay Reber: We're so glad you got married.

Leonidas Reber: Because if you didn't we wouldn't exist.

Ari Reber: We like you.

Summer Schlink: Thank you for teaching us how important it is to show up. You always showed up for family, whether that meant coming to our concerts and events, or organizing visiting or yard work days for our great-grandparents. You showed us how to show up for the Lord and magnified your callings, went on missions, and taught us home evening lessons about following promptings and showing love. I've always felt loved and welcome in your home and cherish opportunities to sit and visit with and learn from you. I love you both so much and will always be grateful you followed the prompting to get married and build this amazing family that I get to be a part of!

Aaron and Becky Hale: Happy anniversary Papa and Grandma, we love you guys! Hi Grandma and Grandpa! We're so grateful for all your examples and for all the hard work you guys have put in over the years to help us to build a strong family, for home evenings, and for your examples of missionary service. We love you so much. We appreciate you and we look up to you. We hope to be just like you.

Heavenly Hale: I love you and happy anniversary!

40. Our Posterity

Sherilyn "Sheri" Wheeler: Aug. 28, 1955–Sep. 30, 2020
Mike Hale: Mar. 14, 1955–Apr. 29, 2018
Married: Dec. 30, 1976

Aaron: 1977
Summer: 1979
Autumn: 1982
Spring: 1984
Winter: 1985
Season: 1988–2013
Rainy: 1989

Aaron Hale: 1977
Becky: 1976
Married: May 14, 1999

AJ: 2000
     AJ Hale: 2000
     Sarah: 1998
     Married: Jan. 23, 2021
          "Arie" Aaron III: 2022
          Evelyn: 2024
Aroet "Aro": 2002
     Aroet "Aro" Hale: 2002
     Jenna: 2000
     Married: Sep. 20, 2021
          Aroet Jr.: 2024
          Son expected 2025
Aceson: 2003
Hannah: 2005
Haleigh: 2009
Hinzlee: 2011
Andersen: 2012
Harper: 2014
Heavenly: 2018
Ryker: 2019
Ruston: 2019

Sheri and Mike, cont.

Summer Hale: 1979
Nathan Schlink: 1977
Married: Jan. 11, 2003

Nathan: 2004
Ethan: 2005
Liberty: 2006
Belle: 2008
Faith: 2009
Hope: 2011

Autumn Hale: 1982
Jason Crawford: 1983
Married: Jun. 12, 2004

Leah: 2008
Alice: 2011
Vaughn: 2013

Spring Hale: 1984
Cory Theobald: 1979
Married: May 17, 2003

Abigail "Abby": 2004
Margaret "Maggie": 2005
George: 2007
Frederick "Freddy": 2008
Eleanor: 2015
Henry: 2017
Michael: 2019
Cory Jr.: 2021
Christian: 2023
Son expected 2025

Winter Hale: 1985
Kyle Freebairn: 1983
Married: Jul. 15, 2005

Mary: 2007
Owen: 2008
Blake: 2011
Dylan: 2012
Carter: 2012

Sheri and Mike, cont.

Season Hale: 1988–2013
Ian Barnett: 1983
Married Jul. 11, 2009

Brecken: 2011
London: 2013

Ian Barnett: 1983
Erin: 1991
Married: Dec. 3, 2016

Watson: 2019
Elliott: 2021
Rowan: 2024

Rainy Hale: 1989
Brandon Christensen: 1989
Married: Dec. 18, 2010

Oliver: 2012
Sawyer: 2014
Hyrum: 2016
Annie: 2018
Elizabeth: 2021
Penelope: 2022

Pamela "Pam" Gale Wheeler: Oct. 15, 1956
Dale Garner: Dec. 29, 1955
Married: Oct. 8, 1977

Tara: 1978
Nathan "Nate": 1980
Mandi: 1981
Tanner: 1983
Benson: 1985
Hunter: 1987
Brittany: 1988
Brookley: 1991
Kourtney: 1992

Tara Garner: 1978
Spencer Rowland: 1978
Married: Mar. 22, 2014

Nathan "Nate" Garner: 1980
Heidi: 1978
Married: Jul. 12, 2002

Maesyn: 2004
Jacob: 2006
Mikah: 2009
Benjamin: 2012

Mandi Garner: 1981
Clint Acedo: 1972
Married: Nov. 11, 2005

Reagan: 2007
Aubrey: 2009
Lincoln: 2014

Tanner Garner: 1983
Shelly: 1981
Married: Apr. 11, 2008

Jun.: 2009
Allie: 2011
Noah: 2013
Adelynn: 2016

Pam and Dale, cont.

Benson Garner: 1985
Sarah: 1986
Married: Jul. 17, 2008

Abigail: 2011
Harper: 2013
Whitman: 2015
Quincey: 2020
Ellis Grace: 2022

Hunter Garner: 1987
Natalie: 1985
Married: May 29, 2009

Henry: 2015
Indy: 2017
Brody: 2019
Beck: 2021

Brittany Garner: 1988
Chris Boynton: 1983
Married: Sep. 21, 2012

Scout: 2014
Jayden: 2016
Rockwell: 2019
Morgan: 2021
Catcher: 2022

Brookley Garner: 1991
Nicholas Hansen: 1992
Married: Sep. 25, 2015

Graham: 2018
Bridgette: 2019
Marshall: 2023

Pam and Dale, cont.

Kourtney Garner: 1992
Tommy J Stewart: 1992
Married: Dec. 12, 2015

Emerey: 2017
Bridger: 2018
Heber: 2020
Colter: 2021
Sawyer: 2023

Richard "Rick" Wayne Wheeler: Nov. 26, 1957
Debbie: Mar. 17, 1960
Married: Dec. 11, 1981

Trevor: 1982
Justin: 1985
Chase: 1989

Justin Wheeler: 1985
Ashley: 1989
Married: May 31, 2013

Indy: 2016
Gunnar: 2018
Brooklyn: 2020

Chase Wheeler: 1989
Sarah: 1989
Married: Mar. 3, 2011

Hadley: 2012
Graham: 2014
Cooper: 2016
Beau: 2018
Piper: 2021

Dale Brent Wheeler: Sep. 4, 1959
Tracy: Jun. 1, 1963
Married: May 12, 1983

Sarah: 1984
Laura: 1992
Austin: 1995
Brent: 1998

Sarah Wheeler: 1984
Kenny Allred: 1987
Married: Nov. 13, 2009

Ella: 2011
Carter: 2015

Austin Wheeler: 1995
Ashleigh: 1996
Married: Feb. 11, 2017

Zoey: 2019
Emmet: 2023

Brent Wheeler: 1998
Sydney: 1997
Married: Dec. 1, 2023

Lawrence "Larry" Todd Wheeler: Aug. 17, 1965

Kyrene: 1990
Jordan: 1991
Kiri: 1994
Bethany: 2000
LaRisa: 2003

Kyrene Wheeler: 1990

Kinzley: 2009
Prezley: 2014

Kiri Wheeler: 1994
Jason Pudney: 1986
Married: Jul. 6, 2020

Kadnce: 2009
Bella: 2012
Lilliann: 2020
Kiaya: 2022
Oakley: 2023

Laura Lee Wheeler: Oct. 5, 1968
Bill Gregory: Apr. 1, 1970
Married: Nov. 22, 1991

Kianna: 1992
Harrison "Kyler": 1996
Kaden: 1997
Kallen: 1999
Kazlan: 2002
William "Kutler": 2003
Kelton: 2005

Harrison "Kyler" Gregory: 1996
Ashley: 1997
Married: Mar. 5, 2016

Wyatt: 2022
Briggs: 2024

William "Kutler" Gregory: 2003
Ellen: 2003
Married: Oct. 20, 2023

Kelton Combs Gregory: 2005
Madeline: 2000
Married: Nov. 19, 2024

Sawyer: 2025

Meilyn Eagar: Oct. 8, 1968
Rob Bushman: Oct. 26, 1962
Married: Jul. 2, 1987

Chelsea: 1989
Jonathan "Jon": 1991
Zachary "Zac": 1993

Chelsea Bushman: 1989
Andrew DiLello: 1988
Married: Mar. 19, 2013

Molly: 2016
Gabriel "Gabe": 2017

Kari Eagar: Nov. 24, 1970

Ciara: 1990
Evan: 1993
Taylor: 1995
Paityn: 1999
Ryann: 2010
Kyson: 2012
Canaan: 2014

Ciara Earlywine: 1990

Ryann: 2010
Kyson: 2012
Canaan: 2014
Everleigh: 2020

Evan Earlywine: 1993
Bryauna: 1992
Married: Jun. 23, 2019

James Dean: 2016
Bradleigh: 2018

Taylor Earlywine: 1995
Nick Wheelis: 1993

Millicent: 2018
Lorette Fay: 2022

Rebecca "Becky" Amy Wheeler: Jul. 10, 1971
Bill Cox: Aug. 31, 1969
Married: Nov. 22, 1991

Ashley: 1992
Josh: 1994

Josh Cox: 1994
Bailey: 1997
Married: Jun. 11, 2016

Jaxon: 2017
Brantley: 2019
Barrett: 2022

Michael "Mike" Eagar: Apr. 6, 1973
Cindy Lawlor: Nov. 26, 1975
Married: Nov. 6, 2021

Ashton Lawlor: 1997
Alexa: 1998
Aubrey Lawlor: 1999
Ethan Lawlor: 2000
Cole: 2000
Chase Lawlor: 2003
Jason: 2005

Ashton Lawlor: 1997
Hayden Palmer: 1996
Married: March 7, 2020

Posey: 2023

Alexa Eagar: 1998
Josh Smedley: 1995
Married: Dec. 22, 2018

Aubrey Lawlor: 1999
Dakota Roberts: 1996
Married: July 10, 2023

Bryan "Buckwheat" David Wheeler: May 2, 1974
Christina: Dec. 23, 1977
Married: Jul. 22, 2011

Baily Wahl: 1997
Austin Wahl: 1998
Kassidy: 1999
Kinley: 1999
Blake Wahl: 2000
Lorelei Wahl: 2002
Brynn: 2002
Slade: 2005
Amelia Wahl: 2005

Baily Wahl: 1997
Tanya: 1991
Married: May 13, 2023

Alice Smelser: 2012

Austin Wahl: 1998
Tatum: 2003
Married: Oct. 28, 2023

Lorelei Wahl: 2002
Layton Kriloff: 2002
Married: Aug. 1, 2023

Ivy: 2024

Brynn Wheeler: 2002
Bryson Murset: 1999
Married: Jan. 8, 2022

Breckyn: 2022
Molly: 2024

Joshua "Josh" Eagar: Feb. 16, 1975
Kristie: Nov. 15, 1975
Married: Oct. 14, 1995

Jacie: 1997
Jacob: 2000
Kylie: 2004

Jacie Eagar: 1997
Austin Packard: 1995
Married: Mar. 11, 2017

Nova: 2022

Tami Eagar: Sep. 27, 1976
Devin McCoy: Apr. 14, 1977
Married: Nov. 25, 1998

Hannah (stillborn): 2000
Ryleigh: 2001
Liam: 2003
Meghan: 2008

Julie Eagar: Jul. 7, 1978

Gavin Spahr: 2002
Gunner Spahr: 2004
Griffin Spahr: 2006
Gage Spahr: 2010
Grady Spahr: 2018

Kristen Wheeler: Apr. 22, 1983
Ty Reber: Jun. 13, 1981
Married: Aug. 25, 2007

Leonidas: 2008
Jay: 2010
Jaxon: 2013
Ari: 2015

41. Closing

By Dick and Fay:

Well, you've reached the end of this book! Hopefully, you've also had a chance to read the other two we wrote. You might be wondering—why three books?

We wrote the first two to tell the stories of our early lives and help each of our children to get to know the parent they lost. Some of our children don't remember their parent who passed away, so those books are our way of keeping alive the memories of our first spouses and showing our children just how deeply they were loved.

When we got married, all 14 of our children gained not just a new parent but also new brothers and sisters; then Kristen came along to complete our family. We wrote the third book to help us all celebrate our combined family, remember the good times and moments that shaped us, and learn from the challenges we faced together.

Some of our favorite memories as a family were made on the road and in the places we visited together. Traveling across the United States in the motorhome with Grandma and Grandpa Coombs was an adventure filled with incredible sights and experiences. We made so many wonderful memories in Pinedale. Those were moments we cherished—along with countless others. Most of all, we loved simply being together.

We've already said it many times in different ways, but as we close this book, we want to reiterate the two things that are most important to us.

First, we love the gospel of Jesus Christ and know that The Church of Jesus Christ of Latter-day Saints is the only true Church on the earth. We are grateful for our prophet, President Russell M. Nelson, and for the guidance and blessings the gospel brings.

Second, we love each of you and your families. We want all good things for you. We are proud of each of you, pray for you every day, and are so very grateful to have you in our lives. You are so precious to us!

With all our love,
Mom and Dad, Grandma and Grandpa